学汇中外 语通世界

WODE CHENGDIANMENG

我的『成电梦』

——电子科技大学外语专业本科生论文习作

（第三辑）

主编 楚军
副主编 姚连兵 林何 王倩

电子科技大学出版社
University of Electronic Science and Technology of China Press
·成都·

图书在版编目（CIP）数据

我的“成电梦”：电子科技大学外语专业本科生论文习作. 第三辑 / 楚军主编. —成都：电子科技大学出版社，2018. 12

ISBN 978-7-5647-6710-5

Ⅰ. ①我… Ⅱ. ①楚… Ⅲ. ①英语－毕业论文－写作－高等学校－教材 Ⅳ. ①G642.477②H315

中国版本图书馆 CIP 数据核字（2019）第 004826 号

我的“成电梦”——电子科技大学外语专业本科生论文习作（第三辑）

主　编　楚　军

副主编　姚连兵　林　何　王　倩

策划编辑　谢应成

责任编辑　谢应成

出版发行　电子科技大学出版社

成都市一环路东一段 159 号电子信息产业大厦九楼　邮编　610051

主　　页　www.uestcp.com.cn

服务电话　028-83203399

邮购电话　028-83201495

印　　刷　成都市火炬印务有限公司

成品尺寸　185 mm×260 mm

印　　张　9.75

字　　数　250 千字

版　　次　2018 年 12 月第 1 版

印　　次　2018 年 12 月第 1 次印刷

书　　号　ISBN 978-7-5647-6710-5

定　　价　48.00 元

树立精英意识·优化育人环节·培养精英人才

电子科技大学外国语学院　冯文坤

学生主动选择一所大学，意味他们认同一所大学的价值，意味他们对“我将成为什么样的人”有了一种期待，尽管这种期待在一个大学生那里还十分朦胧，但他们却从此接受这所大学对他们未来的一种承诺。“我是谁？从哪里来？到哪里去？”这是古希腊哲学家苏格拉底提出的问题。古希腊哲人认为，人活着就是为了弄清楚这三个问题。“我是谁？”“从哪里来？到哪里去？”这三问不仅是哲学中询问“人”的意义的问题，也可以是一所大学应该首先思考“培养什么人”和“如何培养人”的问题，因为大学是青年人自我塑型和自我形成的地方，是向社会许下未来和承诺美好价值的地方，因此，大学责无旁贷，应率先帮助学生去思考“我从哪里来”“我是谁”“我将到哪里去”这三个问题，并在教育过程中回答学生对人生的建构。

两年前，言荣校长在“关于我校本科人才培养的思考”的报告中，全面总结了学校人才培养所取得的成绩、存在的问题和今后人才培养的目标与实现路径，至今令人振奋，发人深思，催人改进和革新，尤其是言荣校长直逼大学“要培养什么人”和“如何培养人”的发问，并立足电子科技大学，提出了未来电子科技大学精英人才培养目标定位，体现了言荣校长枕于忧患、着眼于未来的教育战略思维和一位教育家的人才培养观，更体现了秉持科大“追求卓越，大气大为”之校训精神的办学理念自信、发展自信和责任自信。精英培养，引领大众，服务于社会是大学的崇高使命，更是对电子科技大学几代人崇高使命的继承和发扬。根据校长讲话，结合外语学院办学实际，围绕精英人才培养定位谈几点愚见和忧思。

一、创新人才培养模式，孕育精英人才成长

要成就精英人才之办学目标，要明确人才培养的模式定位。要使学生明确知道“我成为谁”“我要到哪里去”，要以学生成才或培养效果或标准为终极目标。也就是说，效果或标准重于环节，环节推动人才成长，要把**有效教学、有效学习和有效评估**统一起来。今天，我们的教学管理过程，学习管理过程，似乎每个环节都做到了，有的环节还非常严苛，我们的精力都用来应付这些环节，形式大于内容，学生成长实际效果如何却没有给予充分重视，因为对人才终端之效果如何担责的问题十分模糊，也是十分复杂，但背后折射出的却是大学之全体责任。法

不责众，更何况是一个庞大的机构。生产线上的不合格产品可以退回，可人不同于物。拿外语人才培养来说，一个学生通过 4 年学习，他是不是实现了当初选择的专业人才愿望，是不是达到该专业人才所应有的要求，如外语交际能力、外语写作能力、系统的学科知识以及认知能力等，还是仅仅入了大学，遵循了每个环节，蹲满了学分，最后成为“毕了业的人才”。就我个人愚见，大众教育重通识，精英教育更重研究能力和创新思维。大众教育造就学生“成人”，精英教育造就学生“成为杰出的人”或成为具有精英意识的人。

二、创新课程体系，适应精英人才培养

要培养精英外语人才，就要遵循外语学科的系统性和人文人才培养规律，要实现语言的人文性和工具性的高度统一，要实现中国情怀和国际视野在一个外语人才身上的结合，要在把握语言工具性的过程中含化人文教育，要实实在在把语言转化为学科性学习和向外拓展的工具理性。由此，应该反思我们现有的外语课程内容体系：缺乏学科系统性、内容片段化、破碎化和随意性；操作性、技能训练占到接近 80%、内容倒转为技能服务；课程体系性不衔接，课程层级不分明，课程目标不清楚；特色原本是学科体系中的特色，却一言以蔽之，外语加特色，其结果是特色性遮蔽专业学科属性，不伦不类。

由此产生三大后果、引发三大整改：外语人才学科定位不清楚，专业兴趣游移，效果不明确，标准不清楚，不利于杰出专业人才成长，因此，应强化学科专业定位和人才培养目标的课程体系建设；仅仅为技能而设计的课程体系就如有“矛”无“盾”，有驾照无车开，开花不结果，因此，应将操作性、技能性训练溶于内容系统性传达、素养含化和学科培养目标之中；目前课程体系只具有指标意义，如专业基础课、专业核心课程和专业选修课，它们在多大程度上是服务于外语学科专业人才“成才”是值得我们思考的，因此，应以人才效果和标准为鹄的，加强以“人才培养为中心，以成才为目标”的专业课程体系建设，应推进课程内容调整，建设由 How to Speak English 向 What to Speak with English 转变的课程内容体系。

今天，略举一例，一个十分怪异的事实是：外语文学专业的学生少有读完一本英文原著，一个较长时间从事文学课教学的老师却鲜见他或她读完读透几本原文著作。我一直觉得由体系性课程教学推动学科性研究，进而推动学科人才培养和学科平台建设是自然而然的。可事实则是，一批教师应急而上课，且续且止，留下许多僵死课程，到头来，科研与教学二元对立，元音与辅音永远靠不近。作为学院派的外语学科教学，我们不能让外语教学内容在浅层次上循环，我们的教

师不能在浅层次上经年循环，最后自我矮化，语言用语格式化。我们虽然不能教会学生像奥巴马那样讲英语，但我们可以培养像奥巴马那样运用思维的人。总之，精英人才有各样的，但精英人才一定是有内涵的。大学中的外语专业应该培养“精通外语的精英人才”，不是培养“没有内涵的外语人才”。这是大学院系外语学科人才培养体制与新东方语言培训方式的本质区别。

三、创新人才培养评估体系，适应精英人才成长效果评估

要培养精英人才，反思和调整现有评估机制非常迫切。“以人才培养为中心，以学生成才为目标”，重在成才效果，重在学生“成为谁”“到哪里去”。这一目标对学校、教师要求特别高，心理压力特别大，因为这意味教与学之间无间隙的接触、无间隙的全员投入和无间隙的关怀。这不仅仅是一个规定教授每周在指定时间与学生面谈所能完成的，或循规蹈矩，完成教学各环节，因此做到无教学事故了事。“以学生成才为目标”，把老师的日常意识变成日常责任，时时牵挂，萦于心际，教师就如参加大赛的领队，直到最后一刻，方才身心委地。优化生源，减少师生比，小班授课是完成学生成才的路径，同时还要有若干系统路径，如创新目前的评估体系：建立以学生成才为依据的有效学习路径体系与有效教学综合效果指标体系，如课程内容体系、教/学环节（硬性与灵活结合）、资源体系、学科教学团队；建立以学生成才为目标的“一体两翼”的培养机制和评估机制（学生选、育、评一体化），教师个体（遴选、考核、评价）和教学团队（团队考核个人）；采取**内部和外部相结合的评价和测试办法——内部评估指学科体系评估、教、学评估、课程和课程内容评估；外部评估指学生外语水平认证评估、行业用人评估、国际化水平评估等**。

四、建立全程导师制，落实全员育人

建立全程导师制，形成贯穿四年的学业指导、科研训练、成人成才“三位一体”的引导学生全面发展的指导制度；形成教师团队与学生班级相融合的团队式教与学模式；形成学生（思想工作）与教学一体化的学业、成长、成才体系。从2013年开始，外语学院在全体本科生中落实导师制，对学生的学业过程、学业规划发展、成人成长等进行指导。接下来，学院将实施班级教授导师制，专业教学团队责任制（探索中），基于“基础、提高和发展”的大学外教学团队责任制，以及已经实施并取得显著效果的指导各类外语大赛的“外语实践教育团队”等。

五、学、研、训一体化，在思辨与运思中成长

建立贯穿学生培养全过程的研究方法论课程群、学期论文、学年论文、科研训练等一体化研训机制，培养具有方法论的思维模式与批判性思维能力；根据本科学生毕业走向（直接就业或继续深造），进行差异化的论文或毕业环节训练等；实施“外语写作课程”贯穿四年不下课，培养学生规范写作，独立思考，考量心理变化历程。

今天的大学生似乎并不缺乏知识，一键网络天下，大数据时代的一个重要特征是我们只需要知道“what it is”，而不需要知道“why it is”，可这恰恰指出我们大学在当今的使命：更应该去培养学生的判断能力、逻辑思维能力，从相似性、类似性、联想性和模糊性中去培养学生的选择能力和判断能力。

据观察，大多数具有创新思维能力的人都具有类似性思维、联想性思维和关联性思维等特征，能从两件表面上毫无联系的事情上发现其关联性，一般被人戏称“发散思维”，其实是他们省略了线性逻辑，而直接地领悟到其内隐逻辑。人们常说，有些人无学历却能干大事，如知名企业家，而那些搞量化经济学的却并非能够对市场做出准确的预测，也没有成为企业家。问题的关键是，做出的固化数学建模尽管来源于经验观察所取得的数据分析，却永远也取代不了直观洞察力、类似性思维、关联性思维以及想象力，后者的所有者就是创新性人才。

六、“学科内培养，学科外发展”

人们常讲，育人者应“授人以渔”，要育人者授人可以临深渊而渔之的本领。“授人以渔”与“授人以鱼”是对操作型人才和社会适应性人才的暗喻式诠释。言荣校长讲，当今社会发展，产业更新，变化快于规划，今日就业明日失业，我们的教育应为学生的第二次转岗打下基础，这话讲得简单却深刻，说出了一个教育家“道术合一”的崇高信念和面向未来、与时俱进的责任感和发展观。大学既要培养满足社会行业阶段性需要的应用性人才，又要使学生具有应对变化挑战、掌控变化以及人生变化的适应性人才。前者是学科内培养，后者需要通过培养学生的综合人文素质，厚基础、宽口径，以培养学生的持续再生产能力。前者是培养学科专业精英，后者是造就具有精英意识的商界精英、政治精英和社会贤达。一言以蔽之，培养精英人才，以造就学科领域大师、专业方向领军和行业界翘楚，而培养具有精英意识的大学生则惠及全体学生之终生和全社会之发展，这或许就是我们对大众中的精英教育的最好诠释。

学院组织和推动研究生和本科生文集出版，这是一种记载和书写学生成长中的记忆。湖泊中的涟漪总是由振荡而来，微风过林，七窍玲珑心。我相信这里记录的是同学们的认知自信、成长自信。

前　言

岁月荏苒。每逢 9 月，寒窗苦读的莘莘学子带着新鲜好奇的眼神，怀揣美好的人生梦想来到美丽的成电校园，加入温馨浪漫的外院大家庭；学在成电，度过丰富多彩的四年大学生活，在成电校园留下难以忘怀的、深深的成长足迹；再插上“成电梦”的翅膀，扬起人生的风帆，充满自信地朝着成功的彼岸遨游！

《我的“成电梦”》——电子科技大学外语专业本科生论文习作（第三辑）展现在大家面前的就是同学们学在成电的脚踏实地的学业足印，是从同学们的学期论文中遴选出的优秀篇章，其中，有对目标语国社会文化的领悟与思考，有对语言文学和语言教育话题的志趣与研讨，有翻译理论与实践的分析与探索。

具体地讲，本书包括语言教育、语言文学、文化和翻译几个部分。

“文学研究”部分收录学期论文 6 篇。伍亚茜对 *Love in a Fallen City* 中的“他者”形象进行了探讨；熊安琪和余杨分别对作品 *The Cement Garden* 和 *Fortress Besieged* 进行了较深入的研究；张蕊对经典名著 *Pride and Prejudice* 中的跨阶层的婚姻进行了批判性分析；范诗雪和李玉分别对作品 *A Tale for the Time Being* 做了尝试性研讨。

“翻译研究”部分收录相关学期论文 6 篇。汤朝菊教授指导的袁典同学对中国古典名著《西游记》的书名在不同时期不同英译版本中的翻译进行了深入分析；李清分析研究了《水浒传》的赛珍珠译本；魏荣对《故都的秋》的原文和张培基的汉译本做了比较研究；邓静、向张玉洁和朱博涵分别对习语、政治术语和诗歌翻译进行了探讨。

“语言研究”部分收录了习作 4 篇。颜淑芳对广告中的模糊语言现象进行了探析；朱珈璇对汉字“臣”的反义同形现象做了较有意义的探索；汤朝菊教授指导的贾淞同学的学期论文关注了汉语词汇意义的历时演变现象；柳依同学对网络社交礼仪语言使用中句末句号的缺失现象进行了研讨。

在“教育研究”部分，曾楚奇探讨了通过 MOOC 进行翻译教学的问题；仇筱萱对英语专业课堂教学中同学间的合作学习话题进行了研讨。

“文化研究”部分收录了两篇习作。韩子钰比较分析了《功夫熊猫 2》和《波西杰克逊与魔兽之海》两部电影；日语系的杨芷玥、周小萱和欧宇玲三位同学对中日女性时尚杂志的封面做了对比研究。

目前，学校推进“双一流大学”建设，实施本科精英人才培养战略，着力提升同学们的“新四会”能力，培养学术精英、行业精英和创业精英，学院切实采取各项外语专业本科人才培养举措，以增强同学们的学业自信和成长自信，本书的出版也可视为诸类措施的具体体现。

由于时间仓促，加之本书中的作品都是出自外语专业在校本科同学之手，文中错误和不当之处在所难免，诚望读者批评斧正！

《我的“成电梦”》（第三辑）学生习作得以出版，感谢电子科技大学本科人才培养“特区建设”项目“外国语学院菁英人才工程计划”的资助，感谢英语系、翻译系和日语系导师们的悉心指导，感谢姚连兵、林何和王倩三位系主任对学期论文的遴选编辑和辛勤付出，感谢电子科技大学出版社编辑们的辛勤劳动。

编　者

目　录

文学研究

The Image of the Other in Eileen Chang's *Love in a Fallen City* .... 伍亚茜 2
The Allegory of the Cave in *The Cement Garden* .... 熊安琪 8
The Dilemmas of Fang Hung-chien in *Fortress Besieged*: A Prototypical Case in Early 20th Century .... 余　杨 15
A "Doomed" Happy Ending in *Pride and Prejudice:* A Critical Analysis of Cross-class Marriage between Darcy and Elizabeth .... 张　蕊 26
Exploring the Meaning of "Time being" in *A Tale for the Time Being* .... 范诗雪 34
Human Existence in *A Tale for the Time Being* .... 李　玉 41

翻译研究

Context and Disambiguation: A Case Study of Translating Idioms .... 邓　静 49
All Men Are Brothers: An Oriental Approach to Pearl S. Buck's Translation of *Shui Hu Zhuan* .... 李　清 57
A Contrastive Study of Chinese and English Grammatical Structure in *Autumn in Peiping* .... 魏　荣 64
Translation of Political Terms under Eugene Nida's Functional Equivalence Theory: A Case Study of "Belt and Road" Translation .... 向张玉洁 70
Discussion on Different English Versions of Book Title of *Xi-you-ji* .... 袁　典　汤朝菊 78
Discussion on the Standard of English Lyrics Translation .... 朱博涵 84

语言研究

Reasons for the Existence of Vague Advertisement Language .... 颜淑芳 92
Pragmatic Study of the Chinese Contronym Word "Chen" .... 朱珈璇 98
浅谈汉语词汇意义历时演变中的常规与非常规表现 .... 贾　淞　汤朝菊 104
句末句号的缺失：网络社交礼仪 .... 柳　依 108

教育研究

A Case Study of Translation Teaching through MOOC .... 曾楚奇 115
Cooperative Learning in English Major's Classes at UESTC: Problems and Solutions ..... 仇筱萱 122

文 化 研 究

The Fatalism Narrative Model in Films: *Kung Fu Panda 2* and Posey Jackson and the Sea of Warcraft......韩子钰 133
中日女性时尚杂志封面对比研究......杨芷玥　周小萱　欧宇玲 139

文学研究

The Image of the Other in Eileen Chang's *Love in a Fallen City*

伍亚茜

摘　要：张爱玲的小说不仅以丰富饱满的人物形象而知名，更因其中所蕴含的女性主义达到了新的艺术高度。张爱玲塑造了一系列受男权社会压迫的血肉丰满的女性角色，她们身上所呈现出的委曲求全，与法国女权运动的先驱者——西蒙娜・德・波伏娃在《第二性》中所提出的“他者”有着相似的特性。本文选取张爱玲小说中的一名典型“受压迫”的女性人物——《倾城之恋》的白流苏，将她置于波伏娃女性主义的语境中，通过分析她对于男性的物质依附与精神依附，试图探求她成为“他者”的原因。最终得出结论，男权社会对女性的压迫使得女性逐渐丧失自我意识，自愿成为“他者”。深入探讨这个问题有助于推动新时代女性主义的发展，并对现代社会中女性主义作品的创作大有裨益。

关键词：张爱玲；波伏娃；他者；女性意识

Abstract: In the feminist writer Eileen Chang's works, some similarities on feminist consciousness are shared with the pioneer of French feminist movements—Simone de Beauvoir, and some woman characters show the feature of the *Other* which is mentioned in *The Second Sex.* With the terminology and theory of Beauvoir's, this paper will demonstrate a typical "opposed" woman called Bai Liusu in Chang's novel *Love in a Fallen City* and try to figure out how she is made to be the *Other* by exploring her material subordination and mental subordination. Finally, it attributes the woman's tragedy to patriarchal culture and society, in which women lose their self-consciousness and become the *Other*. Discussing this question in depth can promote the further development of Chinese feminist and serve as a guideline on the creation of feminist works in modern society.

Key words: Eileen Chang；Simone de Beauvoir；the *Other*；Feminist consciousness

1　Introduction

Eileen Chang, a female writer in the last century whose literary output not only constructs an aesthetic literary world but also reveals the historic fate of Chinese women, concerns the lives of the tragic and oppressed women in her works with her penetrating eyes. In her works, we can find that some women are devastated by the surroundings and the society such as Bai Liusu. They are inessential and subordinate to men without self-consciousness, which makes them become the *Other* as Simone de Beauvoir mentioned in her book.

As one of the most influential feminism authors, Simone de Beauvoir's study on woman has brought her the credit. In *the Second Sex*, Beauvoir made her argument that "He is the Subject, he is the Absolute—she is the *Other*." (Beauvoir, 1949, p. 26) In Beauvoir's theory, the reason why women become the *Other* is because of their submission which was formed as a result of the rule of patriarchal society for thousands of years. Hence, the change of the situation requires the establishment of women's self-consciousness.

"One is not born, but rather becomes, a woman." (Beauvoir, 1949: 330) Chang and Beauvoir both agree that women are subject to their marriages and their men. In their works, they argue that marriage is like transaction between bodies and money, and if a woman wants to win her independency, the economic independency is the prerequisite. The female images of Chang's works reflect the dependency on males if from the perspective of the *Other* mentioned in *The Second Sex*. In this work, Beauvoir claims women the *Other* in patriarchal society, which is not born with women but enforced by the patriarchal culture. In spite of the gender differences between male and female, women cannot be defined as the inessential, nor as the *Other*.

Analyzing Chang's works with Beauvoir's eyes can help us better understand Chang's characters' historical tragedy and her unique understanding of women's destiny. Without grand historical background, focusing on trivial daily lives, the women characters in Chang's novel are ordinary but melancholy and can arouse reader's infinite compassion. They are the victims of the ages. In this paper, the writer will define the images of the *Other* and how they become the *Other* in a novel from Eileen Chang—*Love in a Fallen City*, using the theory from Simone de Beauvoir. The image of the woman character—Bai Liusu in Chang's works will be illustrated. How is she made subordinate to men? How does she become the Other? To find out the answers, the character's material subordination and mental subordination will be analyzed.

2 The "Other" in Chang's Works

Both Eileen Chang and Beauvoir admit that women are subordinate to men in marriage in patriarchal society. Chang argues that women have an inborn subordination to men, due to their intrinsic servility. In her opinion, women's lives are revolving around men, and women's mental defect is to blame for it. "Women were subdued and became the salves of patriarchy because they had less physical strength than men did. However, in the natural process of 'survival of the fittest,' why the males were not conquered by lions and tigers since men were weaker." (张爱玲, 1944, p. 67) Instead of physical defect, Chang attributes the oppressed status of women to their mental servility. Unlike Eileen Chang, Beauvoir is against the statement of women's defect, "...the types of behaviors denounced are not dictated to woman by her hormones or predestined in her brain's compartments: they are suggested in negative form by her situation." (Beauvoir, 1949, p. 724) Therefore, it is the social conditions that make women subordinate to men, and Beauvoir divides this subordination into mental subordination and material subordination. Read from the perspective of Beauvoir, Chang's novels reveal these two subordinations of women.

2.1 Mental Subordination

As Beauvoir mentions in *the Second Sex*, "One is not born, but rather becomes, a woman." (Beauvoir, 1949, p. 330) Women tend to shape themselves as the gender expectation suggested by the patriarchal society, and meanwhile accept the values of patriarchal culture — "Women resign themselves to their lot without attempting any action."(Beauvoir, 1949, p. 182) What conduce to it is that "she will gain value in the eyes of males not by increasing her human worth but by modeling herself on their dreams."(Beauvoir, 1949, p. 402) The patriarchy not only deprives women of self-consciousness and makes them ignore the fact that they have become the *Other*, but also compels them to participate in the reproduction of the patriarchal culture. In Chang's novel *Love in a Fallen City*, the heroine shows no personal autonomy on their destinies.

In *Love in a Fallen City*, Bai Liusu got rid of a suffering marriage by divorce and was received by her family just because of her fortune compensated by her ex-husband. When her brother and sister-in-law exploited all her money, they humiliated her, attempting to muscle her out of the family. Having divorced and lost all her wealth, Bai was in panic for her precarious condition.

In this case, as Beauvoir said, "marriage was her only means of survival and the only justification of her existence." (Beauvoir, 1949, p. 503) Fortunately, Bai met a wealthy but sophisticated man— Fan Liuyuan. Since then, Bai had been betting her youth for the rest of her life. Bai persisted in her efforts to seize Fan in order to regain her social status by a marriage, while Fan, who only considered women as the mud on the earth, never thought of marriage but wanted a lover. They began a competition. Bai's weapons were her exquisite appearance, educated manners and soft tender; Fan conquered bai with his wealth, maturity and his flip-flop attitude from chilly to warm. Without the fall of the city, the calculating couple would never be together. The courtship of Bai was adventurous, in which, on one hand, she had to maintain the intimacy with Fan otherwise she would never fulfil her hope of a marriage; on the other hand, she contrived not to become Fan's exclusive lover and detract from her dignity or it would come to no avail. She thinks "if a woman cannot obtain male's love, she cannot gain other women's respect. Women are that mean." (张爱玲, 1943, p. 171)Being "mean" is to submit to the dominant patriarchy, in which the only approach for women to win respect is by marriage. Likewise, Beauvoir also indicates, "the wife finds her dignity only in accepting her vassalage." (Beauvoir, 1949, p. 551) In this society, Bai Liusu was meant to be the *Other*.

Actually, without men's love, Bai was also afflicted with her struggling family condition. Beauvoir claims "the destiny that society traditionally offers women is marriage." (Beauvoir, 1949, p. 502) Bai is one case in point. When Fan sent her home and left Hong Kong, the whole family was in an invisible rage. "If a woman is duped by a man, she'd better die; if a woman wants to trick a man, she must be immoral; if she fails to trick him but is tricked by him, then she is extremely immoral…" It is because "marriage is the only way to be integrated into the group, and if they are "rejects," they are social waste." (Beauvoir, 1949, p. 504) Her family was ashamed of her, which imposed more pressure on her. When the second change was brought to her, Bai cried. At that moment, she knew she submitted to not Fan's charm or gentle conducts but to the pressure from her family which she defined as "the most suffering part." (张爱玲, 1943, p. 192) Finally, she won, but seemingly. She was totally subordinate to marriage and her husband in order to be received socially. She lost her self-consciousness and became the *Other*, despite of Fan's unfaith in marriage, for she had got received. What the marriage brought her was infinite sorrow.

Even in modern society, women cannot get rid of the historical fate. They are forced to get married when they are over a certain age. In conformity with the tradition, if a woman cannot marry a man when her age exceeds a limit, she will be regard as a "leftover". The situation has not been changed after about a century, and marriage is still the way for women to be respected.

2.2 Material Subordination

Besides, the material control leads to women's subordination. In Chang's novels, the women characters' condition relies on sexual relations and marriage. Out of selfish motive, their plans for the future revolve on the benefits they can gain in the relationship, and marriage is just an approach. About themselves, they have no spiritual pursuit and even lose their self-consciousness. The powerful patriarchy not only forces women to be received by marriage, subordinate mentally, but also restricts women's economy to win their material subordination. In Beauvoir's point of view, for some women, "there is an art to 'catching a husband': 'keeping' him is a profession."(Beauvoir, 1949, p. 572) A profession is the source of one's living foundation. The fact that some women treat marriage as an occupation reflects their dreadful dependence on men.

In *Love in the Fallen City*, Bai's first marriage was based on finance. In this marriage, she was abused by husband and his family, concealing that this kind of marriage is of no love but a trade of body and money. When Bai is in the courtship with Fan, what she thinks is to have economic security. When Mrs. Xu tried to comfort her, she said, "What can I do? I did not get well-educated; my shoulders and hands cannot carry any weight." (张爱玲, 1943, p. 165) Although life of luxury had impoverished her family, Bai did not want to degrade her family's fame by a demeaning job. There is an old saying in China, "ignorance is the virtue of a woman." Spurred by this kind of value, many women at that time cannot undertake a decent job due to its requirement on education. For some noble family, it was ashamed for the women to work outside, which completely confined the future of Bai Liusu. Without the economic dependence, especially when her money was occupied by her family, she had to count on the marriage and Fan Liuyuan was her only hope. She thought, "Fan is adorable, but her goal is for economic security, which he can absolutely guarantee." (张爱玲, 1943, p. 192) Bai planed and contrived, transacted her youth with a stable life, while achieving it made her brood over her sorrow. Without the dependence on finance, Bai became very passive. She had to be tolerant towards her husband's unfaith. It is foreseeable that there would be a sad finale to her seemingly comfortable life. The reality compelled her to consider marriage as a mean of livelihood, which determined her complete dependency on men. As Beauvoir indicates, "he is a citizen, a producer, before being a husband; she is above all, and often exclusively, a wife". (Beauvoir, 1949, p. 551) Bai Liusu considered herself as an inborn wife for she could not afford her own life. Marriage was a profession, especially in the age that there was not enough profession prepared for women. With no other choices, Bai Liusu became the captive of the economic marriage, became subordinate to man, became the *Other*.

In Chang's age, the women in her writings were not expected with self-independency and self-consciousness. In the capitalist country that Beauvoir existed and explored, women were still oppressed by the patriarchal culture. The situation was worse, for a woman who was in a society of the remaining evils of feudalism. Therefore, unlike Beauvoir's rational criticism, Chang's work is full of emotional tolerance. In her novels, Chang manifests sympathy and sadness for her characters. Meanwhile, as a woman, she knows the necessity of economic security for those women. Hence, Beauvoir and Chang both touch women's nerve— economic status. Since matriarchy was substituted by patriarchy, women's condition as the *Other* has been decided. The material subordination determines women's subordination in family and in society. In Beauvoir's opinion, economic independence conduces to women's social independence and motivates women to fight. However, in Chang's works, we cannot find a woman who has a clear evaluation of her social condition, let alone to combat with it. In other words, it is them who internalize patriarchal values and are willing to become the *Other*. It is the intrinsic reason why there is always a melancholy embracing Chang's novels.

3 Conclusions

Bai's tragedy was implicit, which was seemingly in accordance with her ideal — getting marriage with one who had fortunate. However, her marriage was more like a trade between youth and wealth. Although Chang didn't continue Bai's marriage life, we can imagine it. Controlled by her material desire, she withstood all her husband's unfaith, doing her best to keep up appearances in front of her snobbish family, in which she would gradually lose her self-consciousness, finally become the *Other*. If the fulfillment of an "enviable life" is in exchange for the consciousness of being the *Subject*, the consequence will be devastating.

Analyzing Eileen Chang's novel from the perspective of Beauvoir intensifies the historical profundity of Chang's works. Her understanding on female fates, without grand historical background, pays attention to trivial daily life but unveils women's inescapable tragedy. The powerful patriarchy governs women's thoughts, imposing man-dominance on them. However, nowadays, even after over half a century, the women are still being oppressed by patriarchal culture without being aware of it. In the information and the internet age, more and more so-called feminist network literature emerges on the internet which only takes advantages of feminism but with the core of patriarchy. These kinds of false feminism only degrade the hundreds of years' efforts on feminist and infuse subordination into women. Fortunately, with these feminist writers like Eileen Chang and Beauvoir, women were heard and started to change their situation. However, the achievement of the real liberation of female requires consistent efforts. The development of feminism is vibrating between two tough situations: on one hand, female's consciousness is being arousing; on the other hand, some women are still trying to be subordinate to men, materializing themselves. How to eliminate women's unconscious subordination and willingness to being the *Other* is still a question.

References

[1] Beauvoir, Simone de. Trans. Constance Borde, & Sheila Malovany-Chevallier. *The Second Sex*[M]. New York: Vintage Books, 2011.

[2] 方珏. 波伏娃存在主义的女性主义哲学思想渊源探析[J]. 山东社会科学，2008（12）：38-41.

[3] 黄晓东. 西方女性主义视野中的张爱玲小说创作[J]. 当代文坛，2010（3）.

[4] 贺燕蓉. 试析张爱玲作品中的女性意识[J]. 妇女研究论丛，2002（3）：45-49.

[5] 蒋书丽. 跨越时空的契合——张爱玲和波伏娃的女性意识比较[J]. 东北大学学报（社会科学版），2010（3）：278-282.

[6] 鲁建平. 凋零的“玫瑰”：张爱玲小说中的病态女性形象[J]. 现代文学，2010（11）：92-95.

[7] 刘岩. 西方文论关键词：第二性[J]. 外国文学，2016（4）： 88-99.

[8] 颜毓洁，崔莹. 试论波伏娃《第二性》中的女性意识[J]. 芒种，2014（22）：149-150.

[9] 张爱玲. 倾城之恋[M]. 北京：北京十月文艺出版社，2015.

[10]赵思奇. 论西蒙娜·德·波伏娃的“女性气质”——从《第二性》谈起[J]. 山东社会科学，2016（5）：51-55.

The Allegory of the Cave in *The Cement Garden*

熊安琪

摘　要：《水泥花园》是伊恩·麦克尤恩的第一部具有代表性的长篇小说，故事以锋利残忍的笔触刻画了一系列性心理畸变与生态异化衍生出的伦理悲剧情节，发行之后引起了广泛争议。本文以麦克尤恩的《水泥花园》为研究对象，通过柏拉图的洞穴理论，深入分析了二者相互对应之处，最终得出洞穴里囚徒们的生存状态正对应了杰克一家荒原般的地理环境与原生态的心理欲望这一结论。本文共分为六个部分，第一章包括文献综述以及对水泥花园和洞穴隐喻概念做简要介绍。第二章细致分析水泥花园里人物的心理状态。第三及第四章随着洞穴理论的深入，描写洞穴内外或家庭内外文明的侵入与拒斥。第五章探讨外界文明对杰克一家拯救的失败原因，最后对全文加以总结，提出自己的希冀。

关键词：《水泥花园》；洞穴隐喻；文明；原始；拯救

Abstract: *The Cement Garden* is Ian McEwan's first representative novel. The story depicts a series of ethical tragedies derived from sexual psychological distortion and ecological alienation with sharp and cruel lines. The publication of the book caused widespread controversy. This paper takes *The Cement Garden* as the research object, and through Plato's cave theory, aiming to analyze the mutual correspondence between *The Cement Garden* and cave metaphor. A further conclusion is drawn that the geographical isolation and psychological primitive state of the Jack family is a manifestation of the prisoners in the cave. This paper is divided into six parts. The first chapter includes literature review and a brief introduction to *The Cement Garden* and the concept of Plato's cave. The second chapter carefully analyzes the psychological state of the characters in the cement garden. The third and fourth parts describe the invasion and rejection of civilization inside and outside the cave or the world. The fifth chapter discusses the reasons for the failure of the external civilization to save the Jack family. Finally, it summarizes the full text and puts forward hopes.

Key words: *The Cement Garden*; Allegory of the Cave; Civilization; Original; Salvation

1　Introduction

The Cement Garden tells that the four children who were in the season of love are unconscious, indulged and eventually lost themselves after their parents have passed away. The Jack family lives in an old house that seems to be isolated from the world. They have few relatives and neighbors. "Our house had once stood in a street full of houses. Now stood on empty land where sitting nettles were growing round torn corrugated tin." (*The Cement Garden,* Shanghai Translation Press, 2012, p. 208, the citation from the book will no longer be marked) The harsh father died of a sudden heart attack while he repair his garden with cement, and the mother died shortly after her son's 15th birthday. To keep the family from being taken over by outsiders and being forced to separate, the children buried their mother's body in a large mental cabinet in the cellar, and lied about it as "a dog's body."

The earliest version of *The Cement Garden* was published in 1978, and foreign research on it began in the 1970s. In 1979, Tom Paulin pointed out that McEwan's attempt is to create a fable in a dead public society and a thriving personal world.(Tom Paulin, 1979) After the 21st century, foreign studies on *The Cement Garden* have become more comprehensive and deeper. People began to interpret *The Cement Garden* by comparing McEwan's other works. Domestic research on *The Cement Garden* lags behind. It was not until 2007 that the first Chinese translation by Feng Tao was published. In 2009, Xia Lingxiang published the article "*Ethical dislocation on the Island of Ice: An Interpretation of Cement Garden from Freud's Theory of Personality Structure*". (夏凌翔, 2009) The article analyzes Freud's id, ego and superego.

However, most scholars focused on discussing the ethical dislocations and the psychological distortions of adolescents in the book. In recent years, several articles have studied the ecological significance, including natural ecology, social ecology and spiritual ecology, but many unexplored areas are still waiting to be explored. For instance, *The Cement Garden* has not yet been interpreted from the perspective of Plato's cave. This paper takes a new perspective on the basis of previous studies. The author has linked the truth and moral education reflected in the cave theory with the character fate of the characters in the cement garden, and has reached new conclusions.

2 The allegory of the cave

The cave metaphor is put forward by Socrates' mouth when Plato discusses "the essence of an educated and uneducated person" in Volume 7 of *The Republic*.(Plato, 2002) Imagine human beings live in an underground cave since they were born, "And have their legs and necks chained so that they cannot move and can only see before them, being prevented by the chains from turning round their heads." Behind them is a low wall. Above and behind the low wall there are burning fires. Between the low walls and the fire, someone lifts the puppet up high and projects it in front of the prisoners. Since they haven't seen anything real, the prisoners would believe the authenticity of what they see. Until a prisoner walks out of the cave under the chance, he knows the true world after a short period of discomfort. He felt sorrow for his former self and all the prisoners in the cave. Therefore, he did not want to return to the cave and live in prisoners. As the book says, "He would rather endure any bitterness than living as prisoners again."

Plato's cave theory is intended to illustrate the following points: the feeling is not necessarily true; the process of finding truth is hard; the ignorance of man is terrible; the cultivation of virtue is necessary... the question of humanity and truth and the significance of education contained in it has great significance for modern society.

The four siblings are like the prisoners who live by a faint fire as they live in a small, dark house with no constraints. They never care about or question the authenticity of their world just like those prisoners in the cave. The door of the small dark house could have been pushed through easily, but they never tried. They won't tolerate the man who came back from the outside. For four siblings in the story, Derek is a completely outsider which brought only harm and threat. They have a strong vigilance against the outside world. In order to cover up the secrets of the parents' death, to prevent the house from being demolished and the younger siblings from being adopted, they built the mother's body in a metal cabinet. In their eyes, society is the enemy, the aggressor, rather than a place of friendship and mutual assistance. In this vast world and even the vast universe, they can only use each others' body temperature to warm each other. There, the taboo of moral ethics has long been melted by the darkness. In the cave only lighted by fire, day after day, what are the prisoners alive for? If people give up thinking about the meaning of life, then there is no meaning in living.

Due to remote geographical location, deserted relationships and parents' premature death, children's sexual psychology has undergone deafening changes. Masturbation, incest, heterosexuality, transvestites and severe Oedipus complexes are all derivatives of the lack of social conventions and ethical education, just as the ignorant prisoners in the cave. The island-like house is just the cave in Plato's mouth. There is no moral chains in the house, but only the original emotional chains that are distorted burning and colliding. In an interview, Ian McEwan said frankly, "I found myself wanting to describe a child in a closed world without any power constraints." Whether it was a prisoner or Jack and his brothers and sisters, they were all to be Bound willingly. Led by their own original desire, they are always vigilant and keeping distance from the external civilization represented by Julie's boyfriend Derek, who would be talked about later.

3 The original desire like chains to the persons in the house

At the beginning of human survival, inbreeding was normalcy. Regardless of Zeus and Hera in Greek mythology, or the Nu Wa and Fuxi in Chinese legends, incest phenomenon exists for a very long time, and it is a prominent feature in human society's primitive culture. Morris, a human and animal behaviorist, believes that the production of incest taboos is due to biological reasons, rather than a restrictive measure of early human culture. With the development of human civilization and scientific knowledge, incest has gradually become a taboo, and it is firmly resisted by the social moral and ethical rules. This taboo is the restriction of modern civil society on instinct and unconscious desire. (Zhang Helong, 2003, p. 40-46)

In the whole novel, Jack's entire chaotic youth period are accompanied by the sprouting of sexual consciousness and the anomaly of sexual psychology. Jack's face was devastated by acne. He abandoned all the rituals of personal hygiene. "I no longer washed my face or hair or cut my nails or took baths. I gave up brushing my teeth." (207) Even so, he can gaze at himself in the mirror for an hour. He is narcissistic, melancholic, insane, and often unable to explain his behavior himself; he is indifferent, selfish and jealous. Step by step, he walks to the misunderstanding of life and sex. At the beginning of the story, they played a game: "I" and my sister Julie played the role of scientists, stripping Sue's (the little sister) clothes and examined her body as a space specimen. (197-198) This game provokes "me" a strong libido impulse and fantasy. After the first taste of the pleasure brought by masturbation, Jack got out of hand. However, the gentle and loving mother did not play a correct guiding role while realizing Jack's behavior. She said to Jack, hesitatingly, "Every time you do that, you lose the blood of two pints." From Freud's point of view, child's sexual desire is a kind of sleepy factor. It can be made public and cause catastrophic results because of adult's interference and obstruction. In the article, in such a closed family where parents are not "strictly disciplined", his (Jack) sexual consciousness is completely free from the intrusion and interference of social consciousness. Moral and behavioral norms are outside his world. His desires and impulses cannot accept the discipline and integration from the outside. Thus, he is in a spontaneous and dangerous primitive state at any time. (Zhang Helong, 2003, p. 40-46) And eventually Jack had an incestuous act with her sister Julie.

The youngest brother, Tom, is no different from the prisoner in the cave. He is afraid of communicating with the outside world. In a certain period of time, he wants to be a girl, dresses like a girl and does what girls do. Later, he even lingered on a huge copper crib and became a veritable baby doll under the care of Julie who play the role of mother. He is unwilling to grow up and ignores whatever changes in the outside world and uses transvestites and heterosexuals to wrap up his original desires. All he wants to do is to return to his fantasy state of protection and harmlessness.

4 Indifference and escape of love like the shadows in the cave

In the Oxford Advanced English-Chinese Dictionary, the first interpretation of the word love is a strong feeling of deep affection for somebody/something, especially a member of your family or a friend. It can be say that love is one of human's most basic emotions, which accompany and instruct people to choose how to live. Love has been postulated to be a function to keep human beings together against menaces and to facilitate the continuation of the species. (Helen Fisher, 2004) Life without love will be filled with violence and distortion, and eventually will go to destruction. In *The Cement Garden*, the indifference and escape of the Jack family to love is consistent with the prisoners' fear of the sun. Because the prisoners have never seen the sun, the fragile fire has become their most trusted friend. The four children did not feel normal love and warmth from beginning to end, so they could not understand the meaning of love.

In the book, the response of the four brothers and sisters to the death of their mother is particularly true and shocking. In the struggling process of Tom, "Mother toppled sideways in a frightening, wooden sort of way, her head struck the bedside table and the clock and the glass of water crashed to the floor. Her head remained waged between the bed and the table, and now one hand was visible by the pillow." (242) Jack didn't know whether he should push the corpse into an upright position, but he finally gave up and ran out of the room. Facing the death of mother, for Jack, The joy of freedom is more than the pain of the loss. He said, "When mother died, beneath my strongest feelings was a sense of adventure and freedom..." Afterwards, when the mother's body began to emit rotten odors, he explained to Derek that it was a dog's body. This illogical feeling and behavior Proves not only Jack's poor love for his mother but the selfishness of human nature. What most tragic is that they never try to modify their love and hate in a normal pattern, because they had never realize that their emotions is unusual.

5 The person who breaks the chain and walks out of the cave

In the novel, Julie's boyfriend, Derek, is clearly "the prisoner out of the cave" and "the moralized self". He lived with his parents, getting along well with his father like friends. His mother was strict with him and he had to wash his hands before even drinking tea. For Jack, his father had no end of silence but to sneer at his acne. Derek's instinctive desire is under the strict monitoring of adult society, and the environment does not allow him to make unethical behavior. In the process of associating with Julie, he had a keen interest in this wilderness-like family and wanted to integrate and possess. For Jack and Julie, they rapidly got used to play the role of father and mother after the death of their parents, but Derek's appearance broke the delicate balance of this family. They thought the obtrusion of Derek would threat the stable and harmonious world. Therefore, Drake's appearance finally became one of the decisive factors in accelerating the incestuous relationship between the Jack and Julie. At the end of the novel, after seeing the incest between Jack and Julie, Derek said, "It's sick... he is your brother." (322) The resentment led him to open the tin box in the cellar and told the secret of this family to the outside world. The story ends in the blue light twinkling on the wall and the arrive of the police.

It is not difficult for us to find the correspondence between the allegory of the cave and Freud's theory. In Freud's "tripartite personality structure" theory, the id is the instinct; the ego is the realized instinct; and the super-ego is the moralized self. The battle between the three is endless. The various instinctive impulses of id that do not conform to the social patterns are suppressed by the ego under the guidance of the super-ego. This creates contradictions between repressing oneself and resisting oneself. Therefore, these instinctive impulses must be manifested in the unconscious field through unconscious spiritual processes. (Freud, 1987, preface)The prisoner who walks out of the cave experienced a transition from id, self, and superego after the journey of seeking truth. When he returned to the cave again and tried to persuade the remaining prisoners into the outside world—the civilized society, the difficulties and injuries he would face are unpredictable.

6 Invasion and Rejection of Civilization

It is not difficult to infer that the adult (outside) world will enter this wilderness-like place in an irresistible manner. All obscenity and distortion, mistakes and confusion, naivety and innocence will be domesticated and meet the standards of the so-called civilized world. It can be seen that under the influence of modernity, it is an inevitable trend for closed cave to open up. Caverns under modernity have new dimensions and new changes. In order to achieve the closed society opening to the outside world and to avoid conflicts and moral vacuums, we need both "returning to the roots" and "opening new ones." (Zhao Sijun, 2016) Freud said that humans created civilization through sublimation. Nowadays, civilization are synonymous with city, convention, order, technology, and so on. With the development of civilization, the alienation of ecology, spiritual alienation, and the alienation of human relations are like accessories, and the severity is increasingly highlighted. There are many reasons that cause modern people to feel uneasy, but the fundamental reason is the incompatibility between human nature and the civilization he created

7 Failure of salvation and its causes

The appearance of Drake from the outside world broke the isolation of the Jack family and gave them an opportunity to go to normal life. But it is clear that Jack and Julie refused with fierce action. The ways and motivations of their rejection have been mentioned above, so I won't go into details here.

In my opinion, there are three reasons for failure. First of all, Derek's "invasion" is not deep. He only asks things with a curious eye, and obviously does not pay much attention to the abnormality of Julie's family. For example, under Jack's lie that "the smell is from a dog body", although he knows the truth, he pretends that he didn't know and even helps to fill the cracks. Second, unlike the prisoner who escaped from the cave and wanted to save other prisoners, Derek had his own desire for power. Before he knew Julie, his life was under the strict constraints of social rules, and he could never let go of his desires in outside world. And in the house without parents, if he can marry Julie, then he has control over not only the house but also everyone. Although the family is very strange, the yearning for power still makes Derek want to join in. He is so eager to become a leader and do whatever he wants. The last point is also very important, that is, the psychology of Julie and Jack and their younger siblings have been severely distorted and cannot be recovered. At the end of the story, the reveals of secret did not cause panic among the four children. Instead, they talked about the past with a terrible calm. They went into emotional at the beginning and psychological misunderstandings and eventually failed to get out.

8 Conclusions

In my point of view, *The Cement Garden* is just like the photocopy of Plato's cave. The lucky one will return to the cave. Convinced or threatened, the entrance door will eventually be opened. The prisoners will be exposed to the sunlight, facing an uncertain fate in the future. Because the power of civilization is strong. Civilization can introspect itself but prisoners in the cave will not. The closed environment and the pitiful curiosity made them lack the introspective chips. They don't want to understand the changes in their life even the better changes, and they believe what they have being taught in an extreme way. However, stagnation leads to the ruin. Although the development processes of civilization is accompanied by a series of incredible side effects, we also cannot deny that it has something really beautiful and meaningful.

Linking the allegory of the cave to explore the practical significance of the *The Cement Garden*, we can conclude that it is inadvisable that those prisoners who do not want to give up the chains are willing to be distorted and indulged in illusions by the false choices. And so is the practice of Derek, who is in a civilized world but selfish and desperate to have power. The indifference and retreat to the surrounding environment and interpersonal communication is not the beginning of the human's emotional tendency to survive but trust and mutual assistance. McEwan's *The Cement Garden* sounds the alarm for the modern society that is inundated with desires, ethical confusion and moral loss. Meanwhile, education always plays an important role in the replacement of each generation, and we could never ignore and underestimate it.

References

[1] David Malcolm. *Understanding Ian McEwan*[M]. Columbia: University of South Carolina Press, 2002.

[2] Helen Fisher. Why We Love: the nature and chemistry of romantic love[J]. *New York Review of Books*, 2004.

[3] Plato. translated by Guo Binhe and Zhang Zhuming, *Utopia* [M]. Beijing Commercial Press, 2002.

[4] Tom Paulin. Abandoned Prefabs: Recent Fiction[J]. *Encounter,* 1979（1）：49-50.

[5] Zhao Sijun. Restitution and Development of Moral Education: The Modern Thinking of Plato's Cave Theory[J]. Nanjing University, 2016.

[6] 刘春芳.《水泥花园》中的“水泥花园”意象研究[J]. 天津大学学报，2013（1）：72-76.

[7] 王悦，徐靖焱. 麦克尤恩《水泥花园》的不可靠叙述[J]. 三峡论坛，2011（3）：21-25.

[8] 夏凌翔. 水泥荒岛上的伦理错位——从弗洛伊德的人格结构理论解读《水泥花园》[J]. 新西部，2009（8）：135-138.

[9] 张和龙. 成长的迷误——评麦克尤恩的长篇小说《水泥花园》[J]. 当代外国文学，2003（4）：40-46.

The Dilemmas of Fang Hung-chien in *Fortress Besieged*: A Prototypical Case in Early 20th Century

余 杨

摘　要：在《围城》一书中，钱钟书先生运用辛辣的讽刺和深邃的洞察力描述了几个非主流知识分子的经历。他着力于刻画主人公方鸿渐的人生，表现那个年代的知识分子在道德与人格方面的弱点，揭露了急剧的现代化冲击所造成的社会扭曲，也揭示了在中西方文化相碰撞融合的背景下中国社会的特征。本篇论文试图通过介绍和分析方鸿渐的人生经历，包括家庭、学业、职业以及爱情与婚姻四个方面，展现方鸿渐作为一个非主流知识分子代表所遭遇的人生困境。

关键词：家庭；学业与职业；爱情与婚姻；人生困境

Abstract: In *Fortress Besieged*, Ch'ien Chung-shu makes use of biting satire and deep insight to depict the experiences of several non-mainstream intellectuals. Paying much attention to the life of Fang Hung-chien, the main character in this novel, the author presents the weakness of intellectuals in morality and personality, revealing the distorted society caused by the shock of modernity and demonstrating social characteristics under the mixed impact of the Chinese and Western culture. And in this paper, it seeks to give a introduction and analysis of Fang Hung-chien's life experiences, including family, study and career and love and marriage, in order to figure out the life dilemmas of Fang Hung-chien shown in this novel.

Key words: Family；Study and career；Love and marriage；Life dilemma

1　Introduction

Written by Ch'ien Chung-shu, *Fortress Besieged* is a Chinese satiric novel depicting the lives of several Chinese intellectuals and Chinese society in the early Anti-Japanese War. Set between the 1920s to 1940s it follows the misadventures of Fang Hung-chien, the hero of this novel. Fang Hung-chien was the son of a country gentleman. A marriage had been arranged for him, but his fiancée died during the period of his university life before he could see her. His father-in-law was so touched by his letter of condolence that the bank owner subsidized him to study aboard. However, Fang Hung-chien went to Europe where he studied at several universities without pursuing a degree. After being pressured by his family, he bought a fake degree of a imaginary university, Carleton University, from an American Irishman when he had run out of money and must return home to China. The beginning of the novel was set on the boat home, where Fang met Miss Pao and was cheated by her. At the same time, he met his schoolmate, Su Wen-wan. After arriving in Shanghai, Fang Hung-chien lived in the Chous' house and began to work in the Golden Touch Bank operated by his father-in-law, Chou Hou-ch'ing. During this period, Fang Hung-chien won the favour of Su

Wen-wan while falling in love with Su's cousin, T'ang Hsiao-fu, at the first sight. He was busy with dealing with the two ladies at that time. Besides, he met Chao Hsin-mei, a suitor of Su's. Shortly afterwards, the complicated relationship among Fang Hung-chien, Su Wen-wan and T'ang Hsiao-fu was put to an end. Su Wen-wan finally married Ts'ao Yüan-lang, a poet. Chao Hsin-mei eventually knew Fang Hung-chien was not his rival in love. Since then, Fang Hung-chien and Chao Hsin-mei became friends. Gradually, Fang Hung-chien no longer got along well with his former parents-in-law, the Chous and even was driven out of the Chous' house and the Golden Touch Bank. As the Anti-Japanese War broke out, the Fangs escaped from hometown to the concession of Shanghai. Through the recommendation of Chao Hsin-mei, Fang Hung-chien decided to go to the inland San Lü University to work as a teacher together with Chao Hsin-mei, Sun Jou-chia, Li Mei-t'ing and Ku Er-chien. At San Lü University, Fang Hung-chien was enmeshed in the complicated interpersonal relationship and encountered many setbacks. Accidentally, he was engaged to Miss Sun Jou-chia. Before long, Fang Hung-chien and Sun Jou-chia left San Lü University and returned to Shanghai. With the help of Chao Hsin-mei, Fang Hung-chien married Sun Jou-chia and worked at a local newspaper. After their marriage, the contradictions erupted between the new couple, between Fang Hung-chien and the Fangs and between Fang Hung-chien and Sun's aunt and became more acute. Fang Hung-chien resigned from the newspaper and wanted to go to Chongqing, which led to a bitter quarrel between the couple. The novel ended with his wife leaving him alone, while he listened to a clock chiming. Form the brief description of storyline above, it can be seen that the novel is a humorous tale with attraction.

Ch'ien Chung-shu set out to write this novel while he and his wife Yang Chiang were living in Shanghai during the Japanese occupation. According to Yang Chiang, the successful production of several of her plays inspired Ch'ien to write a full-length novel. Many of the characters and much of the plot are taken from the experiences of Qian and Yang abroad and in China. In *Ch'ien Chung-shu and His "Fortress Besieged"*, Yang Chiang (1986, p. 5) wrote, "Chung-shu culled his materials from times, places and social classes familiar to him, but all the characters and plots that form his story are fictional. Some characters may have resonance with someone real, but what happens to them is completely imaginary. Some plot lines may appear authentic, but then the characters are pure fabrication."As the only full-length long novel of Ch'ien Chung-shu, it has won great popularity and high praise since its first publication in 1937. Wu Mi comments it as the "the reflection of the subsistence of the whole human beings". Many critics even call it "The New Scholars". Even today, the book is still popular and of great importance in Chinese literature.

Actually, one of the reasons to explain the popularity and status of the book is that the book has profound significance on modern society as the reflection of life dilemmas. Although its title "Fortress Besieged" derives from the French proverb about marriage, the book is not restricted to a love story. Actually, it is more like an encyclopedia about human life, which shows a variety of paradoxes and dilemmas in one's life through presenting the life experiences of Fang Hung-chien. Nathan K. Mao (1979: preface 24), one of the translators of the English version of *Fortress Besieged*, writes in the translator's preface and says that "*Fortress Besieged* is a book of many thing. It makes us laugh at its dense populace of every social type imaginable. But beyond the mirth and liveliness,

Ch'ien Chung-shu also want us to see the follies, vices, and stupidities of men everywhere; and when we do, the laughter that has been evoked is abruptly silenced. The surface of the book is comic, but at its core we find a relentless satire of twentieth-century Chinese intellectuals, a sobering commentary on the true nature of courtship and marriage, and the sympathetic portrayal of one man, in whom we find a little bit of each of us." In other words, the book is a mirror in which we can see the shadows of our own lives. Form Fang Hung-chien's life experiences including family, study, career, love and marriage, we can find out the common dilemmas faced by modern people.

2 Life Dilemmas of Fang Hung-chien

As mentioned before, the book does not only talks about marriage, but also talks about multifaceted respects of life. The title of the book actually refers to the whole life of Fang Hung-chien. In other words, the whole life of Fang Hung-chien is a besieged city, and Fang Hung-chien is the one who is trapped in it and cannot find his way out. Form Fang Hung-chien's life in the book, we can see the shadows of real life and timeless puzzles faced by the ancients and the moderns, to which we are still endeavoring to search for the keys.

2.1 Family

Fang Hung-chien came from a county located at the south of the Yangtze where "Nine out of ten of the emigrants from this district living in big cities were now either blacksmith, bean-curb makers, or sedan chair carriers. The most famous indigenous crafts were clay dolls; and for young men entering college, civil engineering was the popular discipline. The intractability of iron, the insipidity of bean curb, the narrowness of sedan chairs, and in addition, the smell of earth could be called the local traits; even those who became rich or high officials lacked polish."(8-9) From the three words, "Intractability""insipidity"and "narrowness", the folk climate of Fang Hung-chien's hometown can be clearly seen. And the characteristics of the local people there were also easy to know. Besides, Fang Tun-weng, father of Fang Hung-chien, was a prominent local squire who had passed the second-degree examination under Manchu rule. The identity and education of his father indicates that Fang Tun-Weng was a feudal patriarch whose thoughts were still rooted in the past feudalism. It was in this social environment and against this family background that the compliant and weak character of Fang Hung-chien had formed. And Fang Hung-chien's character, nurtured in such a traditional patriarchal family with his father as the unchallengeable authority, contributed a lot to trapping himself in his own besieged city.

He was surrendered to the authority of his father by unwillingly foregoing his own choice. As a feudal patriarch usually did, Fang Tun-weng arranged Fang Hung-chien's first marriage. Fang Hung-chien's father-in-law, was a manager of a small bank opened by himself together with his fellow villagers. And his fiancée was a girl who didn't even finish her high education. As an educated man who had entered university, Fang Hung-chien should have resisted this engagement, but his character and family prevented him from following his heart. Fang Hung-chien accepted the marriage at the very beginning. He didn't have the awareness of freedom of love and marriage. The most courageous thing he did was just writing a home letter to ask for release from the engagement by making excuse of sickness, which was instantly seen through by his father and scorned by him mercilessly. Although the arranged engagement finally ended up with the death of his fiancée, Fang Hung-chien still stuck in the besieged city built by his family.

He was sandwiched between his original traditional family and his newly-built modern household. Another specific example of Fang Hung-chien's life dilemma in terms of family can be found after Fang Hung-chien's marriage with Sun Jou-chia. There was no firm foundation in the marriage between Fang Hung-chien and Sun Jou-chia. Their conjugal relationship was rather weak and feeble. Under such circumstance, the Fangs did a lot of things either intentionally or unintentionally, either voluntarily or involuntarily, which indeed did harm to the relationship between the new couple instead of making efforts to help them better their marriage. When Sun Jou-chia first came to visit the Fangs, The two sisters-in-law of Jou-chia were not polite. Before they met Sun Jou-chia, the younger sister-in-law said to the elder one that "Sister, you sure are good-natured! Who does Sun Jou-chia think she is, putting on those smelly airs and expecting us to go meet her! I certainly won't go!" (305) And the reply from the elder one is that "She wouldn't come, because she can't. My guess is she's about to give birth and wouldn't dare show her face at her in-law's home."(305) From the simple dialogue, the hostility of the two sisters-in-law to Jou-chia was clear. And when Jou-chia came to the Fangs for the first time, the Fangs exposed their feudal ideas to the new couple, which didn't match the identity and thoughts of new couple. Fang Hung-chien used to study aboard and Sun Jou-chia was a college graduate, so their minds were much more modern than ordinary people. But when they came to the Fangs as a newly-wed couple for the first time, they were asked to conduct a series of feudal obligations' performance. This, on the one hand, was not acceptable to Fang Hung-chien, and on the other hand, he had to defend it for his family. Therefore, "When it was time for them to pay respects, a red carpet was spread before the sacrificial table, obviously intended for Hung-chien and his wife to kneel down before the souls of the Fangs' departed ancestors, Jou-chia stepped stiffly onto the carpet without showing the least intention of kneeling down. Hung-chien, together with Jou-chia, bowed three times and was done. "(310) However, when Sun Jou-chia complained about the Fangs especially Fang Tun-Weng' talking to Sun Jou-chia that she should take the responsibility of taking care of house rather than go to work, Fang Hung-chien could not help defending his father by saying that " There's some sense to what he says."(312)

From those details above, it can be seen that the Fangs is one of Fang Hung-chien's life dilemmas. For his whole life, he was deeply affected by his family. Fang Hung-chien didn't want an arranged marriage, but he still followed his father's willing. Fang Hung-chien did not want to get a diploma from aboard, but he had to buy a fake one under the pressure of his father. And Fang Hung-chien wanted to have a peaceful life together with Jou-chia, but his family became one of the main factors which led to their unhappy marriage. Besides, the Fangs deeply affected his character, which eventually led to a besieged city of his whole life.

2.2 Study and Career

The dilemma of his academic pursuit is that Fang Hung-chien questioned the worth of a diploma produced by a foreign university, however, he was pressured and compelled to acquire one to prove his own worth and satisfy his parents' vainglory. At university, Fang Hung-chien was a worthless sort, who had switched his major from sociology to philosophy before finally settling down as a student of Chinese literature major. At that time, it was popular for someone majoring in Chinese literature to go aboard to acquire a foreign trademark so that the value of Chinese literature major can be proved and even improved. So, financed by his father-in law, Fang Hung-chien had gone to study abroad in Europe. However, during his stay in Europe, Fang Hung-chien did not spend his time on study or acquire a diploma. He even changed his universities for three times. When it came to returning home, he was urged by his father and father-in-law to obtain a Ph.D. At this time, "Finding himself pressured on both sides, Fang Hung-chien finally realized the importance of a foreign diploma. This diploma, it seemed, would function the same as Adam and Eve's figleaf. It could hide a person's shame and wrap up his disgrace. This tiny square of paper could cover his shallowness, ignorance, and stupidity. Without it, it was as if he were spiritually stark naked and had nothing to bundle up in."(12) Without any other ways to help himself out of this awkward situation, Fang Hung-chien finally had to buy a fake one. y Fang Hung-chien was haunted by the academic dilemma. On the one hand, he knew it was ridiculous for a student of Chinese literature major to study abroad. But the current fashion was for a Chinese literature student to obtain a foreign trademark to improve one's worth. On the other hand, Fang Hung-chien looked down upon the worship of diploma in the society and was unwilling to obtain one, but he had to obtain a Ph.D. to show his ability and achievement while studying abroad to his father and father-in-law and most importantly, to satisfy their vanity. Fang Hung-chien did experience the study without making important gains from it. He attended university, but only for a diploma. He studied abroad, but just for killing time. He did not intend to obtain a diploma, but finally bought one. For the whole process of his study experience, there was no goal or positive motivation for his study. After he bought a fake diploma for covering his "shame", the diploma had caused a series of troubles for him. To some extent, this fake diploma actually incurred Fang Hung-chien's career dilemma.

He was plunged into the dilemma of career by virtue of his inner contradiction evoked between his sense of righteousness and the relentless reality, between his great aspiration and his lack of perseverance and stamina. Fang Hung-chien never imagined that the fake diploma would hinder his career and drag him into a dilemma. Although Fang Hung-chien is a person of weakness and compliance, he was still an intellectual with sense of righteousness and conscience. When he had to find a job after returning Shanghai, he did not use the fake diploma to help himself find a job, just as what he had said when he persuaded himself to buy the fake thing. At that time, Fang Hung-chien thought that "Every dutiful son and worthy son-in-law should seek to please his elders by bringing glory to the family. In any case, when later it came time for him to look for a job, he would never include this degree in his resumé"(14). And even though he was recommended by Chao Hsin-mei to Kao Sung-nien, the president of San Lü University as an intellectual with a Ph.D. for a job, he still did not attach his fake degree when he sent his resumé to Kao Sung-nien. And when he knew he was degraded as an associate professor for not having a Ph.D., he even felt released and relaxed, feeling that “his demotion to associate professor was already a blessing from above”(195-196).

However, the society did not appreciate intellectuals with righteousness like Fang Hung-chien, and he was sidelined by Han Hsüeh-yü, who used the same fake diploma from Carleton University to be the director of History Department. Finally, Fang Hung-chien had to leave San Lü University for Shanghai to find a job. In this period, Fang Hung-chien found a job in a local newspaper with the help of Chan Hsin-mei. But, he soon decided to give up the present job to go to Chongqing to find better job opportunities. All these experiences of Fang Hung-chien showed that he was a contradictory person. He bought a fake diploma, but he did not make use of it for career out of righteousness. He had job, but he always want a better one without making efforts. From Golden Touch Bank to San Lü University, San Lü University to Sino-American News Agency and even from Shanghai to Chongqing. Fang Hung-chien could never settle down. His contradictory idea and weak character made him always stuck in the dilemma of career, and he always entered different besieged cities of career one after another. Even his final hope of career in Chongqing was just like a single spark in a total darkness. The hope Fang Hung-chien saw in his career was the faint light a weak person seeking warmth in the cold darkness saw on the road ahead.

2.3 Love and Marriage

“Marriage is Fortress Besieged” is what the title directly refers to. Almost all the characters in the novel are involved in the topic, marriage. In the pursuit of love, Fang Hung-chien’s inner world is the most complicated one. For his pure feeling, Fang Hung-chien seems to want a girl who is neither babe in the wood nor totally worldly exterior in the world. For choosing a wife, he seems to be extremely particular. However, Fang Hung-chien’s reason always cannot control over his feelings. In most cases, Fang Hung-chien just follows his own feelings blindly. In addition, he does not know what his real pursuit exactly is. Undoubtedly in consequence, Fang Hung-chien catches dilemma in his love, and eventually was stuck in the fortress besieged of marriage. All of these can be demonstrated through the relationships between Fang Hung-chien and the five women appeared in his life.

The first important woman for Fang Hung-chien was his deceased fiancée, Miss Chou. Because of this woman, Fang Hung-chien encountered a dilemma between modern sense and traditional obligation. This woman, arranged by Fang Hung-chien’s father, was a more traditional one compared with the other four women. Miss Chou did not finish her high school study and stayed at home to learn housekeeping once engaged with Fang Hung-chien. For an educated man who had been affected by new ideas of love like Fang Hung-chien, Miss Chou was obviously not a good match. However, what he did was just completely subjected to the reality after a futile protestation of pretending being sick. But for Miss Chou died in an early age, Fang Hung-chien might have married her. Form this, it could be seen that Fang Hung-chien actually did not have strong idea about his marriage and love.

The next woman entered in Fang Hung-chien’s world was Miss Pao. It was in this relationship between Fang Hung-chien and Miss Pao, Fang Hung-chien fell into the dilemma between sense and sensibility. Miss Pao was an attractive woman for men. “She was wearing only a scarlet top and navy blue, skintight shorts; her red toenails showed through her white, open-toed shoes…When men students saw Miss Pao, they burned with lewd desire, and found some relief by endlessly cracking jokes behind her back. Some called her a charcuterie--a shop selling cooked meat--because only such a shop would have so much warm-colored flesh naked."(7). From the description, Miss Pao was so attractive to male students that Fang Hung-chien also chased her. One the one hand, the relationship with Miss Pao was so casual that Fang Hung-chien was unwilling to say love to Miss Pao because he thought that she was an immodest woman. One the other hand, he could not help being physically attracted by her out of lust. When he knew that Miss Pao just made used of him, he could only comfort himself that he hadn't suffer any loss and may even have had the better of it. Actually, Fang Hung-chien knew that it was not the case. in fact, he felt "but disappointment, frustrated lust, and wounded pride all refused to settle down, like the doll which always rights itself when over and even wobbles about more vigorously."(23). This showed the blindness of love driven by lust and the weakness of his character. And for lust, Fang Hung-chien made himself fall into a mental besieged city. He could not help being disappointed and suffering from this and desperately tried to comforted himself at the same time. This relationship with Miss Pao actually opened the love dilemma of Fang Hung-chien.

The third one is Su Wen-wan, a qualified girlfriend in the eye of Fang Hung-chien. On this occasion, Fang Hung-chien was in the dilemma between his eagerness for company and his lack of commitment to love and sense of responsibility for love. After being abandoned by Miss Pao, Fang Hung-chien chose Su Wen-wan to accompany him before his returning to Shanghai from aboard. Miss Su liked Fang Hung-chien because he is the best choice around her. In the next several days on aboard, he was intimate with her while claiming in his heart that they two were just like two parallel lines. When departing, he was cheered up by the red cheeks of Miss Su. After returning to Shanghai, he could not help going to see her and kissed her under the moonlight. At the same time, he did not wanted to give a promise to Su Wen-wan and avoided her. Finally, their relationship was out of control because his intimate behaviour with Miss Su made Miss Su think that he would marry her. In the end, he walked into another a besieged city of love. Out of loneliness, he could not helping to approaching Miss Su, but he also wanted avoid her likeness because he did not love her.

The fourth one was the most pure lover cherished by Fang Hung-chien. This love experience brought about his dilemma in a triangle relationship. T'ang Hsiao-fu was Su Wen-wan's cousin. Miss T'ang left Fang Hung-chien a good impression at the first sight and he soon fell in love with her deeply. Meanwhile, he did not made clear with Miss Su and finally formed a triangle relationship among the three people. When he was determined to confess to Miss Su and make a proposal to Miss T'ang, Miss Su had spoken ill of him to Miss T'ang. Suddenly, the relationship between Fang Hung-chien and T'ang Hsiao-fu ended with great pain left for Fang Hung-chien. In this relationship, Fang Hung-chien chased Miss T'ang on the one hand, and maintained intimate relationship with Miss Su on the other hand. He could not deal with the complicated triangle relationship promptly and opportunely and suffered a lot from it. The ending of relationship with T'ang Hsiao-fu not only broke his heart, but also became the fuse of his breaking with the Chous.

The last woman and the most important one in Fang Hung-chien's life was Sun Jou-chia, his wife. The marriage with Sun Jou-chia made Fang Hung-chien suffer a lot from the dilemma of marriage without true love which eventually led him to the suffocating and inescapable fortress besieged. Entering the fortress besieged with Sun Jou-chia was unexpected to Fang Hung-chien. He appreciated Sun Jou-chia with little romantic sentiments and emotions, but the feelings were far from love. He thought that the relationship between him and her was just a joke form Chao Hsin-mei. However, when he thought he had seen through love and cooled his heart, he fell into the trap made by Sun Jou-chia and married her. Although he had feelings to Sun Jou-chia, it was not enough to support him to go through the difficulties in marriage and life with her. Fang Hung-chien wanted real love, but chose a ordinary lover without true love for her. Fang hung-chien wanted to experience marriage, but he is not mentally strong enough to bear it. Therefore, his marriage between Sun Jou-chia became a totally fortress besieged and the couple quarreled a lot and even fought soon after their marriage.

As a matter of fact, the fortress besieged not only refers to the marriage between Fang Hung-chien and Sun Jou-chia, it is just a part of it. Throughout the whole love experiences of Fang Hung-chien's, he is in fortress besieged, entering and going out one after another. The fortress of marriage run out of his energy of fighting his way out, and he had to stay in it desperately. All of these was because of Fang Hung-chien's mishandling of his feelings. Whether it be love or marriage, it cannot confine oneself both physically and mentally. It is that people involved in it has the ability to confine themselves. Fang Hung-chien's weakness and indifference made himself receive the engagement arranged by his father. His desire for lust pushed him to have a short relationship with Miss Pao. His indecision led to his intimate and ambiguous relationship with Su Wen-wan. His cowardice made him miss T'ang Hsiao-fu. His immature decision and impulsion resulted in the fortress besieged of his marriage.

3 Reasons for Fang Hung-chien's Dilemmas

From the analysis above we can see that the whole life of Fang Hung-chien is exactly a besieged city. And almost all respects of his life are trapped in it. However, all the life dilemmas of Fang Hung-chien are not groundless. There are complicated reasons for emergence of his life dilemmas. Among those reasons, his internal character and the external social environment are the main ones.

3.1 Micro Reason：Internal Character

Born in a prototypically feudal family, Fang Hung-chien did not have many opportunities to make decisions on his own during his growth. Having a father who had passed the the second-degree examination under Manchu rule, he got accustomed to relying on his family to make decisions for him, which eventually led to the weakness and indecision in Fang Hung-chien's character. Once there was no one for him to rely on, his life would be a mess. What's more, coming from a feudal family and having received modern education, he became contradictory in character as well. Fang Hung-chien's family background and life experiences shaped his character. All of the characteristics in his character constitute as a significant factor that finally leads to his life dilemmas. It could be easily found that each dilemma Fang Hung-chien suffered in his life is closely related to and deeply affected by his character.

3.2 Macro Reason: External Social Environment

Karl Marx (1888: 2) used to express that idea that "the essence of man is no abstraction inherent in each single individual. In its reality it is the ensemble of the social relations." People always live under specific social background, so social environment always has a profound impact on people in society. Fang Hung-chien's life dilemmas have its profound social reasons.

The novel was set between 1937 to 1939, a period of political instability. There were both domestic trouble and foreign invasion under the rule of the Kuomintang. During the period of war, Shanghai was like a fortress besieged in which everyone was trapped. Under this situation, Fang Hung-chien could nor find a good job or plan for his future, so he had to temporarily work at the Golden Touch Bank operated by his father-in-law. However, unstable political situation also affected interpersonal relationship. The relationship between Fang Hung-chien and the Chous soured, which compelled Fang Hung-chien to leave Shanghai for San Lü University located at inner land to work as a teacher, which was the first turning point in Fang Hung-chien's career. But,higher education was in darkness and corruption in Kuomintang-controlled areas in the early Anti-Japanese War. Fang Hung-chien could not find his future and was sidelined by those hypocritical colleagues and superiors at San Lü University. When Fang Hung-chien left San Lü University and went back to Shanghai and found a job at a local newspaper, the political situation in Shanghai worsened rapidly and "Political terrorists incidents occurred nearly every day. Men of good will were so depressed that, like the transportation lines in major Western cities, they slowly began to go underground"(316; ch.9). Fang Hung-chien resigned from the local newspaper because Shanghai was on the point of falling into enemy hands. Therefore, Fang Hung-chien wanted to leave Shanghai for Chongqing to seek better job opportunities at the end of the novel. In short, the political situation actually was the main factor which brought career dilemmas one after another to Fang Hung-chien.

Meanwhile, the war seriously hindered the normal development of economy, further worsening Chinese economy. "In Shanghai, commodity prices, like a kite with its string broken in the wind, soared high above the ground as though they had achieved Nirvana and immortality. Public workers struck again and again. Trams and buses wished they could have hung out 'Full House' signs like movie theaters and hotels. Copper and nickel coins were all confiscated. Stamps were temporarily put to a new use as supplementary currency. If only people could have been sent like mail, then the painfully crowded conditions on public buses could have been avoided. The struggle for survival was gradually stripped of mask and ornament to reveal a primitive brutality. A reasonable sense of shame was not cheap at all; many could not afford it."(315). In this economic situation, the Fangs' economic situation became worse as time passes, which meant that Fang Hung-chien could not obtain financial support form his family. Meanwhile, the Suns also were not very rich, and Sun Jou-chia's parents were cool toward her affairs to the point of indifference. Therefore, Sun Jou-chia had to seek support from his aunt. In the end, the Fangs and the Suns looked down upon each other.

Sun Jou-chia could not get along well with the Fangs. And Fang Hung-chien could not get on well with the aunt. The contradictions between Fang Hung-chien and Sun Jou-chia's aunt, and between Sun Jou-chia and the Fangs intensified. At the same time, because Fang Hung-chien did not earn much, his relationship with the Fangs deteriorated. Besides, Sun Jou-chia's salary was higher than Fang Hung-chien, leading to frequent quarrel between them. All of these contradictions accumulated and finally contributed a lot to the family dilemma and marriage dilemma of Fang Hung-chien, especially his marriage dilemma.

In addition, this period witnessed the coexistence of emerging Western capitalism and the hovering feudalism. Fang Hung-chien was the best example of this ideological situation. For one thing, he studied aboard and received advanced education. He sought for love and freedom. For another thing, he grew in a feudal family and was under the pressure of feudal patriarch. He was still influenced by feudalism and some feudal ideas still affected his mind. In this situation, he was sandwiched between the two completely different ideology. In marriage, he wanted both freedom and the obedience to his family. In life, he wanted to follow the modern lifestyle preferred by his wife and at the same time consider his parents' preference. Fang Hung-chien could not seek peace between the two sides. No matter which side he took, he would contradict with the other one and fell into "fortress besieged". Therefore, Fang Hung-chien was always in dilemmas.

Political darkness and corruption, economic slackness and disorder and cultural convergence and clash, all of these made the people's lives at that time become uneasy and even vagrant. People in such macro social environment were unable to lead normal lives, not to mention finding ideal future according to their plans. Most people had to silently suffer from the social instability and lead aimless lives without hope for the future. However, there was difference between intellectuals and ordinary people. Intellectuals were the pioneers and also lone souls in struggle with social reality sometimes just because of their sensitivity. And their awareness of dilemma where they were trapped and other struggled was not always shared by others, which made them all the more lonely and painful and further trapped in their life dilemmas. Therefore, most ordinary people might just accept the social reality blindly without any painful struggle while the intellectuals wanted to find their ways out of the social reality. Under such situation, the dilemmas of intellectuals became much more prototypical in the society of early 20th century. Fang Hung-chien, as one of the intellectuals, was aware of the social disorders and contradictions and was willing to rush out of the fortress besieged of the society. However, the social reality was too inescapable to get rid of, his perseverance was not strong enough to battle with it, and his loneliness was strong enough to destroy his efforts. So, Fang Hung-chien was certain to meet various dilemmas in his life because of his identity of being a sensitive intellectual in a society in chaos. Fang Hung-chien's personal dilemmas actually reflected the life dilemmas of a group of Chinese intellectuals and even ordinary people as a prototypical case in the early 20^{th-}century.

Throughout Fang Hung-chien's whole life, he was in various dilemmas due to the social environment he lived in. On the one hand, the social transformation that modernity is introduced into traditional China and grafted on this ancient civilization caused Fang Hung-chien's family dilemma and contributed greatly to his love and marriage dilemmas. On the other hand, the social instability including political confusion and economic depression and inflation led to Fang Hung-chien's study and career dilemmas. Besides, the identity of being an intellectual who had studied abroad in a distorted society with unhealthy atmosphere also made Fang Hung-chien fall into various dilemmas one after another.

4 Conclusions

Fortress Besieged written by Chien Chung-shu is a masterpiece containing profound ideological philosophy. Through paying attention to introducing the life experiences of Fang Hung-chien, the author, with superb literary and cultural attainment, shows his great insight in life and human beings. Although there is specific background for *Fortress Besieged*, its meaning does not restricted to the specific times. Although this novel focus on the life of Fang Hung-chien, it does not confined to this single character. In the preface to *Fortress Besieged*, Chien Chung-shu (1947: preface 1) writes, "In the book I intended to write about a certain segment of society and a certain kind of people in modern China. In writing about these people, I did not forget they are human beings, still human beings with the basic nature of hairless, two-legged animals." This indicates that Fang Hung-chien and many other characters in the novel are the certain kind of people picked by the author to present the the common nature of human beings, and to show the common dilemmas people faced in modern society. Even today, we can see the shadows of contemporary society from the book. For modern people who is still faced with life dilemmas in modern civilization, it is still of great importance to read the book. In addition, Chien Chung-shu's philosophical thoughts in the book on society, human beings and their lives have immeasurable significance to modern society and modern people, which gives a enlightenment to modernization and encourages people nowadays to reflect on these matters.

References

[1] Ch'ien, Chung-shu. *Fortress Besieged* [M]. Jeanne Kelly & Nathan K. Mao. Shanghai: Foreign Language Teaching and Research Press, 2003.

[2] 田丽阳. 围城・人生——试论小说围城的现代主义意蕴[D]. 郑州大学，2007.

[3] 王琳琳. 从《围城》中的女人们说开去——传统女性婚姻心态的现代审视[J]. 浙江师范大学学报(社会科学版)，1999（4）：120-121.

[4] 汪涛. 《围城》中方鸿渐围城人生的原因[J]. 文学教育(上)，2009（12）：62-63.

[5] 宣杰. 人性的围城[J]. 云梦学刊，2002（2）：64-66.

[6] 解志熙. 人生的困境与存在的勇气——论《围城》的现代性[J]. 文学评论，1989（5）：74-78.

[7] 杨绛. 记钱钟书与《围城》[M]. 长沙：湖南人民出版社，1986.

A “Doomed” Happy Ending in *Pride and Prejudice*: A Critical Analysis of Cross-class Marriage between Darcy and Elizabeth

张　蕊

摘　要：《傲慢与偏见》是英国女作家简·奥斯汀的代表作。在这篇小说的最后，达西和伊丽莎白缔结了美满的婚姻。但是，他们真的能幸福地生活在一起吗？从性格、地理差距和社会差距三个角度来看，他们都存在太多不可调和的矛盾。从这些实际出发，他们的美好结局注定不会如此美好。因此，本篇论文将会从性格、思想和阶级对其跨阶级的婚姻进行批判。

关键词：达西；伊丽莎白；婚姻；阶级

Abstract: *Pride and Prejudice* represents the masterpiece of British authoress, Jane Austen. In the end of the novel, Darcy and Elizabeth obtain a happy ending. But can they indeed have a fulfilled marriage and lead a happy life? From viewpoints of personality, geographical distance and social distance, they have too many irreconcilable conflicts. Practically, their happy ending will be doomed. Therefore, this paper will question their cross-class marriage critically from personality, mind and class.

Key words: Darcy；Elizabeth；Marriage；Class

1　Introduction

1.1　Introduction to Pride and Prejudice

Pride and Prejudice consists of 61 chapters with the opening line famously announcing: “It is a truth universally acknowledged that a single man in possession of a good fortune must be in want of a wife.” (Austen 1) This sets marriage as a central subject and a central problem as well for the novel. Meanwhile, it demonstrates that marriage takes economy into account. Altogether, the novel displays four major marriages respectively between Mr. Darcy and Elizabeth Bennet, between Mr. Bingley and Jane Bennet, between Mr. Wickham and Lydia Bennet, and between Mr. Collins and Charlotte Lucas. And it is widely accepted that their marriages are intertwined with true love, moral charming, impulsion and interest correspondingly.

To be more specific, Darcy and Elizabeth are two foremost protagonists, their marriage is a thorny road. Although they begin the novel as hostile acquaintances and unlikely friends, after a series of dramatic episodes they eventually work to understand each other and themselves so that they get together. As for Jane and Bingley, Jane is a pretty, elegant and kind lady. She attracts Bingley greatly, however, due to Darcy and his family’s dissuasion, they have also experienced a long process to marriage. Interestingly, it is still Mr. Darcy that contributes to their marriage to a certain extent. With the progress of plots, we can see that Wichham is a selfish, hypocritical and dishonest guy. Even so, he allures Lydia and afterwards Lydia elopes with him. With the intervention of Darcy, he agrees to marry her. In the case of Charlotte and Collins, their marriage lies in the comfortable economy of their household. All of these distinct marriages ultimately allow readers to question on what foundation a conjugal relationship should be established, especially when it comes to class, wealth and personality. This is also the reason why so many researchers focus on the topic of marriage in this novel.

In addition, *Pride and Prejudice* employs the narrative technique of free indirect speech. By using this narrative, it invites readers to follow the particular character's viewpoint, sharing her/his speeches and thoughts. Besides, irony is known to be frequently used throughout the novel, which makes the novel vivid, interesting and thought-provoking as well.

Pride and Prejudice has become one of the most popular novels in the world with long fascinated readers, consistently appearing near the top of lists of "most-loved books" among both literary scholars and the public. What's more, it has engendered a variety of adaptations, such as notable film versions, televisions versions, etc. *Pride and Prejudice* deserves its global reputation and the representative of Jane Austen.

1.2 Introduction to Jane Austen, the Author

Jane Austen (1775—1817) was an English female novelist known primarily for her six major novels, which are *Sense and Sensibility* (1811), *Pride and Prejudice* (1813), *Mansfield Park* (1814), *Emma* (1816), *Northanger Abbey* (1818), and *Persuasion* (1818). These works interpret, critique and satirize the British landed gentry at the end of the 18th century with successful use of biting irony, along with social commentary.

Though her four previous novels were published anonymously and brought her little fame during her lifetime, she has achieved big success as a prolific and celebrated writer with her another two published novels in her real name in 1818 after her death. These achievements of Austen have inspired varieties of critical essays, films and dramas, having earned her great fame around the world.

For much of Austen's life, her father served as the rector of the Anglican parishes and lived in the country town, so she generally led a peaceful and modest life, which influenced her writing style to some degree. In addition to this, one big event also affected her greatly.

When Austen was twenty, Tom Lefroy became her neighbor from December 1795 to January 1796. Austen described Lefroy as a very gentlemanlike, good-looking, pleasant young man. It is clear from Austen's letters to her sister Cassandra that they spent substantial time together: "I am almost afraid to tell you how my Irish friend and I behaved. Imagine to yourself everything most profligate and shocking in the way of dancing and sitting down together." Obviously, Austen was genuinely attracted to Lefroy, however, the Lefroy family intervened and sent him away. Austen wrote to Cassandra, "The day will come on which I flirt my last with Tom Lefroy and when you receive this it will be all over. My tears flow as I write at this melancholy idea." Both Lefroy and Austen must have known marriage was impractical as Lefroy had little money and was dependent on a great-uncle in Ireland to finance his education and establish his legal career. Nevertheless, in November 1798, Lefroy was still on Austen's mind as she wrote to her sister she had tea with one of his relatives, wanted desperately to ask about him, but could not bring herself to raise the subject. In old age, Lefroy admitted that he had been in love with Austen: "It was boyish love."

Therefore, it can be understood that Austen never married but wrote down the ideal marriage between Darcy and Elizabeth in *Pride and Prejudice*.

1.3 Introduction to This Paper

This paper expects to explore the continued development of the marriage between Darcy and Elizabeth after the ending of the book. Will they have the capability to lead a fulfilled marriage? From author's own experience, she experienced an unsatisfactory love story because of reality. She created a happy ending and an ideal marriage for Darcy and Elizabeth in *Pride and Prejudice*, but maybe she herself would not believe that they would have a fulfilled marriage afterwards, so she just ended the book when they get together. From viewpoints of personality, mind and class, great differences exist between Darcy and Elizabeth: Darcy's obstinate character, his broader experiences and his noble origin from the upper class are all inconsistent with and even contrasted with Elizabeth's impressionable disposition, her narrow mind and her humble origin of lower class. Due to these reasons, the happy ending for the marriage between them in *Pride and Prejudice* is doomed from a realistic perspective.

2 A "Doomed" Happy Ending between Darcy and Elizabeth

To begin with, it is necessary to explain that the four marriages illustrated above all obtain relatively good endings, in the book or in the movie. Wickham and Lydia live together and Lydia still shows off her marriage sometimes. Besides, Collins and Charlotte live comfortably and are going to have a baby. Bingley and Jane, Darcy and Elizabeth live closely and enjoy themselves. These four marriages, good or bad, all gain peaceful results; obviously, the ending of the book is overwhelmingly beautiful and romantic. However, the questions and doubts amongst modern readers towards their marriages are evoked whether it is credible to be happy thereafter and forever life with such salient differences and discrepancies in reality. Therefore, the happy ending between Darcy and Elizabeth is questionable and seemingly incredulous.

Undoubtedly, *Pride and Prejudice* includes certain realistic issues, such as wealth, society, etc., but this book is romantic as a whole. If plots continue to develop after the end, the marriage between Darcy and Elizabeth will invariably incur problems. This paper will focus on three main reasons accounting for this phenomenon. The explanation of these reasons will be classified and interpreted as follows.

2.1 Incompatible Personality

Though handsome, tall, and intelligent, Darcy lacks ease and adheres to his opinion obstinately. Comparatively, Elizabeth is lively, playful, and witty but with a tendency to be suspicious and judge on first impressions. Both of them are stubborn and less likely to understand each other. Their incompatible personality will be one potential threat of their ill-fated ending.

To describe in details, Darcy is too self-conceited while Elizabeth is inclined to suspect others. For instance, Darcy thinks vanity is a weakness but pride will be always under good regulation where there is a real superiority of mind, while Elizabeth turns away to hide a smile. After one dinner, Darcy and Elizabeth talks much, Darcy says, "There is, I believe, in every disposition a tendency to some particular evil, a natural defect, which not even the best education can overcome." Then Elizabeth says, "And your defect is a propensity to hate everybody." "And yours," Darcy replies, with a smile, "is wilfully to misunderstand them." (Austen 49) At a party, Elizabeth questions whether Darcy never allows himself to be blinded by prejudice, and Darcy answers, "I hope not." Subsequently, Elizabeth satirizes, "It is particularly incumbent on those who never change their opinion, to be secure of judging properly at first." (Austen 81) From these examples, it is evident that the personality of Darcy is different from that of Elizabeth greatly.

To some degree, Darcy and Elizabeth hold totally different values towards certain things. When they have conflicts, they tend to trust their own opinions. In this book, a variety of examples can illustrate this. Darcy considers poetry as the food of love while Elizabeth is convinced that one good sonnet has the efficacy in driving away love. In Nether field, Elizabeth says, "To yield readily—easily—to the persuasion of a friend is no merit with you." Darcy responds, "To yield without conviction is no compliment to the understanding of either." (Austen 42) Even some fundamental views, Darcy and Elizabeth think differently, which is easy for them to argue with each other.

Moreover, Elizabeth is prone to be influenced by others' speeches while Darcy is reluctant to explain unless it becomes serious. After hearing what Wickham describes, Elizabeth cries, "I had not thought Mr. Darcy so bad as this—though I have never liked him. I had not thought so very ill of him—I had supposed him to be despising his fellow-creatures in general, but did not suspect him of descending to such malicious revenge, such injustice, such inhumanity as this!" (Austen 70) This intensifies Elizabeth's prejudice towards Darcy and her misunderstanding lasts for such a long time until Darcy's explanation. As for Darcy, actually, he gets many chances to explain himself but his conceit and confidence precluded him from confession. Until he proposes to Elizabeth, only to be blamed and criticized by her, he starts to interpret the truth, writing a letter and leaving. After reading the letter, soon Elizabeth cries again, "How despicably I have acted! I, who have prided myself on my discernment! I, who have valued myself on my abilities, who have often disdained the generous candour of my sister, and gratified my vanity in useless or blameable distrust! How humiliating is this discovery! Yet, how just a humiliation! Had I been in love, I could not have been more wretchedly blind! But vanity, not love, has been my folly. Pleased with the preference of one, and offended by the neglect of the other, on the very beginning of our acquaintance, I have courted prepossession and ignorance, and driven reason away, where either were concerned. Till this moment I never knew myself." (Austen 172) From her change, it can be seen that Elizabeth is used to making prudent judgments instead of cultivating the habit of proving. After talking with Wickham, she believes in his one-sided story without investigating. After reading Darcy's letter, she changes her idea easily again. Hence, if similar situation happens, it is more likely for her to misunderstand Darcy even after their marriage.

Everyone's personality is not simple to be changed. Darcy's and Elizabeth's easy-to-conflict personalities will be one factor threatening their marriage.

2.2 Horizontal Geographical Distance: Dissimilar Local Cultures

Mind plays a vital role in the marriage. Similar minds, thoughts and values can promote the happiness while dissimilar ones are likely to destroy the marriage. As for Darcy and Elizabeth, somehow they diverge regarding their values and beliefs owing to dissimilar local cultures which nourish their minds and personal experiences which shape their thoughts. This reality will be another enormous obstacle confronted in the marriage between them.

From the book, Darcy and Elizabeth come from different places: Elizabeth and her family live in Longbourn which is a relatively small and conservative village, on contrary, Darcy comes from Pemberley in Derbyshire. Different places give rise to different local cultures and absolutely result in regional disparity. Just like Darcy says, "The country can in general supply but few subjects for such a study. In a country neighbourhood you move in a very confined and unvarying society."(Austen 36) But Mrs. Bennet should hold the view that London has no great advantage except the shops and public places over the village. Even Elizabeth admits that there are more kinds of people in the town than in the country, however, Mrs. Bennet answers that, "I believe there are few neighbourhoods larger. I know we dine with four-and-twenty families." (Austen 37) As for Elizabeth and her family, they are restricted to their small circle, and thereupon, their vision and mind are unable to be expanded beyond their everyday life and to transcend beyond their daily triviality, which leads to such ignorant remarks above made by Mrs. Bennet even thinking that 24 families are big. Geographical distance without convenient transportation impedes people from different localities from effective communication and meaningful interaction, social integration therefore becomes impossible. Long-time isolation and separation is fated to tear society apart, increase more misunderstanding and breed more prejudice and discrimination.

The place Elizabeth and her sisters often visit is Meryton, only one mile from Longbourn, to see their aunt. Most of their life is spent in the village, that is also the reason why Elizabeth feels excited when she has the precious chance to travel with her aunt and uncle. In contrast, Darcy comes from a different place and has a much wider and upper social circle with a large party of friends. He travels around many places, like London, Pemberly, Nether field and so on, instead of staying in one place for much time. As a result, he has broader experiences than Elizabeth and her family. Geographical mobility, especially long-distance travel, which is almost unlikely especially for lower class and which is only available for a handful of noble and rich men seems to further barricade the communication between the former and latter, with the former more narrow-minded and the latter more open-minded. Given this difference, effective communication between Darcy and Elizabeth is more difficult.

In addition to geographical distance, different personal behaviors and minds influenced by local cultures between Darcy and Elizabeth can also have a great effect on their marriage. As for Elizabeth, her youngest sister's elopement, her mother of mean understanding, her family of complexity, they all can influence their marriage at any time. What's more, the reality of the society and the environment in which they live pose threats to their marriage as well. Gender discrimination is pretty serious during their period. For instance, the estate of Elizabeth's father estate, Longbourn, is only entailed to the male line. Mr. Collins is just Mr. Bennet's distant second cousin but the heir to Longbourn House. At that society, the status of women is much lower than men. That is the reason why obsequious and pompous Collins has the courage to talk to Elizabeth, "Pardon me for neglecting to profit by your advice, which on every other subject shall be my constant guide, though in the case before us I consider myself more fitted by education and habitual study to decide on what is right than a young lady like yourself." (Austen 85) Even Collins, an obsequious guy, can be so confident in that social environment while female has to struggle for their life. It is thought that Elizabeth's independent thoughts on love are precious, but it is exactly due to the truth that women rely on men greatly. After the marriage between Darcy and Elizabeth, there is no doubt that Elizabeth needs to follows customs no matter how dependent she wants to be.

Darcy and Elizabeth might reconcile for a while when they are in love, affectionate and passionate; however, they cannot shield from the reality forever. Differences triggered by geographic distance will make the contradiction eventually irreconcilable in their marriage.

2.3 Vertical Social Distance: Unbridgeable Gap Between Social Classes

The class between Darcy and Elizabeth differs widely, one is superior while the other is inferior. The first appearance of Mr. Darcy is described in this way: "Mr. Darcy soon drew the attention of the room by his fine, tall person, handsome features, noble mien, and the report which was in general circulation within five minutes after his entrance, of his having ten thousand a year. The gentlemen pronounced him to be a fine figure of a man, the ladies declared he was much handsomer than Mr. Bingley, and he was looked at with great admiration for about half the evening, till his manners gave a disgust which turned the tide of his popularity; for he was discovered to be proud; to be above his company, and above being pleased; and not all his large estate in Derbyshire could then save him from having a most forbidding, disagreeable countenance, and being unworthy to be compared with his friend." (Austen 7) Putting his manners away, Darcy is a pretty noble man. He belongs to the upper echelon of society and the most superior class in the novel. He is the wealthy owner of the renowned family estate of Pemberley in Derbyshire. In contrast, Elizabeth represents a poorer daughter of the gentility: Her father, Mr. Bennet owns the Longbourn estate, but his property is entailed on a distant relation, meaning that five of his girls cannot inherit it; her mother, Mrs. Bennet only has four thousand pounds from her father. In addition to the wealth, there also exists educational and other differences between them.

When Darcy proposes to Elizabeth, he should cite their economic and social differences as an obstacle his excessive love has had to overcome, "He spoke well, but there were feelings besides those of the heart to be detailed, and he was not more eloquent on the subject of tenderness than of pride. His sense of her inferiority, of its being a degradation, of the family obstacles which judgment had always opposed to inclination, were dwelt on with a warmth which seemed due to the consequence he was wounding, but was very unlikely to recommend his suit." (Austen 157) Distinct social classes between Darcy and Elizabeth will not disappear even after their marriage. Actually, the opinion of social class is deeply rooted in those characters during their period, namely from the end of the 18th century and the beginning of the 19th century. The more Elizabeth fights for it, the more profound effect it shows.

Later, Darcy's aunt, Lady Catherine de Bourgh remarks their differences more straightforwardly and expressly, "I will not be interrupted. Hear me in silence. My daughter and my nephew are formed for each other. They are descended, on the maternal side, from the same noble line; and, on the father's, from respectable, honourable, and ancient, though untitled, families. Their fortune on both sides is splendid. They are destined for each other by the voice of every member of their respective houses; and what is to divide them? The upstart pretensions of a young woman without family, connections, or fortune. Is this to be endured! But it must not, shall not be. If you were sensible of your own good, you would not wish to quit the sphere in which you have been brought up." (Austen 297) Ridiculously, Elizabeth even insists she and Darcy are equal. Moreover, Lady Catherine conveys what Elizabeth's marriage to Darcy will become in particularly harsh terms: "Are the shades of Pemberley to be thus polluted?" (Austen 298) Even as the novel closes, Lady Catherine refuses to accept Darcy's actual marriage to Elizabeth.

Like Catherine implies, the social distance between Darcy and Elizabeth will pose a fatal threat for their marriage. As described above, the author of *Pride and Prejudice*, Jane Austen herself experienced a romantic love story but surrendered to the material reality which is ripped apart by different social classes. Compared with her own love story, the happy ending in this book is like castle in the air without mentioning how they genuinely overcome different social classes.

Furthermore, George Bernard Shaw described marriage as an institution that brings together two people "under the influence of the most violent, most insane, most delusive, and most transient of passions. They are required to swear that they will remain in that excited, abnormal, and exhausting condition continuously until death do them part." At last, the marriage will just become sustained not by love and emotions but on the basis of economic security and value compatibility. Nevertheless, the marriage between Darcy and Elizabeth lacks the matching of these conditions, which buries an enormous dangerous seed.

According to numerous researches, at home and abroad, the marriage between similar social classes is more likely to sustain stability. Particularly, in the era where Darcy and Elizabeth live, social environment is far more exclusive than now, their cross-class marriage will be pretty unrealistic and have an "ill-fated" happy ending.

3 Conclusions

The romantic novel *Pride and Prejudice* provides an insight into various kinds of marriage. By reading this book, everybody will have his or her own understandings about the marriage. Darcy and Elizabeth, Bingley and Jane, Wickham and Lydia, they all have their own marriage attitudes albeit to changeable degrees. Even at present, their distinct personal experiences are common among all.

As a whole, Jane Austen writes marriages in a relatively romantic way in *Pride and Prejudice*, which leaves many questions in the marriage between Darcy and Elizabeth. From incompatible personality distance, horizontal geographical distance and vertical social distance at their time, their marriage must be infested with many problems, and their future road must be bumpy and tortuous. Therefore, the happy ending for their marriage in the book is destined to be doomed. It is said that marriage without love is wrong. Nevertheless, marriage without considering reality is stupid as well.

With the development of politics and economy, nowadays, persons' thoughts have become increasingly open and inclusive; however, social class still plays an important role in the marriage. Even now, it still limits the choices of the marriage. Therefore, faced with marriage, everyone needs to be realistic and think clearly. From this novel, readers need to understand no marriage is perfect but ought to take it seriously.

References

[1] Austen, Jane. *Pride and Prejudice*[M]. Oxford: Oxford University Press, 1991.

[2] *Pride and Prejudice* (Movie). United Kingdom, 2005.

[3] https://en.wikipedia.org/wiki/Jane_Austen. 2018 年 7 月 7 日获取.

[4] https://en.wikipedia.org/wiki/Pride_and_Prejudice. 2018 年 7 月 7 日获取.

[5] 孟洁，姚文娟，谢芸. 简·奥斯汀《傲慢与偏见》中婚恋伦理观研究[J]. 语文建设，2016（33）： 65-66.

[6] 孙玉华.《傲慢与偏见》婚姻观的社会文化意义[J]. 作家, 2008（22）：104.

[7] 奥斯汀. 傲慢与偏见[M]. 王科一译. 上海：上海译文出版社，2006.

[8] 吴若芳.《傲慢与偏见》中的婚姻观解析[J]. 语文建设，2013（12）：45-46.

Exploring the Meaning of “Time being” in *A Tale for the Time Being*

范诗雪

摘　要：在学术界，探究时间和存在的关系历久弥新,不会消逝。哲学家们总是会用时间和存在的关系去探讨我们生命的意义。露丝·尾关的《不存在的女孩》一书的开篇中，主人公奈绪提出一个重要的概念——时在，它的出现既是对整部书的主题的推动，也是生命的意义的反映。本文旨在结合小说文本分析“时在”这一概念。“时在”的含义并不能简单地拆分为时间和存在，从开始到结束，在本书中至少有七种直接或间接性的描述。“时在”是指存在经历时间、时间本身存在、量子力学中的部分概念这三个方面的内容。本篇论文将会分析这三个方面的含义及具体内容，并通过这三个方面探讨人生及生命意义这一主题。

关键词：露丝·尾关；时间和存在；时在；《不存在的女孩》；生命的意义

Abstract: Time and being has always been a fascinating topic among scholars and philosophers. Philosophers often use time and existence to explore the meaning of our life. Ruth Ozeki’s book *A Tale for the Time Being*has put forward an important term “time being”. This concept has an important impetus for the theme of the whole book, since it reflects and refers to the meaning of life. Here the meaning of "time being" is not directly divided into two words: time and being. From the beginning to the end, there are at least seven direct and indirect descriptions in the time. The meaning of time being involves existences in time, time exists (time is materialized), and some concepts in Quantum mechanics. I will also explore the author’s intention and analyze the meaning of life through these parts.

Key words: Ruth Ozeki；Time and Being；Time being；*A Tale for the Time Bei*ng；Meaning of life.

1　Introduction

1.1　The introduction of the novel

The novel “*A Tale for the Time Being*” is divided into two parts, which are the odd chapters and even chapters. The old chapters are involved around Nao and the even chapters are involved around Ruth. In another word, in the novel, the main character of the odd numbered chapter is Nao and the protagonist of the even numbered chapters is Ruth. The even ones tell Ruth’s story which mainly describes her thoughts on Nao’s views. The odd chapters focus on a Japanese girl named Nao suffered some misfortune. Her father had been expelled from the company, once bought a platform ticket and committed suicide to the central fast line of Shinjuku, while her mother was addicted to the aquarium jellyfish, with a cold and harsh character. And she was bullied at school, and even she works part-time as a prostitute. She escaped from reality and tried to get rid of all misfortune. When her grandma knew her misfortune, she told her the philosophy of time, and guided her confused mind. Nao harvests lots of philosophical thought from her grandma's actions and words, and time being is one of these philosophies.

1.2 Layout of paper

First, this paper will introduce time being in general. Through the relationship of time and being to explain and explore time being. Second, I will find some interpretations of "time being" in the novel. In the interpretation of the word "time being", meanings of "time being" are divided into the following aspects in the novel: existences in time, time as existence, and some concepts in Quantum mechanics. Through the interpretation of time being in the text, we analyze, the meaning of "time being" and life expressed in the novel, and I will find the connection of life with the meaning of time being. The author's intention is explored through the analysis of text and its context, which is related to the theme of life in the novel.

2 "Time Being" in the Novel and Their Relation

In *A Tale for the Time Being*, time being, as a prominent term, plays a role in deciding the structure of the novel. When we talk about time being, we need to understand what the relationship of time and being is. As is known that time and existence interact. Time affects existence, and existence affects time. Specifically, time is a manifestation of material movement, and continuity and order of change, "Materialization of Time is realized by human's behavior and transformed into the existence that can be felt directly. One is to make the abstract time depend on the natural phenomena and objective laws which have summarized attached on the carrier that can meet the needs, and present it in the form of products and things." (Wang Xuan & Huang Kai, 2017) Dasein is not an isolated individual, but is always deeply influenced by the Western spirit thereby deeply rooted in the history of Western history. (Wen Han, 2016, p 43) So we can also say being has timeliness.

Their relationship also expresses in other ways. In physics, everything is all moving, and the things that exist are made up of molecules, atoms and particles, which are closely connected as time. And the explanation that all being is time has more poetic in the novel, "She sat back in her chair and gazed out the window at the tiny stretch of horizon that she could see through a gap in the tall trees." A pine tree is time. "Dark clouds hung low in the sky, forming an almost indiscernible line where they met the still, dull sheen of the ocean." Oceans are time. (Ruth Ozeki*,* 2013, p. 30) That is because existences are the manifestation of time. In philosophy, being is time that is same to Heidegger's point of view. Heidegger believes that if people want to think about being, they must go through being. (Heidegger, 1962) In these parts, we know time being roughly, when we know the relationship of time and being by and large, and then I will talk about "time being" specifically in the novel base on their relationship.

3 "Time Being" and Its Meaning in the Context

3.1 Existences in and Through Time

"Time being" is something that existences can go through for time and then cease to be. Nao,the protagonist of the novel， explained that "time being" is the person who lives in the time. "A time being is someone who lives in time, and that means you, and me, and every one of us who is, or was, or ever will be". (Ruth Ozeki, 2013, p. 2) That meaning of Nao is same to Ma Cheng Chang's thought like "the present is related to us, and it is now called time is facing us - people - and stay". (Ma Cheng Chang, 2009) These views here show that existences through time and these also express the relationship between human beings and time. Time and being are inextricably linked. Heidegger's ontological philosophy inquires into existence itself, and its philosophical basis is to inquire into the special existence of human beings. (Yang Run Dong, 2018) The sentence reflects that people are being. And this sentence is also exploring the specific relationship between existence and time. In general, "time being" is that some existences in time. We all know life is the process of human beings from birth to death. In general, time being is life.

Another part also express the meaning of time being that existences through time. The novel displays the relationship of time and being through Jiko's talking. Jiko who is Nao's grandma tells Nao the words and stories are time being. Talking Stories and words is the sequential manifestation of existence. "Language is the house of being." (Ruth Ozeki, 2013, p. 345) Words and stories have the property of time. We need spend some time to tell the story. It is clearly pointed out that existence is through the baptism of time. Without some existences in time, existences will not exist in the world. In other words, the characters of existence is timeliness, time is not outside of us and not separated from our life.

Our life is the sum of our time. We all know that we should treasure time, seize the time and make use of the limited time in our life. Thus, time is of great significance to our life. Heidegger once mentioned that time is combined with our existence, and when we understand the meaning of our existence, we also understand the meaning of time. (Heidegger, 1962) Therefore, the view of time being that existences through time has important guiding significance to our life, and it is not difficult to understand why the author put it in the beginning of the article in the tone of Nao.

3.2 Time and Its Existence as Things

Time exists and at the sometime it manifests. The problem that time exists or not is dependent upon how it is materialized.In her diary,Nao talked about a book which is called *Shōbōgenzō*, or the *Treasury of the True Dharma Eye.* She cited a few sentences like "Time itself is being, ... and all being is time ... In essence, everything in the entire universe is intimately linked with each other as moments in time, continuous and separate." *Why time itself is being? Maybe, we can find traces left by time through something being.* As the novel wrote, *Dōgen* said that "*A pine tree is time,and bamboo is time. Mountains are time. Oceans are time ... (*Ruth Ozeki, 2013, p. 30)

Why the tree and bamboo is time? It is because time is the changing process of things.We can say time exists, but since it has no factual body, it is a concept of sensibility. Time itself has a great significance, and the novel say *"if time is annihilated, mountains and oceans will annihilate."* (Ruth Ozeki, 2013, p. 30) *In a word, if time* does not exist, we will not exist in the world. In this world we look for the meaning of existence and look for the meaning of survival. From the above, we have known the relationship between time and being, so when we talk the meaning of our life, time is an unavoidable topic.

Another way of talking about time is materialization of time in our world or in our daily life. When we speak of the present, we have hinted at the existence of time, so time is materialized. "Now" is transient. Once it appears, it disappears. In another word, while talking about "now", it has be gone, this is almost similar to suicide to the word "now", so that it is so certain that "now" exists actually. There are different opinions on this phenomenon in the novel. If you whispered now! ... Now! ... Now! ... Over and over, faster and faster, into the wind as the world whipped by, trying to catch the moment when the word was what it is: when now became NOW. (Ruth Ozeki, 2013, p. 102) In a moment, it's a very small unit of time, like a particle. So, it explicates the granular nature of time. In the novel, it mentioned 6,400,099,980 moments that constitute a single day. (Ruth Ozeki, 2013, p. 432)

3.3 Time and Its Existence as Segments

When we talked about the concept of "Now", it can involve an extended concept. That concept is a view of instant.

Hocking mentioned that time itself does not exist. Time is only a concept created by human beings, but the measurement of time is added according to the changing process of things. Hocking says, "however, the discovery that the speed of light appeared the same to every observer, no matter how he was moving, led to the theory of relativity-and in that one had to abandon the idea that there was a unique absolute time. Instead, each observer would have his own measure of time as recorded by a clock that he carried: clocks carried by different observers would not necessarily agree. Thus time become a more personal concept, relative to the observer who measured it". (Stephen Hocking, 1988, Chapter 9 The Arrow of Time)

Hocking's view is similar to Old Jiko's idea of time in the novel. Old Jiko is super careful with her time. She does everything really slowly, even when she's just sitting on the veranda, looking out at the dragonflies spinning lazily around the garden pond. "She says that she does everything really slowly in order to spread time out so that she'll have more of it and live longer…" She thinksthat she does everything really slowly in order to spread time out so that she'll have more of it and live longer. So that is the different between the Smart people and ordinary people. Maybe people are the same age but smart people arrange time better, so they have more time. In *Sand and a Distant Star*, a dramatic role named Ye Ying said: "There are two definitions of time, one belongs to everyone, moving forward forever, the other belongs to oneself, freezing at the most important moment in one's life." (Lai Shengchuan, 2003, 3' 28"-48")

Time has different meanings for different people and people will dominate their time according to their own circumstance. Just like in the novel, Old Jiko is the enlightened person of Nao's life.

The idea of using Old Jiko's idea of time is to convey the meaning of life in this book: to cherish all the time. Just like the concept of "fragmentation of time", which we have learned before. The view of instant has a similarity of the concept. In the appendix, the author mentioned Zen moments. It reads as follows: One day is made of 6,400,099,980 moments. A snap equals sixty-five moments. When you finish up your 98,463,077th snap, you will experience the truly intimate awareness of knowing exactly how you spent every single moment of a single day of your life. (Ruth Ozeki, 2013, p. 431)

More than once the parents and teachers tell me to cherish the time, and the past is irreparable, the future is also very difficult to predict. They inspire us on the road of life and strive to realize their social values in life (Social value can be seen as the status of the society).Then the realization of the value of time is inseparable from the realization of the value of existence. If we want to really live to find our social value, we mustunderstand how fast the time goes by. We should try to seize every moment whether the moment is sorrow or joy, and appreciate every time we have, so as to cherish every time. This is the time that I understand which can give us a sense of meaning. As the author says, "sadness is to prevent all moments from wasting."

3.4 Revelation from Quantum mechanics

The last mention of time being is quantum mechanics. In science, quantum mechanics is thought as time being. The time being in Quantum mechanics is also talk about their relationship. In the second appendix of the novel, three principles are put forward.

The first one is the superposition that a particle can be in two or more places or states at once (i.e., old Jiko and; Nao and me; Nao and me). (Ruth Ozeki, 2013, p. 433) "Superposition: by which a particle can be in two or more places or states at once (i.e., Zen Master Dōgen is both alive and dead?)."Whether people are alive or dead, they have the opposite sides, so whether Nao was alive or dead, she actually existed in the world. So time is not a boundary.

The second one is the principle of Entanglement. Entanglement: by which two particles can coordinate their properties across space and time and behave like a single system (i.e., a Zen master and his disciple; a character and her narrator; old Jiko and Nao and Oliver and me?)

No matter what time and space is existence can be leapfrog which meaning is two particles can across space and time. Just like Nao and Ruth, they come from different space and time, but they are linked through a dairy. Ruth was influenced by Nao's experience, and Nao's dairy change her behavior and the perception of life. For example, we knew old Jiko's ideal of time about moment which is influenced Ruth's attitude towards time and life. Ruth's write "Time interacts with attention in funny ways. At one extreme, when Ruth was gripped by the compulsive mania and hyper focus of an Internet search, the hours seemed to aggregate and swell like a wave, swallowing huge chunks of her day. At the other extreme, when her attention was disengaged and fractured, she experienced time at its most granular, wherein moments hung around like particles, diffused and suspended in standing water."

The third principle is the measurement problem "the act of measuring or observation alters what is being observed (i.e., the collapse of a wave function; the telling of a dream?)." For example,

Ruth's three dream. That is to say, Ruth and Nao exist in different time and space, but some measurement activities can change the mind of the surveyor, the thoughts will affect existence. After Ruth read old Jiko's thoughts through the dairy, Ruth met Old Jiko and talked to her in her dream. That's phenomenon shows the third principle.

The first principle tells us particles' states, which is related to matter. The second one tells the relationship of time and being. The last one tells about measurement that is similar to the second principle. In summary, the author combines his view with physics to show that time and existence is inseparable. Nao's life can influence Ruth's life by crossing time and space. And they connect through a journal.

4 Conclusions

In Nao's life which is full of time and space, she went through much time being. In her study life, she was oppressed and bullied at school. She has a sorrow life neither in her school or her family. Then we find she and her father change their life affected by Old Jiko. "I just want you to know that me and my dad are really okay, now that I finally know what kind of man he is, and even though we haven't actually discussed the topic of suicide, I'm pretty sure that neither of us is thinking along those lines anymore". (Ruth Ozeki, 2013, p. 414) A sorrow is also one part of time which belongs to our life, thus we can't to escape our sad life. War, suicide, bullying, family history are all a small part of our life. Narrowing it down can be regarded as an instant. In countless moments, we can choose peace, choose courage, choose to change, choose every bright in our life, even we can choose the future. Because there are many possibilities in the future, which will make today better, and there will be countless times that bad situation can be changed. We have known that time have a great significance in being. When we grab your time and cherish your time, life which is made up of being has a far-reaching influence. The elements of crow, forest and dream in the novel are two space-time connections between Ruth and Nao. The young people of every age have their own loss and confusion, the life that Nao was bullied, the age of the first half of her grandmother and the latter half of her life, the war of genocide and the solemn and tragic resistance of the coming death in her uncle's age, all these time being are conveyed to Ruth through some channels, bringing thoughts to Ruth's and our life. Ruth witnessed the rebirth of Nao. She and her father found the answer to life, and both she and her father had countless moments of choice. When they were serious for their ideals, they would eventually find their own way, because they were "reborn". The girl who was sad, depressed, painful and nonexistent finally accepted this "no existence" because she had existed in another existence which has no sorrows, and she did not need to endure the "death", and she could choose to "live".

The novel through a view of instant and existence is timeliness to let us perceive every moment of life and tell us choose what you want to do at every choice. And eventually you will become the person you want to be. Time and being constitute the meaning of life, if we don't to want to waste our life, we should grasp time and existences (whether these existences are good or bad). This is the meaning of life that we need live in the present.

In short, time being is a very important part of our life. We need a deeper understanding. The relationship between time and existence, time itself, being itself and quantum mechanics, which are include the view of life expressed by the author. For Nao, her grandmother's idea of time and existence influenced herself and her father's path; for Ruth, Nye's notebook and Ruth's husband, mother, and her life had an important influence on her life. Just like Old Jiko said in Ruth's dream: "Everything in the universe is constantly changing, and nothing stays the same, and we must understand how quickly time flows by if we are to wake up and truly live our lives. That's what it means to be a time being". (Ruth Ozeki, 2013, p. 432) The meaning of time being is also the meaning of life. Therefore, we should seize time being and grasp our life.

References

[1] Lai Shengchuan. https://v.youku.com/v_show/id_XNTYyNzk2NzM2.html. 检索日期: December 6th, 2018.

[2] Martin Heidegger. *Being and time*. Published by State University of New York Press [M]. Albany, 1996.

[3] Ruth Ozeki, *A Tale for the Time Being*[M]. New York: Penguin books, 2013.

[4] Stephen Hocking. *A Brief of History of Time*. United Kingdom: Bantam Dell Publishing Group, 1988.

[5] 马成昌. 以时间论存在——谈海德格尔《时间与存在》中的时间观[J]. 哈尔滨学院学报，2009（5）：5-8.

[6] 王旋，黄凯. 时间的具象化与设计[A]. 设计艺术研究，2018（1）：54-58.

[7] 文晗. 存在的意义如何转向存在的真?——论海德格尔的思想转向[J]. 北京社会科学, 2016（2）：41-47.

[8] 杨润东. 认识你自己——以海德格尔存在分析为中心的考察 [J]. 汉字文化，2018（13）：51-54.

Human Existence in *A Tale for the Time Being*

李 玉

摘 要：这篇文章借助对“人的存在意义”的思考来分析美国作家露丝·尾关的《不存在的女孩》的意义。本文通过将“人的存在意义”与文本相结合分析其中主要人物实现自己存在意义的方式，得出作品意义即人的社会属性是实现人存在意义的主要途径。本文将结合《不存在的女孩》分析人存在意义的具体内涵，并解释人的社会属性的定义以及其重要意义，并结合文本与存在主义理论，运用马克思哲学中的存在论理论来分析作品的意义，即“社会属性是实现人存在意义的主要途径”。

关键词：《不存在的女孩》；人的生存意义；社会属性

Abstract: This article uses the thinking about the “the meaning of human existence” to analyze the meaning of the work of *A Tale for the Time Being*. By combining the meaning of “human existence” with the text, this paper analyzes the way of main characters realizing their own meaning, and concludes the meaning of the work, that is, the social attribute of the human being, is the main way to realize the meaning of human existence. This article combines the text and the theory of “existentialism” and the ontological theory in Marxist philosophy to derive the meaning of the work, that is, “social attributes are the main way to realize the meaning of human existence.”

Key words: *A Tale for the Time Being*; Human existence; Social attributes

1 Introduction

The Japanese-American writer Ruth Ozeki (1956—)’s new work *A Tale for the Time Being, 2013* won praises from all walks of life and won the American Library Association Best Novel Award. The *New York Times* annual good book and many other important European and American literary awards, included in the short list of the Bukke Award, the US National Book Reviewer Awards list inside the cover. As a new book, its various charms and features need to be further explored.

The content of *A Tale for the Time Being* is made up of two first-person narrators. One is a 16-year-old American Japanese girl, Nao Xu. She left her hometown in California with her frustrated father. She was suicidal because of the depressive family atmosphere and the bullying of her classmates. But she decided to write her great-grandmother before she finished everything. Another narrator is Ruth, a Japanese writer living on a secluded island in North America. She accidentally found Nao’s diary on the beach and the relics of her grandfather as a pilot of the Second World War. The world of the two narrators is thus linked. In general, the novel contains a variety of themes: the value of human existence, war and humanity, campus bullying, suicide culture, Zen and quantum mechanics, feminism…And the “value of human existence” will be used as this article key research objects. The main characters in the novel: Nao, Ruth, The old Jiko, Haruki… all reflect the value of human existence.

2 The Meaning of Human Existence

Before talking about the meaning of human existence, we must first understand what is human existence. Marxism believes that man is the most veritable social animal. The “sociality” of human beings is equivalent to “super-biological”, which means that people exist beyond other creatures and have special social attributes. (马克思, 恩格斯, 第 23 卷, 1997, p. 669)The philosophy of existentialism points out that human survival is a life activity with self-productiveness. The way people live is the way of life and experience of people who live in the world. It is the way of “production” and “reproduction” of the world of people and people. Human survival is different from animal survival. Animal activities are instinctive activities, and human activities are “productive” activities that people consciously and actively carry out. The reason why this kind of living is different from the living activities of animals is that this kind of living activity of human beings is not only “produced” by human beings, but also has self-creation, and its “production” is in accordance with the possibility of the object. At the same time of people’s own needs and abilities, it depends to a considerable extent on people’s life experience, survival comprehension and life beliefs, and makes people’s sense of existence grow. (恩格斯, 1997, p. 113) Heidegger thought “existence” itself, whether it is due to its own unique truth, which leads to its involvement in human nature; or, when metaphysics departs from its foundation, can it prevent in advance: the existence of human involvement may come from this Involvement itself produces a kind of light—a kind of light that leads people to belong to existence? (海德格尔, 2018, p. 64) The phrase “The Destiny of Heaven” has a special meaning. “Humanity comes from heaven” because heaven limits the “existence” of human beings, and nature and humanity are bound by inevitability. Here, people may notice three important meanings: （1）Although sex is limited by nature, the growth of nature is the nature of nature, so the revealing of nature is essentially the natural realization of heaven. process. （2）While sex and ontology are identical in ontology, they also differ in phenomenology because they enrich and display themselves in different ways. （3）“Life” means both human activities and superhuman processes: both the subjective aspect of existence and the objectivity aspect of existence.According to the above explanation of “human existence”, we can draw the “existentialism” philosophy in the West, the existential thought in Marxism, Heidegger’s “existence” thought or Confucius’ “human existence” Understanding. They all show the existence of human beings is inextricably linked with the surrounding world, and the existence of a single isolated person is inseparable from its surrounding world.

3 Human Social Attribute

Human existence is the second level of human existence. Man is not only a natural being, has the nature of nature, more importantly, man is a social existence, with the social nature. Due to human characteristics. In fact, insisting that man is the unity of natural existence and social existence, natural attribute and social attribute points out that the natural attribute of the actual human being is the natural attribute of socialization, which is the important difference between Marxist theory of human nature and other abstract theories of human nature one.

Strictly speaking, society is a community of individual interactions, a unique group developed in accordance with different laws of biology, while "social" refers to social forms that are different from those of biological forms and all that is derived from them. In other words, "social" refers to the supernatural, and social attributes essentially refer to superhuman attributes or supernatural attributes. Therefore, "social" is only for people, "people are real social animals."(奥古斯丁, 2010, p. 144)

Only in society can people exist and develop. The animal exists only naturally, so it has only its own body. Its inherent characteristics are "innate" and doomed. Its entire life is to manifest its genetic result. However, people have their social existence, society determines his consciousness and will, decides his motivation and reason, and thus decides all human behavior.Social existence is not an instant addition to itself, but social existence is the result of socialization. Social existence is the basic point that characterizes the existence of human beings and the nature of human activities.The existence of human beings can only be achieved from social existence. Society is just human society, it is the sum of the actual personal relationships and activities.

Man is a social being, which determines that he must have its own social essence.(恩格斯, 第1卷, 1997, p. 77) Marx believes that social life is multifaceted and that social relations are rich and varied. These rich and varied social relations do not exist disorderly, but are organized according to a certain law and have a specific structure of the organic system. According to Marx, the essence of man is "the summation of all social relations" in its reality. This means that it is not one-sided but all social relations that stipulate the social essence of man.From the perspective of the relationship between the main point of view, it can be manifested as individual, group, class, nationality and so on.

In class society, the class nature of people is a manifestation of the concentration of personality. Individuals in different positions in social relations have different material interests and have different demands, thoughts and feelings, so their essences are different.(蓝荣策, 2001) In the *A Tale for the Time Being*. Due to the Nao, the Haruki#1 and the prostitutes in the maid cafe belong to different classes, so their demands are different. Nao is a child, what she wants is a happy family, a school environment which is free of bullying. Murashu-1 is a soldier, because he was struggling with "obligations" and "righteousness" in his heart and he did not want to die with the enemy, he chose to suicide. As the prostitutes in the maid cafe in order to meet their own needs, economy is his demand.

Nationality is also an important aspect of human social attributes. The nation is a stable social community formed in history with common language, common ground, common economic life, common culture and common psychological quality.(张曙光, 2001) Therefore, people's nationality always reflects people's daily activities of production, distribution, exchange and consumption, reflecting certain national psychological habits and behavior characteristics. The "Samurai" spirit of Haruki#1 and the suicide of Haruki#2 described in the book all belong to a certain extent to the national character of Japan.

"The Bushido is the Road to Death." This is a famous phrase in the famous Japanese warrior

Sutra book *The Book of the Red Leaf.* Warrior, with loyalty, reputation, martial arts as a code of ethics. Japanese martial arts since ancient times, there is a strong desire for warriors. The moral values associated with "Wu" and "Bushido" are highly valued.Samurai culture has a special form, also has a high status. Samurai is taken as a shame when captured or killed by another knife, and "cutting the belly" is the highest embodiment of the warrior loyalty and a warrior tradition."Jade Broken" (mass suicide), known as "the essence of Bushido." Japanese have always regarded the defeated suicide as a act of " known the shame," as the essence of Bushido. "Bushido" has always been used by the ruling class. After the early Meiji period, the "cut belly" was regarded as the center of "Yamato sprits" The first of the "military metaphors" promulgated in 1882 stipulated that soldiers must suicide when necessary. Soldiers are taught that death itself is a spiritual victory. During the war, there was not a well-trained rescue team or a complete medical system in the entire Japanese army. In some crisis situations, the wounded could be slaughtered or committed suicide. In the late World War, driven by militarism and "warrior road", large-scale suicide military operations such as the meatballs of the Japanese "Kamikaze" agents, the "jade fragments" of Japanese military and civilian groups on the Pacific islands, one hundred million Jade broken. In the *A Tale for the Time Being*, the Haruki#1 was to ordered to carry out the suicide attack. "During the physical examination in October, the recruiting officer ordered us to 'switch off our hearts and minds completely.' He instructed us to cut off our love and sever our attachment with our family and blood relations because from now on we were soldiers and our loyalty must lie solely with our Emperor and our homeland of Japan." (Ruth Ozeki, 2013, p. 265) This demand that the military cut off the love of the family only allegiance to the emperor is the best manifestation of the spirit of "Bushido" during the war and is also a part of Japan's unique national character. Through this unique national character, Haruki#1 really exist in that particular history.

And the suicide culture is another kind of Japanese unique national character. Japan is one of the countries with the highest rates of suicide in the world. Except for the war period, the number of Japanese people who died in their own hands far exceeded the number of who died in the hands of others.Since the 1980s, Japan has committed suicide on average every 20 minutes and has broken through the mark of 20,000 deaths each year for more than 10 consecutive years. Japanese scientist Kato said: "The theme of suicide has its special importance in Japanese culture. "It argues that death is not the opposite of life, but perpetuity as a part of life. The Japanese usually think that life and death are not completely opposite, and that death is a continuation of life.After the death of the soul can get the soul, continue to survive in "other world." This 'soul' can return to the motherland and hometown, guarding the 'living people'. In the *A Tale for the Time Being*, Nao and Haruki#2 chose the suicide at the same time. "Somewhere I read that men born between April and June are more likely to commit suicide than men born at other times of the year. My dad was born in May, so maybe that explains it. Not that he's succeeded in killing himself yet. He hasn't. But he's still trying. It's just a matter of time." (Ruth Ozeki, 2013, p. 42) Due to Japan's unique culture of shame, Murakami was shamed to choose to commit suicide after being in business because he could not realize his worth and was unable to provide his wife and daughter with a good living environment.

Therefore, we can also prove that Nao and her family really exist in the presence of humanity.

4 Social Attribute Is the Main Realization Factor of Human Existence

Becauseman is not only a natural being, has the nature of nature, more importantly, man is a social existence, with the social nature. Due to human characteristics. In fact, insisting that man is the unity of natural existence and social existence, natural attribute and social attribute points out that the natural attribute of the actual human being is the natural attribute of socialization, which is the important difference between Marxist theory of human nature and other abstract theories of human nature one.Combining the definition and connotation of human existence, we can conclude that human social attributes are the main realization factors of human survival value.

4.1 Nao's Writing Method of Crossing Time and Space

At the beginning of the novel, the voice of the first narrator, Nao Xu, is created, creating a dialogue atmosphere between the narrator as a character and the implied reader and the real reader:

Hi!

My name is Nao, I am a "time" (time being).

Do you know what is "time"?

Well, if you give me some time, I will tell you. (Ruth Ozeki, 2013, p. 2)

Facing such eager and mysterious greetings, readers expect that the next will be a relaxed and interesting dialogue but find that the voice of the narrative comes from a girl who is preparing to commit suicide, so the reader's heart suddenly hangs up, eager to understand the cause of suicide and possible outlets. Nao's suicidal sentiment stems from her sudden return to life after returning from the United States to Japan. After the father was unemployed, he tried many times to commit suicide. The classmates of the school even completely despised and obliterated her existence by giving me a funeral prank. She therefore suspected that she really became a ghost. Her only spiritual comfort comes from the legendary great-grandmother, who is eager to resist the anxiety of the time, experience the value and reality of existence by describing the life story of the old man.

Thus, in the process of writing her own son, she opened up a space for dialogue, letting the wisdom of the old child moisturize her lonely heart and resist the temptation of death. The diary used by Nao also created a unique dialogue space. The diary was converted from Marcel Proust's Remembrance of the Year. The diary shop neatly cuts all the contents of the book, leaving only the cover, which is stuffed with blank paper. Nao used the "hack" culture (hack) born in the Internet age to describe this approach and thought that writing with such a book "is like a real publication", and that it is "excellently confidential" sex can prevent students from peek or put it on the Internet .From this we can find that the story of preventing Nao's suicide from giving birth to Nao is the story of writing the old one is the interaction with the old one. The unique dialogue space created by Nao also opens up a communication channel with strangers.

4.2 The Old Jiko's Dialogue Across Time and Space

Through the narrative of Nao, the legendary life of the old Jiko came to us and formed a multi-party dialogue space full of Zen wisdom. When Nao began to write a diary, the old man was over 100 years old and lived in a deep mountain temple. When Nao has a “philosophical problem,” she sends an email or text message to her old friend. From time to time, the long-distance return of the old Jiko and Nao Xu and the readers form a unique multilateral dialogue relationship. For example, when Nao Xu is ready to introduce the reader to the meditation method that the old Jiko taught her, she tells the readers while sending text messages to the old ones for comments: Well, wait a minute. I haven’t actually asked her if she can tell you about it. Now that I think about it, I should probably ask her first. Ok, I sent a text message to her and asked if she could tell my friend how to participate in Zen…Oh, wait. Cool! My son just replied to my text message, she said that as long as we are both serious, not in the hustle and bustle, then I teach you how to participate in Zen is no problem. I am not fooling around, what about you? I don’t think you are in trouble. At least, I will imagine that you don’t have it, and then maybe you won’t be. (Ruth Ozeki, 2013, p. 317)

The highly respected character voice of the old Jiko has increased the authority of Nao’s narrative and has a greater impact on the reader’s mind. “I will imagine that you don’t have it, then you may not.” Readers who read this sentence are likely to accept Nao’s psychological suggestion, believe that he is serious, and eager to hear her introduce how to participate in Zen. The “Guide to the Zen” that follows is mostly directed by the second person to explain how the reader wants to operate.This is similar to the three-face-to-face communication that connects the old Jiko with the readers and proves that the existence of the person is related to other things around.

4.3 The Soul of Ruth and Nao Xu

The two narrators of the novel, Ruth and Nao, belong to different communication layers. Ruth, as a reader of Nao’s diary after many years of completion, has no time to meet the time and space of Nao. However, the overall structure of the novel allows them to alternately describe the first person in the form of a first person, resulting in a round of dialogue. In addition, in the narrative order, because Nao Xu’s narrative is included in Ruth’s diary, the novel should first talk about Ruth to the diary, and then Nao’s diary content. However, the opening of the novel allowed Nao’s voice to eagerly greet the reader, and Ruth seemed to respond to the call and appeared, thus highlighting the theme of the dialogue.The dialogue between the two in different stratosphere also verifies the social attributes of people.

Before encountering the precious items of Nao, Ruth also fell into the anxiety of the idle time and the sense of emptiness. Like the author, she is a novelist and filmmaker. In order to take care of the sick mother and husband at the same time, she moved from New York to a small island town with only about 50 residents. When she first saw the towering trees around the house, she cried. “I have never felt so weak.” (Ruth Ozeki, 2013, p. 206) After living on the island for 5 years, she felt that the novels of the novel were exhausted and she turned to her own care. The long years of the mother of Alzheimer’s disease. This turn is like the life of Nao, who is eager to write about his own life. Fifteen years later, Ruth felt that her self-consciousness was further swallowed up by her cockroaches, eager for communication between people and complex and subtle interpersonal relationships. The Nao diary she got was her inspirational resuscitation, helping her and the outside world to communicate across time and space.

5 Conclusions

The social attribute theory of Marxism, Heidegger's "existentialism" and Confucius' "the thought of heaven and man" all point out that the connection between man and surrounding things is the main factor to realize the value of human existence. That is, the social attribute of man is the value of human existence. The main realization factor, in the "non-existent girl", the multi-conversation space between Nao, the old Jiko and Ruth and the way of its existence more specifically explain that the social attribute of human beings is the main realization factor of human existence value. It can be said that the girl who does not exist takes time as the classic and space as the latitude, showing the different ways in which people are connected, thus gaining personal life value.

References

[1] Ruth Ozeki. *A Tale For the Time Being*. Viking: Penguin. 2013.

[2] 奥古斯丁. 论自由意志[M]. 上海：上海人民出版社，2010.

[3] 恩格斯. 费尔巴哈论[M]. 北京：人民出版社，1997.

[4] 海德格尔. 时间与存在[M]. 陈嘉映, 王庆节译. 北京：商务印书馆，2018.

[5] 蓝荣策. 对人类本质的再认识[J]. 现代哲学，2001（1）：46-50.

[6] 刘欣桐, 等. 现代西方哲学[M]. 北京：人民出版社，1990.

[7] 露丝・尾关. 不存在的女孩[M]. 杭州：浙江文艺出版社，2015.

[8] 马克思，恩格斯. 马克思恩格斯全集[M]. 北京：人民出版社，1972.

[9] 张曙光. 哲学生存论的彰显及其意义[N]. 光明日报，2001-11-20.

翻译研究

Context and Disambiguation: A Case Study of Translating Idioms

邓　静

摘　要：本论文的主题是分析语境在英汉翻译选字用词上的价值。本文首先研究了歧义的产生以及语境对英汉翻译的影响，再以成语和习语的英汉互译为例，进一步分析如何处理翻译中的词汇和句法问题，最后，通过强调理解语境对翻译合理性的重要性，呼吁翻译专业的学生以及翻译爱好者提高对语境重要性的关注度，更好地掌握不同语境下词语的具体含义。翻译中一大基本功是对词的处理，即选字用词，它绝不是单凭所谓的语感，而是怎么理性地认识词，合理地处理这些词。因此，我们必须重视语境对词义、语义的影响，充分发挥语境功能在翻译中的作用。

关键词：语境；消歧；成语翻译；归化；异化

Abstract: The topic of this thesis is to analyze the value of context in the selection of words in English-Chinese translation. The paper works on the emergence of ambiguity and the influences of contexts in English-Chinese translation. Take translation of idioms as an example and further analyze how to deal with words and syntax in translation. Then, through emphasizing the importance of understanding context to the reasonableness of translation, appeal to translation majors to grasp the specific meaning of words or phrases in different contexts better. One of the basic skills in translation is the handling of words. The so-called word selection is what this means. However, the processing of words in translation is not only based on the so-called sense of language, but also how to understand the words rationally and deal with the words reasonably. The understanding of the meaning of words cannot be separated from the context. Therefore, we must pay attention to the influence of context on semantics and make full use of contextual functions in translation.

Key words: Context；Disambiguation；Idiom translation；Domestication；Foreignization

1　Introduction

There is a phenomenon of polysemy in both English and Chinese. The meaning of Chinese is fixed and rigorous, and it can be independent of context to some extent, while the meaning of English is flexible and depends on context to a great extent. There is a wealth of virtual means. When a word is used in a new language context, it produces new meanings. One of the basic skills in translation is how to deal with words. Foss, the representative of London functional Linguistics, said "Each word in a new context is a new word", so the translator must pay attention to the influence of context on the choice of words.

Context can be divided into two categories: one is small context, that is, the context that has direct and significant influence on language behavior, and the other is large context, that is, context with indirect and potential effect on language behavior. (Zhou, 2016, p. 47) Contextual ambiguity refers to the explicit semantic content of the expression of the speaker or the writer, while the listener or reader has different interpretations due to the influence of context factors. Contextual ambiguity is generally generated in proverbs' communicative activities.

Idioms are fixed phrases and are semantically indivisible. The cohesion of each word in the idiom is so close that its whole meaning cannot be deduced from the meaning of each word in the idiom. In addition to being able to understand some words or phrases in English according to their literal meaning, they can be understood as fixed or conventional idioms in the long process of language development and language use. Such fixed English phrases or sentences contain both idiom and non-idiom meanings.

Study of the value of context in the choice of words in translation has long attracted linguists' attention. The London School first gave a clear account of the importance of context in language use. The London School believes that human language activities are made up of three levels, namely, the entity, the form and the environment. Bronislaw Malinowski, a Poland human linguist, believes that language is a way of behavior, not an ideological signal, and a close combination of discourse and environment. The language environment is essential to understanding the language. He founded the theory that "complete speech in a speech environment is the real language fact". Rupert Firth, a British linguist. He elaborated the context in the context of "Personality and Language in Society" and starting from *Papers in Linguistics* (1934—1951, London, Oxford), proposed the theory and method of studying the discourse in the speech environment. Later, researchers emerged in endlessly and in recent years, context has almost become the central topic of current linguistic research. Both functional linguistics and sociolinguistics, both psycholinguistics and traditional pragmatics, regard context as an important object of language research. Someone has studied the classification of contextual constituent elements, studied contextual problems, and even reinterpreted context.

This paper aims to study the generation of ambiguity in the translation of idioms between English and Chinese and the value of context in the selection of words in English-Chinese translation. This thesis attempts to focus on the application of cultural equivalence and relevance translation theory in idiom translation. Improve the quality of translation on the basis of analyzing and grasping semantics in the context of specific language. In the selection of idiom translation methods, the choice is mainly discussed from the perspective of literal translation and free translation. (Jennifer Bracken, et. al., 2017) Study mainly collects, collates and finds books, periodicals from libraries and online to reserve theoretical knowledge and choose typical examples.

2 Emergence of Ambiguity in Translation

Translation ambiguity plays a major role in real-life bilingual language processing. So far, there is no clear and consistent answer to the question of what the meaning of a word is. The vagueness of the meaning of the word causes ambiguity in human communication. Especially in different historical and cultural backgrounds, global communication needs people to pay attention to the emergence of ambiguity.

2.1 The Emergence of Ambiguity

Ambiguity is a type of meaning in which several interpretations are plausible. A common aspect of ambiguity is uncertainty. It is thus an attribute of any idea or statement whose intended meaning cannot be definitively resolved according to a rule or process with a finite number of steps. (The ambi-part of the term reflects an idea of "two", as in "two meanings") (Zhang, 2006, p.102) Some researchers believe that the occurrence of ambiguity is caused by the general ambiguity of the speaker in the language unit, the single meaning of the speech unit, and the lack of proper understanding of the characteristics that they can convert to each other under certain conditions. Translation is the process of changing the speech product of one language to the speech product of another language while maintaining the content, that is, the meaning is unchanged. (Anat Prior, Shuly Wintner, Brian Macwhinney & Alon Lavie, 2011) Translation is the equivalence of words in the reception language which is as close as possible and natural to the original information, firstly, equivalence in meaning, followed by equivalence in style. However, due to the different nature of language and different linguistics, ambiguity is more likely to occur in translation.

Indirect mappings of translations across languages pose problems for bilingual language processing and language learning. These mis-mappings occur when one word has multiple translations into another language, creating what is referred to as translation ambiguity. In short, there are many reasons for ambiguity, and this article is mainly based on the influence of context on ambiguity.

2.2 Context Ambiguity

Context may play a role in resolving ambiguity. (Bock, 1978) For example, the same piece of information may be ambiguous in one context and unambiguous in another. Linguistic context can act to reduce lexical ambiguity. As a result, fewer translations may remain appropriate in a given context. Context can eliminate ambiguity and ensure the smooth transmission of information. The use of context can also make ambiguities Translation context is a completely new concept in the field of translation theory and practice. We can make full use of it to deal with ambiguity in translation practice. The most obvious manifestation of the function of context is the interpretation of contextual meaning and the elimination of ambiguity.

Contextual ambiguity refers to the ambiguity of a word in a particular pragmatic environment due to the information gap between the speaker and the listeners.

2.3 The Ambiguity of Idioms and the Uncertainty of Translation

Both Chinese and English are rich in Idioms. Idiom is a language phenomenon with a fixed structure and profound connotation. It is the embodiment and reflection of human history and culture in people's use of language. The fascination of idioms is mainly due to their implicit meaning, extended meaning and associative meaning. The dictionary translation of idioms is different from pragmatic translation in the bilingual context. The former is often isolated and static while the latter is flexible. The pragmatic values of the idioms often transcend their superficial meaning, and in most cases, literal translation does not work, or is not suitable for "foreignization". Otherwise, it will produce ambiguity.

Quine, Willard Van Orman first proposed the topic of uncertainty in translation in the works of *word and object*. An important content in this theory is the determination of meaning. The uncertainty of meaning will inevitably lead to the uncertainty of translation. He said that there are two reasons leading to the uncertainty of Translation: the uncertainty of meaning or connotation and the uncertainty of reference or extension. (Zhang, 2006, p. 102) Idioms have distinct cultural characteristics, and their semantics are polysemous and multi-layered. Therefore, the translator must pay attention to the contextual effects of the understanding and expression of the idioms. It is not easy to assume that any pair of idioms between the two languages has a reciprocal relationship and avoid making mistakes.

3 Context and Semantics

Context and Semantics are related to each other closely. The researchers of language and semantics have been interested in them for a long time. (Jennifer Bracken, et. al., 2017) Here the context is defined as a collection of relevant objects and surrounding influences that make the semantics of an object unique and comprehensible.

3.1 The Elements and Classifications of Context

The concept of context was first proposed by anthropologist Malinowski. With the extension of Firth, context is divided into co-text contextual contexts composed of linguistic factors and situational contextual contexts formed by the relationship between language and social environment. Now, when text is generated, context has both the text context and the subjective and objective environment. Which is a consensus. Mr. Qian Guanlian defines and classifies context: Context refers to the material and social environment on which speech acts are expressed. This environment includes both linguistic context and extra-linguistic context. (Li, 2003, p. 159) The American linguist Dell H. Hymes's statement is very interesting. He summed up the context as SPEAKING: S-Setting and Scene, P-Participants, E-Ends, A-Act Sequence, K- Key, I-Instrumentalities, N-Norms, G-Genres. This thesis mainly uses the classification method mentioned in the introduction-Context can be divided into two categories: one is small context, that is, the context that has direct and significant influence on language behavior, and the other is large context, that is, context with indirect and potential effect on language behavior.

3.2 Meaning of Semantics

Semantics is the linguistic and philosophical study of meaning, in language, programming languages, formal logics, and semiotics. It is concerned with the relationship between signifiers—like words, phrases, signs, and symbols—and what they stand for, their denotation. In linguistics, it is the study of the interpretation of signs or symbols used in agents or communities within particular circumstances and contexts. Within this view, sounds, facial expressions, body language, and proxemics have semantic (meaningful) content, and each comprises several branches of study. In written language, things like paragraph structure and punctuation bear semantic content; other forms of language bear other semantic content (https://en.wikipedia.org/wiki/Semantics) .

4 Translation of English and Chinese idioms

The idioms mentioned here are broad, including set phrases, colloquial expressions, proverbs and locutions. The translation of idioms cannot be treated in a static and isolated way. Only in a dynamic context can it be flexible and reproduced skillfully. Idiom translation is a difficult problem in translation study. Chinese idioms and English idioms are fixed phrases formed over a long period of time. Idiom translation can be classified into two basic categories: dictionary translation and pragmatic translation in literary context. Here mainly study the latter one.

4.1 The Characteristics of English Idioms

Chinese idioms are simple in form, with strong generalization and expressive power. The translation techniques of Chinese set phrases could be roughly divided into three kinds: literal translation, using English equivalent, and translation of the thought. (Xiong, 2015) In the Chinese context, idioms have both broad and narrow meanings: The generalized idioms emphasize the change of their history and the accumulation of history, which is called established expressions; Idioms in narrow sense are often in four-word format and they are mostly from classicism.

4.2 The Characteristics of Chinese Idioms

An idiom is a phrase of sentence whose meaning is not clear from the meaning of its individual words and which must be learnt as a whole unit and is a group of words whose meaning is different from the meanings of the individual words. (*Oxford Advanced Learner's English-Chinese Dictionary*, p.1042)

The sources of English idioms are very broad. Some idioms come from the Bible, mythical stories or some customs, and others come from the experience of people in daily production and life. An idiom is a phrase or an expression that has a figurative, or sometimes literal, meaning. Categorized as formulaic language, an idiom's figurative meaning is different from the literal meaning. There are thousands of idioms, occurring frequently in all languages. It is estimated that there are at least twenty-five thousand idiomatic expressions in the English language. (https://en.wikipedia.org/wiki/Idiom) Idiom in English emphasizes national characteristics and regional characteristics. (Yong, 2010) It does not fully reflect the meaning of idioms.

4.3 Domestication, Foreignization and Neutralization in Idiom Translation

Two of most commonly used methods in translating English idioms: domesticating method and foreignizing method from theoretical point of view. Domestication and foreignization, a pair of concepts first put forward by Lawrence Venuti, an American scholar, in 1995, in *The Translator's Invisibility*, are used to describe two strategies employed in translation. The two strategies have their respective advantages and disadvantages. Historically, foreignization and domestication can be regarded as the conceptual extension of literal translation and liberal translation, but they are not completely equivalent to literal translation and liberal translation. The core issue of literal translation and liberal translation is how to deal with forms and meanings at the language level, while foreignization and domestication breaks through the limitations of language factors and extends the vision to factors such as language, culture and aesthetics.

Domestication refers to the translation strategy of using transparent and fluent style to minimize the strangeness of the original text in translation. It makes the world of the source language close to the world of the target language culture readers as much as possible, thus achieving the "cultural equivalence" between the source and the target language cultures. (Carvalho Henriques, Helena. Foreignness, & Familiarity, 2013) Generalizing in a popular language, domestication requires the translator to move closer to the target readers and to adopt the way of target language used by target readers to convey the content of the original text. Foreignization means to deviate from the local mainstream values, retain the language and cultural differences of the original, or to preserve the foreign language of the original to a certain extent, and deliberately break the conventional translation of the target language. It advocates preserving the source language culture in the translation, enriching the language expression of target culture and target language. (Chen, 2010) Generalizing in a popular language, the rule of foreignization requires the translator to move closer to the author and to convey the content of the original text by means of the original expression corresponding to the author's use.

Let's look at a concrete case: "High buildings and large mansions are springing up like *mushrooms* in Beijing." One translation version is "在北京，高楼大厦如雨后春笋般地涌现" The translation of Mushrooms into a "雨后春笋" is in line with the geomorphic customs and language expression habits of the Chinese country. If foreignization translates it into "犹如蘑菇般",although it embodies the style of the original, it will make it difficult for the target readers to accept it.

Some people think that the core of the so-called "foreignization" and "domestication" lies in the preservation or replacement of images. If we take the understanding as the primary pursuit, it is also a way to put aside the image but directly to deal with the meaning. This is the so-called "neutralization". For example: "to kill two birds with one stone", the foreignization version is "一石二鸟", the domestication version is "一箭双雕", the neutralization is "一举两得". (Zhou, 2016, pp.33-34) In the process of translation, domestication and foreignization should be complementary. We should make the translation find a "convergence point" between the readers and the authors.

4.4 An Analysis of the Case of Idiom Ambiguity

English is heavily idiomatic, English idiom is widely used both in writing and speaking. "Idiom", the word, is originated from Greek; (Fan, p.165) it means "a special kind of expressing way of human language", or "a kind of art of human language". Chinese and English people create a lot of idioms that share the meanings; because of the different location, customs, history or logic thinking, there are more English and Chinese idioms cannot be counterparts each other although they present the same meanings literally. (Fan, p.165)

Therefore, ambiguity often occurs during translation, for instance: "A rolling stone gathers no moss" is translated into "滚石不生苔". In general, it means that it is impossible to grow moss on the stone that has been rolling. In Chinese, it is understood that people need to settle down calmly to precipitate. Similarly, an extension of a meaning is "changing jobs frequently, not getting rich". some people even associates to "流水不腐，户枢不蠹", "生命在于运动".Lock the stable door after the horse is stolen: it is not equal to Chinese "亡羊补牢". In English, the idiom means "take precautions when it is too late". For "birds of a feather flock together", we better translate it as "同种鸟儿一起飞", and if we translate it as "一丘之貉", then we add the flavor of censure to this idiom. For "three is better than one", we can translate it to "三个臭皮匠，顶过一个诸葛亮" or "众人拾柴火焰高".Obviously, the affection tint of the two translations is totally different in Chinese. Looking at this sentence alone, we are not sure what "one" stands for and its real meaning.

5 Conclusions

When linguistics develops to a certain stage, new breakthroughs must be sought, and new breakthroughs must originate from the criticism of the original linguistic theories. With the increasingly close ties between countries in the world, the development of language is becoming more and more abundant, and the challenges faced by translators are more and more serious. Of course, the development of technology has also made Machine Translation's processing power stronger and stronger. Whether it is human translation or machine translation, we should not ignore the importance of context analysis, which is the essential element of semantic existence. Only by analyzing the linguistic context and the cultural context of the source text can the literal and connotative meanings of the original be translated into the target text accurately and on this basis the quality of translation can be continuously improved.

References

[1] Anat Prior, Shuly Wintner, Brian Macwhinney, & Alon Lavie. Translation Ambiguity in and out of Context[J]. *Applied Psycholinguistics*, 2011, 32（1）：93-111.

[2] Carvalho Henriques, Helena Foreignness, & Familiarity. An Investigation into the Effects of Foreignization and Domestication in Translation[J]. *Masters Abstracts International*, 2013.

[3] https://en.wikipedia.org/wiki/Idiom. 检索日期: July, 10th, 2018.

[4] https://en.wikipedia.org/wiki/Semantics. 检索日期: July, 10th, 2018.

[5] Jennifer Bracken, Tamar Degani, Chelsea Eddington & Natasha Tokowicz. Translation semantic variability: How Semantic Relatedness Affects Learning of Translation-Ambiguous Word[J]. *Bilingualism: Language and Cognition* 20（4），2017：783-794.

[6] Jun Fan. English Idiom and Its Ambiguity in Translation[J].*Value Engineering,* 2010（6）：148-149.

[7] Michael Bock.Levels of Processing of Normal and Ambiguous Sentences in Different Contexts[J]. *Psychological Research*, 1978, Vol.40（1）：37-51.

[8] *Oxford Advanced Learner's English-Chinese Dictionary* (The Eighth Edition). Beijing: The Commercial Press, 2014.

[9] Xiao Chen.Domestication and Foreignization: A Unity of Acceptance and Rejection[J]. *Overseas English,* 2010(11): 448-450.

[10] 李丽君. 翻译中的语境和歧义[J]. 湘潭大学社会科学学报，2003，27（6）：159-161.

[11] 熊洁. 翻译中的文化对等性研究[J]. 中外企业家，2015（2）：268-269.

[12] 雍涛. 浅析英语习语的特征及翻译[J]. 网络财富，2010（8）：155-156.

[13] 张万敏. 从奎因的翻译不确定性到翻译的可译性[J]. 长春师范学院学报，2006，25（9）：102-103.

[14] 周劲松. 翻译基础十二讲[M]. 成都：电子科技大学出版社，2016.

All Men Are Brothers: An Oriental Approach to Pearl S. Buck's Translation of *Shui Hu Zhuan*

李 清

摘 要：东方学是一门学科，也是一种象征权力话语的意识形态。本论文以赛珍珠的《水浒传》译本 *All Men Are Brothers* 为研究对象，选取东方学为研究视角，旨在揭示东方学的意识形态对翻译的塑造。通过分析译者赛珍珠的东方学者身份，对比原文与译本的语言特征，论述了译本在东方学视角下所代表的文化意义：一方面促进了东西方交流，推进了文化的多元发展；另一方面，在东方学政治性的影响下，译本也被添上了西方中心主义和文化霸权主义的色彩。

关键词：东方学；翻译；赛珍珠；《水浒传》

Abstract: Orientalism is defined as an academic discipline, and also an ideology, emphasizing the power distance from other cultures to the East. This essay intends to take *All Men Are Brothers*, Peral S. Buck's translation of *Shui Hu Zhuan*, as an example to combine theories of translation and Orientalism by means of contrastive analysis. From the perspective of Orientalism, translation could not only play a crucial and positive role in equal communication between China and the West, but also become a motivation for Western-centrism and expansion of cultural hegemony under the influence of Orientalism.

Key words: Orientalism; translation; Pearl S. Buck; *Shui Hu Zhuan*

1 Introduction

All Men Are Brothers is the first and also the last translation work of Pearl S. Buck. It is the initial English version of *Shui Hu Zhuan* written by Shi Nai'an. Pearl S. Buck buried herself into the translation for five years since the late 1920s with dedication to reading other Chinese classical novels. Since it was published by John Day Company in 1933, (庄华萍, 2010, p. 115) *All Men Are Brothers* has become the greatest hit in terms of its countless reprint and a great number of sales on Amazon and other online bookstores. Its popularity embodies the acceptance and admiration of English readers on Pearl S. Buck's version, and stands for a remarkable accomplishment she has achieved.

However, it was also mired in long-time controversy. Critical judgments and obvious suspicion arose from both China and other countries, either in 1930s when she was awarded the Nobel Prize in Literature, or in 1990s when the release of articles on Pearl S. Buck began to increase exponentially. Lu Xun was the first person who criticized the title of Pearl S. Buck's version in his letter to Xiao Ke in 1934. (马红军, 2003, p.123) Qian Gechuan viewed that translation work as mistranslation, sparking more similar reproaches of other critics. (钱歌川, 1981, p. 10)

Why does a translation work obtain floods of opposite judgments? To answer this question, it is circumscribed to only focus on singular terms, sentences, structures from linguistics. This essay intends to discuss key features of *All Men Are Brothers* translated by Pearl S. Buck, and analyze the clash of different civilizations by comparing it with *Shui Hu Zhuan* from the perspective of Orientalism. Translation could not only play a crucial and positive role in equal communication between China and the West, but also become a motivation for Western-centrism and expansion of cultural hegemony under the influence of Orientalism. Full consideration of Buck's identity as an Orientalist will contribute to a new perspective of her translation study, which indicates the relationship among literary translation, ideology and cultural hegemony and will stimulate translators to consider these factors in translating.

2 Orientalism: A Brief Introduction

Orientalism is a term used to refer to academic discipline or academic field, archaeology, and Eurocentrism. (蒋骁华, 2008, p. 11) In the first place, the term "Orientalist" can refer to the following: a person who is professionally engaged in the study and teaching of societies and cultures, languages, people, history and archaeology in the Near East and the Far East; a person interested in Oriental issues; someone with interest in the East and the clash between it and the West; and more . (蒋骁华, 2008, p. 11) Generally, if someone works on knowledge about the East, writes or researches on the East, no matter whether he is an anthropologist, a socialist, a historian, a linguistic or a sinologist, he is an Orientalist. When it comes to the second meaning, "Orientalism" finds its way to acquire negative connotations in some quarters and is interpreted as the study of the East by Westerners shaped by the attitudes of European imperialism in the 18th and 19th centuries with prejudice. This viewpoint was articulated and propagated by Edward Said in *Orientalism* (1978), a critical history of this scholarly tradition.

Before the application of Orientalism into case study of translation, it is a prerequisite for us to date back to its history.

Orientalism originated from the West in modern times, but with realistic occurrence in the Middle Age. It is universally reckoned that the period from the late 16th century to the 17th century has witnessed the birth and evolution of Orientalism. Oriental studies became systematic during the Renaissance, with the initial domination of linguistic and religious factors. During the 18th century, Western scholars strided in the primary stage, reaching out the mysterious history and the geography of the region, though knowledge of some areas is still absent, like Japan and Tibet. What needs to be noticed is that almost all Orientalists have published their own translations. Therefore, they are called "Orientalist-translators". (蒋骁华, 2008, p.12) With the boom of Western civilization and global expansion of colonialism, a great number of Eastern classics were introduced to Europe, contributing to the fast development of Eastern literature in the West. In the twentieth century, the participation of scholars from the newly independent nations of the eastern region inevitably changed the nature of studies considerably.

As for the influence that Orientalism generates in translation, itis viewed differently from scholar to scholar. Since the publication of Edward Said's *Orientalism* in 1978, much academic discourse has begun to use the term "Orientalism" to refer to a general Western attitude towards Middle Eastern, Asian, and North African societies. In Said's analysis, the West essentializes these societies as static and undeveloped—thereby fabricating a view of Oriental culture that can be studied and reproduced. (Said, 1979, p. 363) Nevertheless, if we set the politics and ideology aside, it is undeniably true that the existence and development of Orientalism promoted most translating practices and improved the cultural communication between the East and the West, which was conveyed by Niranjiana in 1992 and Xu Sumin in 1992. (蒋骁华, 2008, p.11)

3 Contrastive Analysis from an Oriental Approach

In a 1998 article, Robert Wechsler said:" Literary translation is an odd art…Like a musician, a literary translator takes someone else's composition and performs it in his own way." Compared to non-literary translation, literary translation is more concerned with characters, nature, values and imagination instead of facts and information. Normally, the more subjective the source text is, the more difficult it is to reach an agreement among readers of the translation version. Therefore, it makes sense that Buck's style influences her translation of *Shui Hu Zhuan*, the well-known literary masterpiece, and exerts various impacts on different readers. In this part, *All Men Are Brothers* is going to be analyzed from the following three aspects: the translator, the titles and formalities, and elements of language. The perspective of analysis is Orientalism, and the analyzing method is contrastive analysis, maintaining linguistic analysis as well as my comments from an Oriental approach.

3.1 The Orientalist-Translator: Pearl S. Buck

Pearl Sydenstricker Buck was an American writer and novelist. As the daughter of missionaries, Buck spent most of her life before 1934 in Zhenjiang, China. Her novel *The Good Earth* was the best-selling fiction in the United States in 1931 and 1932 and she won the Pulitzer Prize in 1932. In 1938, she was awarded the Nobel Prize in Literature "for her rich and truly epic descriptions of peasant life in China and for her biographical masterpieces". (https://www.nobelprize.org/prizes/literature/1938/summary/)

3.2 Analysis on Titles and Formalities

The original text is also known as *Zhong Yi Shui Hu Zhuan*, in which "Zhong Yi" refers to one of the moral virtues being faithful to others, such as your leader, friend or someone who has ever helped you; "Shui Hu" refers to the name of Liangshan Po, a place in Shandong province, which is the geographical background of the whole story; "Zhuan" is a literary form of Chinese classical literature and same as the meaning of "novel" today. As a matter of fact, "Shui Hu" is recorded in *The Book of Songs*, illustrating the revision and boom of Zhou Dynasty. (1046-256BC) It is an analogy with the unity and form of the leading roles in this novel. With so rich cultural symbolic meanings, it is difficult to translate the name of this book into English to help readers of target language comprehend it. "Shui" means water, "Hu" refers to margins or borders, and "Zhuan" can be translated into “novel”. However, the headache is that these words make sense neither when they are put together, nor reflect the original style. Therefore, it is wise of Pearl S. Buck to apply the sentence from a saying of Confucius to the title. The saying, “all men are brothers”, does not only reflect the spirit of “Zhong Yi” of greenwood heroes in the novel, but also bridge the gap between the author and English readers. It can be viewed as an indirect but strong opposition to those negative judgements that criticized her single use of literal translation strategy because she appropriately chooses liberal translation strategy here. As “Shui Hu” is barely repeated in the book, it is too difficult for readers of target language to sketch the image like what the readers of source language do. Consequently, her abandonment of translating “Shui Hu” directly is of great wisdom. Apart from that, it embodies her belief in equality behind the words: everyone will view people around as brothers and the fact has little to do with the nationality, the color, and the hierarchy.

The title of every chapter all follows the rule of antithesis, which is one of the inimitable characteristics of Chinese chapter novels. In the version of Pearl S. Buck, she notices and remains that through neat and balanced structure to restore the Chinese uniqueness of original work. Here are some examples.

Shui Hu Zhuan: 入云龙斗法破高廉黑旋风下井救柴进

All Men Are Brothers: The Dragon of The Clouds uses his magic to vanquish Kao Lian. The Black Whirlwind descends into a well to save Ch’ai Chin.

Shui Hu Zhuan: 及时雨会神行太保黑旋风斗浪里白条

All Men Are Brothers: The Opportune Rain meets The Magic Messenger. The Black Whirlwind fights with White Stripe in the water.

It is obvious that metaphors are used widely in the original text. However, metaphors may cause ambiguity and compromise the clarity of the original intention while translating. Besides, the figurative meaning is often bound to cultural elements, which is another challenge for translators. In this case, Pearl S. Buck chose foreignization to cope with it, which means deliberately breaking target conventions while retaining the foreignness of the original. (Venuti, 2008, p. 273) She was faithful to the syntax and semantics of the original book, including the nicknames of characters. As shown above, “White Stripe In the water” is a vivid presentation of Zhang Shun’s character image, which portrays a man swimming in the water like a fish in the sea. Through analysis above, we can draw a conclusion that although restricted by conditions at that time, Pearl S. Buck has made great efforts to elaborate on the exotic style of the Chinese literature.

Formalities at the beginning and end of every chapter are another prominent symbol of Chinese chapter novels. They are usually sentences or fixed structures without meaning but full of noticeable cultural features and playing a role in guiding the readers to the next chapter or working as a reminder. Pearl S. Buck restored these sentences in her translation, too. Here are some examples.

Shui Hu Zhuan: 且听下回分解。(施耐庵, 2016, p.16)

All Men Are Brothers: Pray hear it told in the next chapter. (Buck, 1933, p. 46)

Shui Hu Zhuan: 且说……(施耐庵, 2016, p.14)

All Men Are Brothers: Let it to be told further. (Buck, 1933, p. 41)

Shui Hu Zhuan: 话分两头……(施耐庵, 2016, p. 2)

All Men Are Brothers: Now the story divides into two parts.(Buck, 1933, p. 1108)

In Chinese chapter novels, stories are comparatively complete in every chapter. In other words, the following four parts are indispensable: beginning, development, climaxand ending. As for transition from one part to another, the author of Chinese chapter novels tends to use formalities to guide the readers to the next chapter till the end of the whole novel. Pearl S. Buck adopted literal translation to remain formalities as well, in order to provide the English-native readers with a sense of freshness and strangeness and strengthen attractiveness of Chinese unique literary form in this version. Furthermore, her translation is likely to break the hegemony of Western literature in the world and work as a cultural medium of friendly interactions between the two peoples.

3.3 Analysis on Elements of Language

According to Roman Jakobson, translation is viewed as interpretation of verbal signs and is distinguished into three labels, namely, intralingual translation, interlingual translation and intersemiotic translation. (as cited in 周劲松, 2016, p.3) When there is a great gap between the source language and the target language, it is a common way for translators to adopt liberal translation as the main translating strategy to entitle the work to more explicit sense. (庄华萍, 2010, p. 116) Nonetheless, Pearl S. Buck's version presents a distinctive translating method that is based on literal translation and is the best reflection of the cultural characteristics of original literary work.

With reference to her translation about the words and phrases, I would like to illustrate from nicknames of heroes and fixed collocations in Chinese. It is one of the most obvious characteristics of *Shui Hu Zhuan*that every hero has his or her own nickname. There are three functions of nicknames: identifying characters, amusing the reader and evoking emotions. Therefore, it could be a challenge for the translator to find the functional equivalence to serve the informative, emotional, creative and aesthetic function of the work. (Nida, 2001, p.87) The key to a good version lies in accurate translation of metaphor and emphasis on Chinese culture. (许燕, 2008, p. 88) As an English translator, Pearl S. Buck still lacks sufficient and comprehensive knowledge about Chinese culture. Priest Hwa, her translation of "花和尚鲁智深" in *All Men Are Brothers*, serves as a strong explanation. There are two inappropriate points here. Firstly, a monk is of course not equal to a priest. Secondly, "花" is mistakenly translated into the first name, which is contradictory to his name, Lu Zhishen. As a matter of fact, "花和尚"refers to the tattoo on his back. As mentioned before, translation covers intralingual translation which is an interpretation of verbal signs by means of other signs in the same language. Therefore, translation like that in Pearl S. Buck's version is likely to hinder the international cultural exchange because of her biased comprehension of the symbolism of the nickname and her over-literal translating strategy.

A great number of fixed collocations in *Shui Hu Zhuan*are shaped by Chinese culture. Translators often fail to find correspondents of those cultural-loaded expressions in another language. Thus, translation requires understanding from a holistic approach. However, Pearl S. Buck acts oppositely so she makes some abrupt and embarrassing mistakes. For example, "叔叔青春多少" is translated into "green spring times"(Buck, 1933, p. 213) and "远恶军州"is translated into "to so evil a place and so distant". (Buck, 1933, p. 152)

As for the sentence structure, Pearl S. Buck abandons tree-like sentence structure in English with emphasis on logic and use of clauses, but remains the bamboo-like sentence structure that is more common in Chinese. (Heaney, 1999, p. 27) As an explanation to this, she chooses to connect the short sentences with "and" for seven times to remain Chinese characteristics in the following sentence.

Shui Hu Zhuan: 原来宋江是个好汉，只爱学使枪棒，于女色上不十分要紧。这阎婆惜水也似后生，况兼十八九岁，正在妙龄之际，因此，松江不中那婆娘意。(施耐庵, 2016, p. 120)

All Men Are Brothers: Because Sung Chiang was originally and by nature a good fellow and he loved only to use weapons and learn the ways of war and the love of women was to him a thing of no great importance. But this P'o Hsi was a woman as unstable as water, and she was but eighteen or nineteen years old, and was in the flower of her youth, and for this she was not pleased with Sung Chiang. (Buck, 1933, p. 317)

In summary, Pearl S. Buck has achieved herexpectation in language style, injecting Chinese cultural elements into her translation to some degree. She translates mainly by means of literal translation, which entitles her version to beauty of mystique and freshness, but her overexertion caused abruptness and misunderstanding for readers of both languages, which has been detrimental to the transmission of the rich meaning of original work and efficient communication between two cultures.

4 Conclusions

The genesis of constant debate about Pearl S. Buck's translation is lurking in her choice of translating strategy, namely, literal translation instead of liberal translation, and foreignization instead of domestication on two hugely different texts.

On the one hand, Pearl S. Buck is an Orientalist-translator, stemming from the fact that she has a good command of Chinese and has published her translation work, as well as remains the Western intellectual paradigm. Therefore, it is a new way to analyze her translation, *All Men Are Brothers*, through a perspective of Orientalism. There is no denying that her translation of *Shui Hu Zhuan*has boosted the intercourse between the East and the West and caused the surge of Western enthusiasm for Chinese culture. We can draw a conclusion that her translation, as a part of all the translating works by Orientalist-translators, has contributed to connection and combination of cultures both in the East and the West for the first time in the twentieth century and laid the ground for further communication on cultural level for two parties in the world.

On the other hand, it deserves to be noticed that Pearl S. Buck is much likely to create a so-called "Oriental literary style". This style is defined from the perspective of an American, indicating the Westerners' deliberate purpose of meeting American expectations on Chinese psychology and culture during translation. Their mindset with prejudice towards Chinese is amphibolic language style. In this way, Buck succeeded in making the readers of target language believe that they are reading the original work by Shi Nai'an. At last, this essay encourages further translation research to explore the cultural elements of famous translation versions without neglecting the impact of politics and ideology.

References

[1] Buck, P. S. *All Men Are Brothers* [M]. New York: The John Day Company, 1933.

[2] Heaney, S. *Beowulf: A New Translation* [M]. London: Faber and Faber,1999.

[3] Nida, E. A. *Language and Culture: Contexts in Translating* [M]. Shanghai: Shanghai Foreign Language Education Press, 2001.

[4] Said, E. *Orientalism* [M]. New York: Vintage Books, 1979.

[5] *The Nobel Prize in Literature 1938*. Retrieved July 6, 2018 from https://www.nobelprize.org/prizes/literature/1938/summary/.

[6] Venuti, L. *The Translator's Invisibility: A History of Translation*[M]. London: Routledge, 2008.

[7] Wechsler, R. *Performing Without AStage: The Art of Literary Translation* [M]. North Haven: Catbird Press, 1998.

[8] 蒋骁华. 东方学对翻译的影响[J]. 中国翻译，2008（5）：11-12.

[9] 马红军. 为赛珍珠的“误译”正名[J]. 四川外语学院学报，2003（3）：123.

[10] 钱歌川. 翻译的基本知识[M]. 长沙：湖南科学技术出版社，1981.

[11] 施耐庵. 水浒传[M]. 长春：时代文艺出版社，2016.

[12] 许燕. 二十年来的《水浒传》英译研究[J]. 山东外语教学，2008（2）：88.

[13] 周劲松. 翻译基础十二讲[M]. 成都：电子科技大学出版社，2016.

[14] 庄华萍. 赛珍珠的《水浒传》翻译及其对西方的叛逆[J]. 浙江大学学报（人文社会科学版），2010（6）：115-116.

A Contrastive Study of Chinese and English Grammatical Structure in *Autumn in Peiping*

魏　荣

摘　要：汉英语言对比是语言学研究的一个热点。本文是建立《故都的秋》原文和译文以及汉英语法结构不同的基础上，主要通过连淑能的《英汉对比研究》中的理论对比分析《故都的秋》原文和张培基译本里面如何体现的中英语法结构的差异，并进一步探讨造成中英语法结构不同的原因。本文将从刚柔性、动静态这两个具体的方面来对比分析汉英语法结构在散文《故都的秋》原文和译文之间的差异，希望能为英汉翻译方法和实践提供一个新的角度。

关键词：汉英语言对比；语法结构；刚柔性；动静态

Abstract: The contrastive study of Chinese and English is a hotspot in linguistic research. In this paper, based on the original text: *Autumn in Peiping* and Mr. Zhang's classic and the different grammatical structures of Chinese and English, the writer will make a comparative analysis to explore and summarize the differences of the two languages in the aspects of rigidity and flexibility, stativeness and dynamicity mainly by means of the theory in Lian Shuneng's book: Contrastive Studies of English and Chinese, then to explore the deeper reasons why they are different in these aspects. This paper aims to provide a new perspective for the method and practice of English-Chinese translation.

Key words: Contrastive study of Chinese and English；Grammatical structure；Rigidity and Flexibility；Stativeness and Dynamicity

1　Introduction

The prose *Autumn in Peiping*, written by Yu Dafu, a famous essayist of China, integrates the sentiment of autumn and the chants of autumn into the text, and expresses his missing for hometown and motherland with strong feelings and beautiful diction. What's more, the English version, translated by Zhang Peiji shows the beauty of the article and the differences between Chinese and English. There have been quite a few contrastive studies of Chinese and English at home and abroad, however, there is a lack of analysis of a particular article in these two aspects. Many researchers focus on the functional linguistics and the grammatical features. As for contrastive study, Wang Sue has conducted an implicit comparative analysis of Xi Jinping's New Year greetings and his translations. (2016, p.159) With regard to abstraction and concretion, In Shao Weiying's paper, he indicates that English tends to use abstract expressions, and Chinese inclines to use specific expressions.(2017, p.102) There are plenty of contrastive studies overseas, such as the functional analysis of English, and the linguistic relativity and language learning, however there are few studies on a specific essay to show the differences between Chinese and English in contrastive linguistics. In this paper, based on the original text and Mr. Zhang's classic, the writer will make a comparative analysis to explore and summarize the differences of the two languages in the aspects of rigidity and flexibility, stativeness and dynamicity, then to explore the deeper reasons why they are different in these aspects.

It is of vital importance to understand the subtler differences between Chinese and English, so as to understand the different ways of thinking between native-English speaker and native Chinese speaker. To some degree, it can provide English learners with some reference, and therefore, help them better understand English. Furthermore, to some extent, the paper can inspire the language researchers and translators in their future study, which will help spread the beauty of Chinese to more countries.

The research method used in this paper is guided by previous theories of predecessor's researches. This paper, from the perspective of Contrastive linguistics, uses the relevant linguistic theories: the methods of the combination of description and interpretation. First of all, the writer will define rigidity and flexibility, stativeness and dynamicity, then make a detailed description of the two texts in English and Chinese and analyze the differences between the two languages. On this basis, the writer will try to sum up the differences between them systematically and explore the deep-rooted reasons of these differences.

2 Rigidity and Flexibility

2.1 The Definition of Rigidity and Flexibility

Chinese is a flexible language, while English is a rigid language. In the chapter two of *The Contrastive Study of English and Chinese*, Lian Shuneng says that English has morphological changes and the sentence is centered by the verb. Its grammar is "rigid". The Chinese language has no morphological change, the sentence is not centered by the verb, and its grammar is "flexible".(2010, p. 51) English sentences take the verb as the center, whose grammar embodies rigidity. Most of Chinese sentences do not take the verb as the center, and the grammar embodies the flexibility. The subject of Chinese can be used as a variety of words and that the Chinese predicate part may not have the verb is the embodiment of Chinese grammatical flexibility, the English subject may use many words to act, and that the English predicate part must have the verb is the embodiment of English grammatical rigidity. (Peng, 2016, p. 102) There are strict subject-predicate structures in English sentences, whose structure is usually composed of noun phrases and verb phrases. The predicate verb is the center of the sentence. Chinese sentence patterns cannot be centered on verbs, and Chinese sentence patterns are diverse, such as topic sentences, agent sentences, descriptive sentences, existential sentences, continuous sentences and so forth.

2.2 The Analysis on the Rigidity and Flexibility in *Autumn in Peiping*

2.2.1 The "de" pattern

"De" is one of the most powerful function words in Chinese.(Li, An, Zhang, 1998, p. 93) There is no "de" patterns in English. In the Autumn in Peiping, the "de" pattern plays the role of adjectives to describe the things or represents a state of being. There are some examples.

（1）Version 1: 秋天，无论在什么地方的秋天，总是好的。

Version 2：Autumn, wherever it is, always has something to recommend itself.

As can be seen from the example, In the Chinese sentence, it has the “de” pattern and it plays the role of an adjective to describe autumn, which means autumn is good. while in English, there is not the“de”pattern, and“好的”is replaced by the verb“recommend”.

（2）Version 1: 江南，秋当然也是有的。

Version2: There is of course autumn in the South too.

In this example, In the Chinese sentence, the “de” pattern represents a state of being, which means the same as the English version, which translates the original sentence as an existential sentence. This is there is autumn.

（3）Version 1: 秋并不是名花，也并不是美酒，那一种半开，半醉的状态，在领略秋的过程上，是不合适的。

Version 2：Unlike famous flowers which are most attractive when half opening, good wine which

is most tempting when one is half drunk, autumn, however, is best appreciated in its entirety.

As can be seen from the example, In the Chinese sentence, it has the “de” pattern and it plays the role of an adjective to express the meaning that it is improper. In the English version, it uses the adjective to express the similar meaning.

2.2.2 The duplicate verb sentence

In the duplicate verb sentence, the predicate is usually a form of the whole which is welded by adverbs or related words, and there are some logical relations between them, such as juxtaposition, progression and causality. The subject can only appear before the predicate. That is, each small sentence is not state the object alone. Then all those who conform to this condition are the duplicate verb sentence, whereas the other is the complex sentence. (Wu, 2000, p.132) There are some examples.

（4）Version 1: 北国的秋，却特别的来得清，来得静，来得悲凉。

Version2: In North China, however, it is particularly limpid, serene and melancholy.

In the example, the Chinese version uses three same verbs “来”, which means coming, while in English, there only can be one predicate in a complete sentence. Therefore, the English sentence uses three paratactic adjectives to express the similar meaning.

（5）Version 1: 脚踏上去，声音也没有，气味也没有，只能感出一点点极微细极柔软的触觉。

Version2: Quiet and [6]

_____, they feel tiny and soft underfoot.

In this sentence, The English version do not translate the Chinese verb “没有”, which means without. The English sentence uses two adjectives “quiet and smelliness” to express the similar meaning.

（6）Version 1: 灰土上留下来的一条条扫帚的细纹，看起来既觉得细腻，又觉得清闲。

Version2: You will discover countless lines left by his broom in the dust, which look so fine and quiet.

This example expresses the ideal well that there is only one predicate in a complete English sentence. The English sentence combine the two Chinese verb "觉得" into one verb "look" and it not only express the similar meaning, but also obeys the English grammar.

2.2.3 Chinese serial-verbs sentence

In the *Semantic Labeling of Chinese Serial-Verbs Sentence Based on Feature Structure*, the writer studies the semantic annotation models of "Serial-Verbs Sentence". He indicates that feature Structure Model provides a different semantic parse approach for Chinese Information Processing, which can represent the complicated semantic relations among the subject, the predicates and the objects of "Serial-Verbs Sentence". (Chen, Ji, Lv, 2013, p. 60) In the *Autumn in Peiping*, we can also learn the semantic relations from the original text and Mr. Zhang's classic. The Serial-Verbs Sentence in this text, it has only one subject, however it has more than one verb to explain the subject's state and action. It is shown in the following examples.

（7）Version 1:一个人夹在苏州上海杭州，或厦门香港广州的市民中间，混混沌沌地过去，只能感到一点点清凉。

Version2: While muddling along all by myself among the urban dwellers of Suzhou, Shanghai, Xiamen, Hong Kong or Guangzhou, I feel nothing but a little chill in the air.

In the example, the Chinese sentence uses three different verbs:"夹""过去""感到", while in English, they are replaced by present participle "muddling", the preposition "among", and the verb "feel". There is only one verb in the English version.

（8）Version 1: 只能感到一点点清凉，秋的味，秋的色，秋的意境与姿态，总看不饱，尝不透，赏玩不到十足。

Version2: I feel nothing but a little chill in the air, without ever relishing to my heart's content the flavour, colour, mood and style of the season.

In the Chinese version, there are three verbs, and they are "感到""看""尝" , which is similar to the meaning of "feel""look", and "taste". In the English one, the sentence only has one verb "feel" and it combines the Chinese verb "看""尝"into one English present participle "relishing".

3 Stativeness and Dynamicity

This chapter focuses on the transformation of several Chinese dynamic features to static features of English embodied in the translation process, including preposition structure, nouns, prepositions, adjectives and verbs in Chinese -English translation.

3.1 The Definition of Stativeness and Dynamicity

Lian Suneng holds the view that "English tends to use nouns, so the narration is static, Chinese tends to use verbs, so the narration is dynamic". (2010, p.133) Quirk and others point out that, broadly speaking, the nature of nouns is static, referring to static entities, whether specific nouns or abstract nouns; on the contrary, the nature of verbs is dynamic and can be used to denote actions, activities and conditions of temporary or change. (Quirk et al., 1973, p.48)There are many Chinese verbs and many English nouns. Chinese verbs are replaced by English nouns, prepositions, or adjectives when translating Chinese into English.

3.2 The Analysis on the Stativeness and Dynamicity in *Autumn in Peiping*

3.2.1 Prepositions denote the meaning of verbs

The expression of verb meaning in prepositional structure is one of the important manifestations of English static characteristics. Because English belongs to the hypotactic language, the inner relation between the sentence and the word mainly depends on the connection of preposition. Therefore, English has always used prepositions to connect the meaning of sentences and words. The structure of different prepositions has a different cohesive meaning. The following are some specific examples of the meaning of prepositional structures expressed in the prose *Autumn in Peiping*.

（9）Version 1: 我不远千里，要从杭州赶上青岛，更要从青岛赶上北平来的理由，也不过想饱尝一尝这“秋”，这故都的秋味。

Version2: To enjoy its atmosphere to the full in the onetime capital, I have, therefore, made light of travelling a long distance from Hangzhou to Qingdao, and thence to Peiping.

As can be seen from the two sentences, The Chinese sentence uses the verb “赶上”, while in the English sentence, it is replaced by the prepositions “from” and “to”. Although they are prepositions, they represent the meaning of verb, which also means going to Qing Dao or Bei Ping. “Excessive use of nouns can make sentences wordy, vague and devoid of vigor.” (2010, p. 135) The English version cannot fully express the motion notwithstanding the expression of verb meaning.

（10）Version 1: 在北平即使不出门去吧，就是在皇城人海之中，租人家一椽破屋来住着，早晨起来，泡一碗浓茶，向院子一坐……

Version2: Suppose you put up in a humble rented house inside the bustling imperial city, you can, on getting up at dawn, sit in your courtyard sipping a cup of strong tea…

Compared with the Chinese sentence, the verb“不出门”is replaced by the preposition “in”, which expresses the similar meaning to the Chinese. What’s more, the degree of the Chinese verb “起来” “泡” has been weakened. Hence the English version is less dynamic.

3.2.2 Adjectives denote the meaning of verbs

Adopting adjectives to express the meaning of verbs is another common manifestation of the static tendency of English discourse. This is closely related to the evolution of English adjectives. English adjectives are new, but most are derived from nouns. Compared with verbs, the number of adjectives in English is more and more large. There are some examples.

（11）Version 1: 北国的秋，却特别地来得清，来得静，来得悲凉。

Version2: In North China, however, it is particularly limpid, serene and melancholy.

In the English version, the Chinese verb “来” is deleted, which has the similar meaning of coming. The three Chinese verbs are replaced by three English adjectives “limpid”“serene” and “melancholy”. Although it expresses the similar meaning, its dynamicity is weakened.

（12）Version 1: 脚踏上去，声音也没有，气味也没有，只能感出一点点极微细极柔软的触觉。

Version2: Quiet and smelliness, they feel tiny and soft underfoot.

The Chinese verb “没有”, which has the similar meaning of “without” is replaced by two adjectives. The two adjectives express the meaning of the verb. Hence, its dynamicity is weakened.

4 Conclusions

This paper is an attempt to contrast the grammatical structure of Chinese and English. Based on the original text: *Autumn in Peiping* and Mr. Zhang's classic and the different grammatical structures of Chinese and English, the writer makes a comparative analysis to explore and summarize the differences of the two languages in the aspects of rigidity and flexibility, stativeness and dynamicity. The whole paper is guided by the theory in the book *Contrastive Studies of English and Chinese* written by Lian Shuneng. According to the contrastive study, it is verified that Chinese is more flexible and dynamic than English. In terms of rigidity and flexibility, in the *Autumn in Peiping,* Chinese prefers to the “de” pattern, the duplicate verb sentence, and serial-verbs sentence, which express more flexibility than English. In the aspect of stativeness and dynamicity, English uses other words to denote the meaning of verbs, such as prepositions and adjectives. Hence, English is less dynamic to some degree. The writer hopes it can bring others some viewing angels to understand the differences between the Chinese and English grammatical structure. The discussion in this paper is only a starting point in the long journey, and the thesis is still to be validated, deepened and extended. The author will continue to try hard in this direction.

References

[1] R. Quirk, S. Greenbaum, G. Leech and J. Svartvik. *A Grammar of Contemporary English*[M]. London: Longman, 1973.

[2] 陈波，姬东鸿，吕晨. 基于特征结构的汉语连动句语义标注研究[J]. 中文信息学报，2013（5）：60-66，74.

[3] 连淑能. 英汉对比研究[M]. 北京：高等教育出版社，2010.

[4] 李讷，安珊笛，张伯江. 从话语角度论证语气词“的”[J]. 中国语文，1998（2）：93-103.

[5] 彭长江. 英汉语法“硬与软”和汉语句型划分——与连淑能先生商榷[J]. 湖南师范大学社会科学学报，2016，45（6）：101-107.

[6] 王素娥. 英汉语显隐性对比——以习近平主席新年贺词为例[J]. 现代语文（文学研究版），2016：（9）：159-160.

[7] 吴松. 复谓句研究：兼论对复杂谓语范围的重新界定[J]. 学术交流，2000（4）：129-133.

[8] 邵惟韺. 抽象化与具体化——英汉表达方法认知对比与翻译中的范畴转换[J]. 华东理工大学学报（社会科学版），2017（3）：102-109.

Translation of Political Terms under Eugene Nida's Functional Equivalence Theory: A Case Study of "Belt and Road" Translation

向张玉洁

摘　要：本文在尤金奈达翻译功能对等理论基础上，探究一带一路术语的翻译版本。文化全球化进程加快，严谨处理文化交流的问题显得更有必要。本文采用“尤金·奈达”的翻译功能对等理论。因此本文将在词汇对等、句法对等、篇章对等、文本对等的基础上展开分析。本文分四个部分。采用了个例分析法和数据分析，结合尤金奈达功能对等理论研究一带一路名称的官方译本，得出结论，即在翻译对等理论指导下的译本更加适合当今政治术语的翻译。

关键词：功能对等；一带一路；政治术语；中国特色

Abstract: This paper explores the translated version of the Belt and Road Initiative based on the translation equivalence theory. Under the circumstance where the culture globalization is faster and faster, it is more necessary to deal with the problems of cultural communications seriously. This paper adopts the translation theory of Eugene A Nida's translation functional equivalence theory. Therefore, the paper's analysis is based on the vocabulary equivalence, the syntactic equivalence, the chapter equivalence and the text equivalence. And the paper concludes 4 parts. It adopts the individual case analysis method and data analysis to analyze the official translated version of the Belt and Road Initiative based at the function equivalence theory. And the analysis can draw a conclusion that the translated version based on the translation equivalence theory suits the political terms' translation nowadays.

Key words: Functional equivalence；The Belt and Road Initiative；Political terms；Chinese characteristics

1　Introduction

This paper is to explore the principle that translation of political terms based on the Eugene Nida's function equivalence theory and it takes the Belt and Road Initiative for example. Therefore it is necessary to introduce some research works about the theory and the policy, which provides the theory base and practice base. And it is beneficial to making further research.

In 2015, China launched the Belt and Road Initiative, aiming to create a win-win future for the world. And the full name of the Initiative is "Silk Road Economic Belt" and "21st Century Maritime Silk Road". As the globalization's pace is fasted and faster, the culture globalization is more apparent. China launched the Belt and Road Initiative in 2015, which means that the political and economic communications will be more frequent. Cultural communication always follows the political and economic communications. Therefore the initiative will bring the new wave of China's external cultural communication. Meanwhile, the cultural communications will affect the political or economic communications in turn because only when the culture is recognized will people recognize the products belonging to the culture. Every country will spare no efforts to advance its culture's going abroad. The one who gets the advantage in culture globalization will seize the priority in the economic zone.

As a result, the importance of cultural communication is beyond doubts. As the role of cultural communication is emphasized, how to make the cultural communications perform better is a question worth working on. The unique language of every country is on behalf of its unique culture. So how to fix the language question is of great significance. And translation will be the significant role in the process.

There are two translated versions of the Belt and Road Initiative that are widely used: "One Belt and One Road" and "the Belt and Road". Basically, the latter one is more frequently used. In the western translation fields, there are a number of translation methods and theories put forward by famous theorists. And function theory is one of them. The theory has been a classical one since it was fully developed by Eugene Nida. There have been some academic works of high tone about the Belt and Road, which will have special reference for translation, such as the definition of the Belt and Road-"China's Belt & Road Initiative: A Game of Thrones? "(Billington, Alexander Ross.2018), "One Belt One Road: China's Nation-Building Initiative".(Zhang, Yizhi Jing Jing, 2017) And there are some valuable works focusing on function equivalence theory of Eugene Nida such as "Discourse in Eugene Nida's translation theory"(Helen, 1993), "Functional equivalent translation of New Testament hortatory discourse into Hill Madia". (Vaz, Christopher Augustin, 2011)

The debates about translation function equivalence have always been the hot spot topic. There have been some remarkable outcomes combined with practice about such as "The Genealogy Development of" Equivalence "Terms and the Construction of Chinese Contemporary Translation Knowledge System", (Liu Runze, Wei Xiangqing 2015) "Introduction to Contemporary Foreign Translation Theory", (Xie Tianzhen 2008) "The Basis of the Legitimacy of the Social System and the Ideological System that Guides Social Action" (Jin Guantao, Liu Qingfeng, 2009) "Equivalence", (Wang Zuoliang, 1963) "Equivalent Translation". (Liu Dan, 1965)

In general, the domestic academic field puts focus on the following topics. But there still exist some problems. According to the statistics from Wanfang Data, we can find: first, the study of translation equivalence theory was in a good situation before 2015, and it has been declining since 2015, but the study of translation functional equivalence theory still exists. And the whole quantity of translation theory reaches up to 68251, and the study of translation functional equivalence theory reaches 10335, which accounts for 15%; second, the study of the Belt and Road Initiative's translation was in an increase tendency during 2004 and 2017, and it decreased from 2017. Third, in the reference type, the translation strategy accounts for 25%, translation teaching accounts for13%, and translation criticism accounts for 62%. Therefore we can see that the translation functional equivalence theory accounts for a considerable proportion, which means that the theory is of model significance as a main stream theory. However, there exists a problem, which is the object or type of translation study is single although it owns a certain number, which confines the horizon of study. So there is space and potential of domestic study of translation functional equivalence theory.

The value of theory: there is an important connection between the significant policy's publicity translation and the conduction of external activities. But there are less monographs of translation theories and translation methods, compared with the literary works. From the perspective of discipline: first, the study of the translation method of external publicity translation based at the "Belt and Road" can broaden the single study field. Second, it is not hard to find most famous translation theories are western translation theories. Therefore, the study is also beneficial to exploring the translation theories with Chinese characteristics. Third, according to some authoritative data base and search engines, the relative studies about Eugene Nida's translation theories are still popular, but most of them still analyze the theory. The study combining theory and object can prove the applicable value of Eugene Nida's translation function equivalence theory nowadays.

2 Translation Function Equivalence Theory

Before analysis, it is necessary to make a brief introduction of the theory. Therefore, the author will represent the function equivalence theory in terms of the development, basic concept and practical use.

2.1 The Development Process of Translation Function Equivalence Theory

The theory can date back to *The Possibility and Limits of Translation Criticism* put forward by Katharina Reiss, which introduced the context function category to translation criticism and connected language function, the type of contexts and translation strategy. In 1984, in *Translation Behavior-Theory and Methodology* written by Justa Holz-Manttari, he mentioned the translation action, which expressed his opinion that translation was the interaction of human driven by purpose and oriented by the result and translation activities replaced translation. In Hans J.Vermeer's work: *The General Translation Theoretical Framework*, he put forward the Skopos Theory centered on the purpose, which made a breakthrough of equivalence theory's restriction and raised a now concept that orientated the translation studies from source languages to target languages. In 1997, Christiane Nord wrote *Objective Behavior-Analysis of Functional Translation Theory* that continued the functionalist tradition enriched the teleology and made up the shortage of teleology.

2.2 The Basic Concept of Translation Function Equivalence Theory

The translation function equivalence theory was put forward by Eugene Nida. "During the process of translating the Bible, he developed a theory, which became one of the classical translation theories." (谢天振，2008) The core concept of the theory is functional equivalence, which means we should pursue the equivalence in function instead of inflexible equivalence on the surface. To form a standard between source language and target language, Eugene A Nida pointed out that the translator should use the most proper, natural and equivalent language to reappear the information of source language from the meaning of language to literary form.

Nida's definition relevant to translation pointed out that translation was not merely the equivalence in vocabulary, but also the equivalence in semantics, style and literary form. What translation conveys contains both vocabulary information in surface and culture information in depth. Dynamic equivalence includes four aspects: vocabulary equivalence, syntactic equivalence, chapter equivalence and text equivalence. He thinks that the meaning is the most important part compared with the form. Form is likely to hide the cultural meaning and make an obstacle in cultural communication. Therefore, in literary translation, translators should show the cultural contents of source language in target language under the guidance of 4 aspects of dynamic equivalence.

In general, the function equivalence mainly discusses his theory based on the four equivalence because he thought there was a huge similarity among all kinds of language frameworks and the deeper framework had more commonality than the surface.

2.3 The Meaning of the Practice of Eugene Nida's Translation Function Equivalence Theory

Working on the translation of political terms under the guidance of translation functional equivalence theory is of great significance. From the perspective of nation, under the international atmosphere where the communication is constantly deepening and the conflict among different countries is increasingly prominent, the priority of culture plays a huge role in the international competition as I mentioned in part 1. "Translation of political terms is more than the translation of pure words or phrases; furthermore, it is the window to convey the domestic message to external world, expressing China's voice and attitude through common language."（潘登，陈艳芳，2016） And the use of translation functional equivalence theory is of great significance for reference because the purpose of the theory conforms a key point of the political terms' translation. The core theory of translation equivalence theory is functional equivalence, which means reaching the same function expected for both source language readers and target language readers. In other words, it means letting people know what we exactly want to express by ourselves instead of being affected by propaganda with some ulterior motives. Furthermore, from the perspective of translation itself, on the one hand, working on the translation of political terms not only contributes to the development of translation of political terms with Chinese characteristics. On the other hand, a theory will develop when it puts into practice. Generally speaking, some translation beginners in college tend to focus on the surface correspondence of words and phrases rather than dig the theory behind. Through the analysis of classical theory, it can help them build theory consciousness, which can make the foundation of further study. Political terms translation with Chinese characteristics needs a theoretical guidance or principle. Through the translation functional equivalence theory, we can have better understandings and promote translation awareness of daily study majoring in translation.

3 The Translation of Political Terms

The principle that translation of political terms should use depends on the features of the texts. The translation of political terms is different from the general translation because of its unique function for external publicity.

3.1 The Features of the Translation of Political Terms with Chinese Characteristics

The study explores the features of political terms with Chinese characteristics. According to different features, there are different translation methods. In the research field, the translation methods of political terms with Chinese characteristics' translation, the criticism of specific political terms. First, from the perspective of the features of political terms with Chinese characteristics, "there are several features as followed: first, they are highly general and concise, close to the time's development, and relative to wide range."(王雪，蔡丽华，2013) And they are oral, so they are easy to understand. Second, from the perspective of translation method of political terms with Chinese characteristics, according to the different features, there are different translation methods. The studies of the field can be concluded into several points. As for the translation of abbreviations, it is suitable to translate after knowing the deep meanings instead of direct translation at the beginning; as for the explanatory translation, it is proper to add annotation; as for new foreign words, the loan-translation and translation through word by word can be adopted; the four-character combination words should be translated under the principle of maintaining the loyalty to the original texts and pursuing the correspondence with Chinese pattern; as for the poems with political features should adopt the transliteration based on the understanding of original contexts to find the proper expressions. Third, from the perspective of the criticism of some specific political terms, some typical words are analyzed such as "China's dream" and "Reform and Opening up". Based on the choice of words and phrases, a lot of articles made comment at the guidance of function equivalence theory.

3.2 The principle of Translation of Political Terms with Chinese Characteristics

The official version should reach its original aim. From what foreign heads of state and government leaders said at the opening ceremony of the Belt and Road Forum, "the words that they used to identify the Belt and Road Initiative are project, framework and cooperation,"(刘润泽，魏向清，2015) which means other the Belt and Road countries do not regard it as a friendly developing chance instead of a threat. And the words they mentioned frequently are cooperation, economic, opportunities, partners, development, etc. From this, we can see that the translated text has reached the aim we expected at the beginning. As a consequence, we can see that the translated text has basically conveyed the core meaning of the Belt and Road Initiative. China is always showing a friendly figure while we always showed figures as friendly emissaries at the ancient Silk Road. Nowadays, China opens up at a larger scale; we are willing to share the interests. The translation should be a strong driving force to help our country go forward. After all, the translation is a direct bridge to connect two different languages. Nowadays, the domestic translation career is developing drastically. There is an interesting metaphor. The famous translator Lin Yutang once said:"translation is like women's wearing stockings, and the translators will give her wear yellow or red stockings. The thickness and color are type and style of a translator". And he pointed out that he thought the closer the translated text is, the better.

4 The Embodiment of Functional Equivalence Theory

To make the theory represented in a more clear way, the author introduces a political term that has been discussed widely in the recent years. And the term is analyzed from 3 perspectives based on the "three equivalence" of the theory because of the limit of the length of the theory. The translated version—the Belt and Road Initiative can represent the essence of the theory.

4.1 The Word Equivalence: The Choice of "Belt""Road" and "initiative"

The reason for choices of "belt" and "road" is similar. The full name is Silk Road Economic Belt and 21st Century Maritime Silk Road. The Chinese name is based on the history and the geographical orientation. According to the Collins Dictionary, belt refers to an elongated region, and road refers to an open way (generally public) for travel or transportation or a way or means to achieve something. And it basically corresponds to the Chinese name in terms of geography and good willing. From the map, it is clear to see the Belt and Road countries form a belt-like area and it also conveys our hope to cooperate together to step into a promising road.

Analyzing the official translation, the deep digging for single words is also necessary. And the choice of the word that describes this initiative is very cautious. In fact, there are several words that share similar functions, such as program, strategy, plan and agenda, etc. According to the Oxford Advanced Learner's English-Chinese Dictionary, "initiative" refers to a new plan for dealing with a particular problem or for achieving a particular purpose. Our purpose is trying to gather countries along the trade routes together to make our economy strive. As a result, the choices of words should represent our wish to increase trade connectivity based on multilateral discussions. "The pursuit is based on extensive consultation instead of single willing. "Compared with "initiative", "strategy" refers to a plan that is intended to achieve a particular purpose, "(孙圣勇，2015) the process of planning something or putting a plan into operation in a skillful way and the skill of planning the movements of armies in a battle or war. First, it is obvious to see that this word has a meaning about military, which is not included in our initiative. Therefore, if we use this word, some foreign commentary media may lead international attention to the aspect that does not exist at all. The USA news institution has once sensationalized that China was fighting for the dominant power of Asia with US in the international society. Second, our purpose is to build a route for economy developing, and it is neither a part of Chinese diplomatic policies, nor the tool of regional combat.

And when we choose the words, we should also consider the historical factors. And, dating back to the original meaning of the word, we can find this word originates from a Greek word "strategos", which means the regional leaders or officers, and it gradually became to mean the military plan. The Belt and Road Initiative is neither a counter of geopolitics nor a battle of seizing the dominant power of countries along the line. As for the word “plan”, it was used in the Marshall Plan, the European Recovery Program that USA dominated. There were some foreign media describing our initiative as the Marshall Plan of China that has a meaning of hegemonism, which is totally opposite to our original purpose.

4.2 The Syntactic equivalence: The Symmetrical Structure

And political terms usually appear in form consisting of four characters even though the expression is not a real idiom. This can help the publicity of the policy and make it clear to understand for people. In fact, Chinese expressions prefer the symmetrical structure, which represents in poems of Tang and Song Dynasty a lot .The tradition of pursuing symmetrical structure may originate from here. From the authoritative expressions, we can see the preference of this form. In Report in the Work of the Government this year, there are 9 expressions in the first paragraph including nouns and verbs, such as “五位一体”“四个全面”“统筹推进”and “协调推进”. From the conjunction—“and”, it is easy to find the translated version is pursuing the correspondence of syntactic equivalence. “Belt” and “road” are divided by “and”, so the form seems to be more balanced and symmetrical. Chinese expressions prefer the symmetrical structure, which represents in poems of Tang and Song Dynasty. The tradition of pursuing symmetrical structure may originate from here.

From the conjunction— “and”, it is easy to find the translated version is pursuing the correspondence of syntactic equivalence. In Chinese expressions, the carefully constructed abbreviations usually complies the principle of concision and symmetry so the expression is catchy and easy to remember. And the article “the” can be regarded as a common use but it can also be regarded as the correspondence of “one” in the Chinese expressions.

4.3 The Text Equivalence: The Original Meaning in Text of Literacy and Text of Politics

In text equivalence, the theory demands the correspondence in language style to express the meaning out of literary words. Only in this way can the translated version represent the style of original works. Therefore the factor of cultural difference is worth focusing on.

In Chinese expressions, we can find that the Belt and Road Initiative is connected to the Silk Road and the Maritime Silk Road in Han Dynasty of China easily. The term intends to enable people to associate the initiative with the ancient beautiful story of the emissary Zhang Qian’s mission to the Western Regions for foreign trade and friendly communication with countries along the route. The “Lu” in the initiative is the same word in the “Si Lu”. It is easy to leave a friendly impression like the ancient route. Accordingly, the translated version should express the spirit of the term. The Silk Road’s image has been a friendly and inoffensive one, which has rooted in foreign readers. So if the translated version is connected with the translation of “Silk Road”. So the translated version also has same effect, which is to get foreign readers to feel the good hope and kindness of China.

5 Conclusions

The analysis above has represented the Eugene Nida's theory and the outcomes have proved his opinion to some extent. But limited by some factors, there is still huge space for the research.

After discussing the political terms' translation and Eugene Nida's translation function equivalence theory, the author analyzes the embodiment of the equivalence theory in the translated version—the Belt and Road. It turns out the translated version has reflected the principle of Eugene Nida's theory, which also has special reference for the translation of political terms nowadays. It turns out that the principle of Eugene Nida's theory matches the demand of translation of political terms. Therefore, the method in the theory can maximize the effect expected. As a consequence, translation of political terms should be based on the translation equivalence theory.

First, the research materials are not of novelty because of the presentation time. Second, due to the limited analysis ability, this paper is lack of more authoritative data. Third, because of the length of the phrase, the embodiment of the theory has not been fully represented. Therefore, the author will keep studying the theory with some realistic cases to improve the knowledge and ability.

References

[1] Allende, Isabel. *A Hammock Beneath the Mongoes* (Margaret Sayers Trans.)[M]. New York: Plume, 1992.

[2] Eugene Nida. *Language and Culture Contexts in Translation*[M]. Shanghai: Shanghai Language Press, 2001.

[3] H.Lehmann & M. Richter (eds). *The Meaning of Historical Terms and Concepts: New Studies on Begriffsgeschichte*[M]. Washington: German Historical Institute, 1996.

[4] Newmark Peter. *A Textbook of Translation.* Shanghai. Shanghai Foreign Language Press, 2001.

[5] Richter, M. Begriffsgeschichte today: An overview. Finish Yearbook of Political Thought, 1999 (3): 11-27.

[6] 金观涛，刘青峰. 观念史研究——中国现代重要政治术语的形成[M]. 北京：法律出版社，2009.

[7] 李蕊. 运用奈达的三步翻译体系实现对等[J]. 翻译研究，2017（9）：115-116.

[8] 刘润泽，魏向清. “中国梦”英译研究再思考——兼论政治术语翻译的概念史研究方法[J]. 中国外语，2015（12）：99-105.

[9] 刘润泽，魏向清. “对等”术语的谱系化发展与中国当代译学知识体系建构——兼谈术语翻译的知识传播与理论生发功能[J]. 中国外语，2015（6）：18-23.

[10] 潘登，陈艳芳. 功能翻译理论视角下的中国时政术语外宣翻译——以“四个全面”为例[J]. 湖北科技学院学报，2016（11）：32-37.

[11] 王雪，蔡丽华. 中国时事政治术语的语言特点及翻译方法[N]. 辽宁科技大学学报，2013（3）：298-301

[12] 谢天振. 当代国外翻译理论导读[M]. 天津：南开大学出版社，2008

[13] 杨明星. 中国外交新词对外翻译的原则与策略[J]. 中国翻译，2014（8）：103-107.

[14] 赵玉宏. 论中国特色词汇的外宣翻译策略——从“中国梦”的英译谈起[J]. 新闻世界，2013（12）：72-74.

Discussion on Different English Versions of Book Title of *Xi-you-ji*

袁 典　汤朝菊

摘　要：作为我国四大名著之一，《西游记》这部小说在国内外都享有很高的声誉。而它书名的英译也在不同时期和不同译者笔下有着不同的版本。我们知道书名翻译的好坏为吸引读者起着不可忽视的作用。之前已经有很多文献表明书名翻译是有着一定技巧的。这篇论文将用到文献研究法、个案研究法和经验总结法，通过《西游记》书名不同时期不同版本的翻译来研究书名翻译方法。在该论文中将主要介绍两个总体方面：一是对于书名翻译的原则和方法，二是围绕《西游记》的不同翻译版本进行分析。

关键词：《西游记》；书名翻译；技巧

Abstract: As one of our four great classical novels, *Xi-you-ji* enjoys a high reputation both at home and abroad. Its title translation differs from countries and translators. And the title of a book makes a great contribution in attracting readers. Previous research has shown that there are many skills for book title translation. In this paper, the methods of literature study, experience summarization, case analysis have been used to look into book title translation by focusing on different English versions of translation of *Xi-you-ji*. The study follows the two general aspects which are principles and methods for book title translation and analysis of different translation versions of *Xi-you-ji.*

Key words: *Xi-you-ji*；Book title translation；Skills

1 Introduction

We can easily find that many translations of book titles are different from what we think. For example, there is a novel named *Wan-yu*（晚雨）and it is translated as *Heavenly Rain* instead of *Late Rain*. And there is no denying that a good title can put the finishing touch to the picture of a dragon so that the translation of a book title really plays an crucial role. So the principles and methods for book title translation are worthy to be concerned. Having a good command of book title translation is of great significance. First, nowadays people have realized that we have been "invaded" by technology and Internet, as a result, there is an increasing advocacy for all ages of people to read books both in Mandarin and foreign languages. Second, with the globalization, a large number of foreign-language books have been introduced and translated into our country and so have ours.

There have been so many papers talking about skills for book title translation. Most of them just follow the pattern of listing principles and some corresponding examples. Different methods have been used in different books but one book can also have different versions of translation. Thus, my study will focus on the translation of the Chinese novel *Xi-you-ji* so that the research can be more targeted.

2 Skills for Book Title Translation

2.1 The Importance of Book Title Translation

As the saying goes, it is hard to create a book title, but it is much harder to translate a book title. The book title, which is the eye of a book and the soul of a book, is created by refining over and over again. As a general rule, a book title should be concise enough to show the core theme directly to readers. At the meantime, we cannot ignore the fact that it plays a very important role in leaving the first impression to readers. Therefore, the translation of book titles should be treated carefully.

2.2 Four Factors in Relation to the Translation of Book Title

There have been four factors to be considered of the book title translation in general: faithfulness, cultural difference, artistic effect and marketing effect.

Faithfulness means to be in accordance with the original one but should not be as equivalent as to be stiff. We have to reproduce the original information in an appropriate, natural and reciprocal way. For example, the famous book *Man-Shy,* written by Australian writer Frank Dolby Davison, was firstly translated as "being afraid of men". However, this book told a story about a small red bull and its partners hid in the mountains, pursuing their free life because of fear of living with human beings. So it is more proper to understand the title as "being afraid of human beings" instead of just "men".

Cultural difference is the second principle that we should pay great attention to. A book carries a lot of cultural information and the book title can be considered as concentrated culture of a society or a country so that translators are supposed to avoid misunderstandings and misleading information caused by cross-cultural communication. When the book *Uproar in the welkin* was popular in Arab, the word "welkin" was translated as "heaven". This inappropriate word gave rise to great anger of Arabians because in their culture, heaven is the most holy place where they show their highest respect to, so it is absolutely an irreverence for a monkey to create such a terrible chaos in heaven and they cannot accept this.

Artistic effect is based on the theory that translation is not only a skill, but also a creative art especially for literature. A successful translation of a book title can always make readers enjoy the beauty of art and arouse a great desire to read the book. Translators had better know the characteristics of both languages and try to give the best play to their advantages to satisfy readers' aesthetic tastes. Famous book *Wuthering Heights* was once translated as *Pao-xiao-shan-zhuang*（咆哮山庄）. Compared with *Hu-xiao-shan-zhuang*（呼啸山庄）, it is deficient in artistic beauty and it is hard for readers to strike a chord towards the tragic love between the hero and the heroine.

The last comes marketing effect. Any translation for books that wants to make a success must get the favor of readers and be accepted by the market. The commercialization of the book market makes it necessary to take the economic factor into consideration. So the translation of a book title roles as the trademark of a book and the attention also should be paid to meeting the demand of our readers.

2.3 Three Treatments for the Translation of Book Title

As for the informative and concise attributes of book title, researchers summarized three treatments in relation to the translation: literal translation, free translation and creative translation.

Some titles can be translated according to its literal meaning. People have common ways of thinking in some ways, which can trigger the readers' common curiosity from the original one. In addition, it is not hard to find exact cultural and linguistic equivalents in both languages. When translated into another language, the new translation can also have the similar effect without misunderstanding despite of cultural differences, e.g. *Ao-man-yu-pian-jian*（傲慢与偏见） for *Pride and Prejudice*, *the Teahouse* for *Cha-guan*（茶馆）.

Free translation is to change something from the original one by adding or subtracting some words on the basis of the original text, and to give more ideas about the book for a better understanding, e.g. *Lu-bin-xun-piao-liu-ji*（鲁宾逊漂流记） for *Robinson Crusoe*.

Creative translation, which is a recreation to separate the translation from its original semantics. People in different countries and different cultural environments have different knowledge towards the entity. As a result, translators can distill information by filtration and screening as much as possible to meet readers' needs. Sometimes, on some occasions, it is normal to break through the restrictions of the original title of a book in the content and form to create better translation versions for the readers to understand and to be interested in, e.g. *Wu-du-gu-er*（雾都孤儿） for *Oliver Twist*, and *Luan- shi-jia-ren*（乱世佳人） for *Gone with the wind*.

3 Analysis Based on *Xi-you-ji*

3.1 Brief Introduction of *Xi-you-ji*

Xi-you-ji（西游记）, written by Wu Cheng'en in the Ming Dynasty, (A. D.1368—1644) is a mythical Chinese novel that is considered one of the four great classical novels. Along with *Heroes of Marshes, A Dream of Red Mansions* as well as *Three Kingdoms,* they all have won popular acclaim from generation to generation. *Xi-you-ji* is a combination of myth parable and comedy, describing the legendary story about a Buddhist monk (Tang Shan-chang) heading for the West in the protection of his apprentices Monkey King, Eight-Commandment Pig and monk Sha. The novel narrates the legends of these people on their pilgrim journey who encountered a bunch of animals with human characteristic. The author focuses on the ever-changing mythical world and embodies the real life in the middle of the Ming Dynasty, which reflects the author's profound exposition and criticism towards the various social conflicts.

Xi-you-ji is renowned in literary across the whole world, and both its language and contents have a unique cultural background and worthwhile to be studied and researched. Its title, which can be treated as a very classic one, is so laconic but doesn't lose any charm. Meanwhile, there is as many as difficulties in its English translation.

3.2 Different Translation Versions of *Xi-you-ji*

The earliest translation version for *Xi-you-ji* is called *A Mission to Heaven*. (*Sheng-seng-tian-guo-zhi-xing* 圣僧天国行, 1913 by Timothy Richard) This version can be classified into free translation. It considers their destination as heaven and the whole process of what the four people experienced as a mission. But as a matter of fact, their destination is known as Sindhu, which is the appellation of ancient India in the early Tang Dynasty (618—907). While heaven means the holy place where everyone finds it very appealing and intend to live there with a very pious heart. So it is not appropriate to exaggerate the holy meaning of the place they were expected to arrive.

Then came *The Buddhist Pilgrims Progress*. (*Fo-jiao-tu-de-tian-lu-li-cheng* 佛教徒的天路历程, 1930 by Helen M Hayes) This version is also a free translation. Compared with the first version, it emphasizes the main characters and defines the four as all Buddhists. However, in the novel, Monkey is created out of a rock, endowed with intelligence and agility both physically and mentally. He not only has the sharp wit and an unruly nature of a monkey but also extra ordinary powers that he uses to overcome demons and monsters. Eight-Commandment Pig keeps with the disposition of clumsiness and he is still a lazy gluttonous pig that needs enjoyment from material comforts. When it comes to trouble he just can not hold his side up so is always call on for help. And monk sha is also a demon from Flowing Sands River. The three apprentices all have magic powers, and to some degree they are not pious Buddhists like the ones who practice abstinence from meat and say prayers.

Later, *Monkey and Pig's magic adventures*, (*Hou-yu-zhu: sheng-mo-li-xian-ji* 猴与猪：圣魔历险记, 1924 by A la Sirene) *Monkey*, (*Hou* 猴, 1942 by Arthur Waley) *Monkey's pilgrimage for Buddhist scripture* (*Hou-zi-qu-jing-ji* 猴子取经记, 1946 Georgette Bone rund MariaNils) and *Magic Monkey*, (*Mo-hou* 魔猴,1994 by Chan Christina and Chan Plat) the four versions are creative translations which paid more attention to the principle of market effect. They all try to express translators' understandings by recreating the title of the book to make it more acceptable for readers because they were the propagandists for Monkey King's spirit and they think Monkey King as the most extraordinary character. But actually, it's a misunderstanding that they all take Monkey King as the core image of the whole book. Translators obviously intend to take readers' psychological acceptance of the book. But this kind of versions disobeyed the principle of being accordance with the original one for they were far away from the main theme and spirit that the author really wanted to show.

Looking through the content and connotation of the original work, these versions of the translation are difficult to reflect the profound literary and artistic attainments of this Chinese classical masterpiece. We know that full of power and filled with spirit as well as being sincere and optimistic in nature, Monkey King is not bothered by suffering and is always ready to face up to new challenges as the most adorable hero in the novel and the character is the main reason that the book keeps reader in thrall. However, like Tang Shan-chang is a monk on a daring mission to find Buddha scriptures, Monkey King's mission is to protect Tang Shan-chang so that the novel put more focus on the whole process of getting Buddha scriptures instead of the adventure or biography of Monkey

King. Besides, Monkey is one of the leading roles but not the only core leading role.

The Journey to the West, (*Xi-you-ji* 西游记,1977 by Anthony C. Yu), *Journey to the West* (*Xi-you-ji* 西游记, 1980 by Jenner, W.J.F) *Travels to the West* (Encyclopedia Britannica, Macropedia in Depth), these three versions are definitely literal translations with good fitfulness. They are perfectly translated in language form which tallies to the original one, but the book's profound moral and artistic mood are not well expressed. No matter "journey"or "travel", they doesn't convey the connotations behind the title because "journey" or "travel" simply mean ordinary travel without pains and catastrophes, it cannot imply the hardships they experienced on the way to the West so that readers would even consider it as a happy and relaxing holiday journey.

Pilgrimage to the West (by Yang Hsien-yi and Gladys Yang), this version is seen as the most excellent version of this book title by many scholars for it not only shows the meaning of "journey" but also implies the characters' devout heart of persistence and the spirit of dauntless. "Pilgrimage" means a journey that a religious person undertaken for religious reasons to a holy place, which is perfectly consistent with the content and spirit of the original book. Successfully instructed by the principle of faithfulness、artistic effect and also the methods of literal and free translation, it not only expressed the meaning of journey but also the pious hearts and spirit.

4 Conclusions

Despite the various treatments for book title translation, from the kinds of translations of the book title of *Xi-you-ji*, it is clear that there are different cultural understanding perspectives reflected from the different translation versions. Just like the saying goes, there are a thousand Hamlets in a thousand people's eyes. By virtue of its profound ideological content and superb artistic achievements, *Xi-you-ji* becomes one of the world's classic literary works. As for the translation of this book title, translators are expected to deliver the implied artistic effect and spiritual value on the basis of its original image. Literary creation is the process of understanding society to reflecting society, it is an aesthetic creation activity while literal translation is the process of understanding the original one to reproducing the original. It is an aesthetic re-creation activity. In this process, translators have to reframe and re-create the works artistically. The reason why our Chinese four great classic novels become the most extraordinary works in our Chinese even the world's cultural heritage lies in their aesthetic value and spiritual charm. So translators must hold an aesthetic attitude to appreciate these masterpieces to comprehend its artistic value. We should try our best to be in accordance with the original one in the ideological and emotional content, artistic aesthetic value, language style as close as possible and consider the acceptance of readers (that is market effect) to have a best translation.

References

[1] Bassneet, Susan, Ander Lefevere. *Translation, History and culture*[M]. Shanghai Foreign. Language Education Press, 2006: 98.

[2] Nida Eugene Albert, Charles Rhett Taber. *Theory and Practice of Translation*[M]. The. Netherlands: E.J. Brill, Leiden, 1982.

[3] Jian Junwang, Su Nihan. An Analysis of Untranslatability between English and Chinese from Intercultural[J]. English language Teaching, 2014（7）：30-32.

[4] Nord, Christiane. *Translation as a Purposeful Activity: Functionalist Approaches Explained*[M]. Manchester, UK: St. Jerome, 1997.

[5] Vermeer, Hans. *A Framework for a General Theory of translating*[M]. Heidelberg: Heidelberg University, 1978.

[6] 安琦. 从语义翻译和交际翻译角度看《西游记》署名的英译[J]. 海外英语（上），2011（6）：195-196.

[7] 丰华瞻. 漫谈书名的翻译[J]. 外国语，1980（2）：17-20.

[8] 孙苗飞. 中国古典四大名著书名英译比较[J]. 上海金融学院学报，2007（4）：63-65.

[9] 王丽娜.《西游记》外文译本概述[J]. 文献，1980（12）：64-78.

[10] 袁荣品. 译书名忌浮躁[J]. 上海科技翻译，2000（3）：23-26.

Discussion on the Standard of English Lyrics Translation

朱博涵

摘　要：当今，许多移动设备上的音乐软件提供英文歌词的翻译。然而，这些翻译的质量参差不齐，风格也大相径庭。在这种情况下，五花八门的歌词翻译往往会导致用户感到困惑，甚至产生误解。因此，英文歌词的翻译标准是一个非常值得探讨的问题。在这篇论文中，我们将探讨歌词翻译标准的三个方面：歌词翻译的现状、其建立的必要性以及可能的改进方式。我们通过调查问卷的形式来调研大众对于这三个方面的看法。结果表明，绝大多数的受试者已经意识到歌词翻译的鱼龙混杂。同时，他们中有超过半数的人期望建立有关翻译内容的标准，并以此能够帮助人们更好地理解歌曲的原意，促进歌词翻译活动向正式职业的转变。

关键词：音乐；歌词；翻译；标准；必要性

Abstract: Nowadays, many music apps provide the translation of English lyrics, the quality of which, however, varies a lot. And this situation usually leads listeners to a confusing zone. Thus, the translation standard of English songs is an important issue to be examined. This paper discusses three aspects of the English lyrics translation: the present situation, the necessity, and the possible improving methods. Questionnaires were designed to survey different groups of people's opinions about those three aspects. The result shows that most of the people have noticed the changing quality of the lyrics translation. And at the same time, more than half of them expressed their expectation of a standard mainly with the content as the focus, which would help people understand the original meaning of songs better and promote lyrics translation a formal profession.

Key words: Music；Lyrics；Translation；Standard；Necessity

1 Introduction

In recent years, with the development of music industry and network information technology, more and more people choose music apps to listen to their favorite songs. Moreover, with the deepening of cultural communications, people can get touch with the music from different countries and different cultures. For example, many Chinese people begin to listen to English songs. However, the results of the translated lyrics are various. Some versions are too simple. Some versions apply the style of Chinese ancient poetry. And in order to make more people understand, other versions use a lot of Chinese native words while the meanings have gone far away from the original ones. What is the function of the translation of lyrics? Is to explain the meaning of the original language, or to pursue the same rhythmic style as the song? (Zhang Chen, 2018) This standard is not to limit the translator's imagination and their styles, but to find a reasonable method to allow the listeners to understand the meaning of the lyrics and not be too confused at the same time.

There are few academic studies on the translation of lyrics in both Chinese and English academic journals. Most Chinese journals still stay in the period of rewriting lyrics rather than translation, which was common many years ago. The rewriting refers to using the original tune of English songs, with the Chinese lyrics which is close to the style of the music, or the atmosphere of original lyrics. (Hu Fenghua, 2007)Some experts hold the opinion that it should be consistent with the principles of literary translation. (Lu Mingyu, 2009) People prefer to call them Chinese versions. However, this does not conform to the mode that we think the lyrics translation should be. Obviously, people want to understand English lyrics nowadays, but not to sing them in Chinese. Translators are often restricted by obeying the rhyme, pursuing the corresponding of tunes and words. They even have to create some words so that the limited number of characters can match the tune. Nevertheless, it is quite easy for the translated version to be different from the original meaning. Lyrics translation is actually similar to what people usually see the words on TV screens when foreigners are singing. That is to explain the meaning of the lyrics in a paragraph, which does not need to conform to the rhyme. But that lyrics translation is too simple. It often ignores many details in order to possess a higher speed while the lyrics translation we need now is that every sentence should to be translated. In foreign language journals, there is little mention of lyrics translation from English to Chinese.

Above all, we can see that there is a certain blank space in the academic field for the lyrics translation we are discussing today. This is actually related to the rapid development of information technology. More and more English songs come into sight of Chinese people. The demand for lyrics translation is increasing at the same time. It is disappointing that the development of language study has not kept pace with the development of science and technology, and as a result, there is such a loophole. Therefore, it is essential to do research on lyrics translation today.

2 Data Collection

In order to understand the public perception of the current situation of English lyrics translation and their views on this phenomenon, we have used the "field study" method and designed the relevant questionnaire. First of all, because the main idea is to get the public's opinion on this issue, there is no age limit and we use the questionnaire in Chinese. As a result, we released hyperlinks to questionnaires on social networking sites to enable Internet users to fill in this questionnaire voluntarily. But as some people still don't use music apps to listen to music today, the first question of the questionnaire is to remove the people who don't listen to music, or the people who don't use apps to listen to music. Similarly, the second question of the questionnaire will exclude the people who have never listened English songs. We designed the relevance logic between questions and questions in order to ensure that those who listen to English songs could continue to answer questions later. Those who do not meet the requirements will be directly terminated by their questionnaires. Only by doing so can we collect truly convincing data.

Next, we divide the following questions into three periods. First, we need to understand the frequency of people using lyrics translation now. Second, whether people have encountered problems in lyrics translation. Third, asking people that whether it is important to establish a standard, and what functions should it have in their opinion. We will analyze everyone's views on lyrics translation first. In these questions, we will divide them into groups based on the familiarity of English songs. Next, we will figure out whether their opinions of lyrics translation is related to the degree of love of English songs. In order to enable the respondents to clearly understand the various phenomena in the translation of the lyrics, I provided as many options as possible and had pictures to explain them. Of course, at the end of every multi topic, I also provided blank spaces for people to fill in as a target to help them express what they want to say and what they think.

3 Data Analysis

3.1 The Necessity of the Standard

In this survey, I have recovered 39 valid responses. In the first and second questions, 5 people did not meet the requirements of follow-up investigation. Some of them did not use music apps to listen to music, while some did not listen to English songs. Specifically, the distribution of people's familiarity of English songs and what experience they have is as follows (Fig 3.1, Fig 3.2).

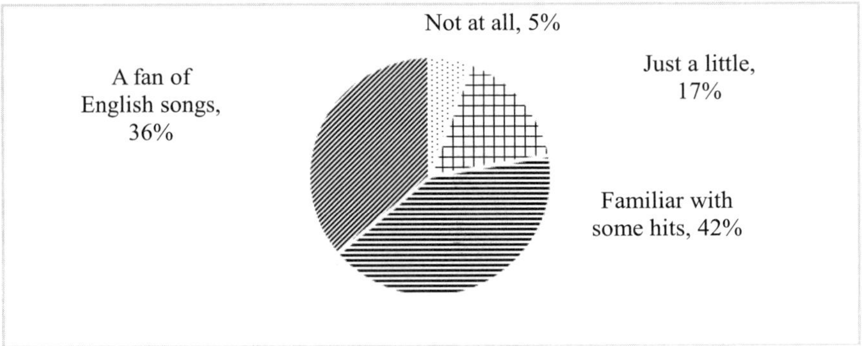

Fig3.1 the result of "Are you familiar with English songs?"

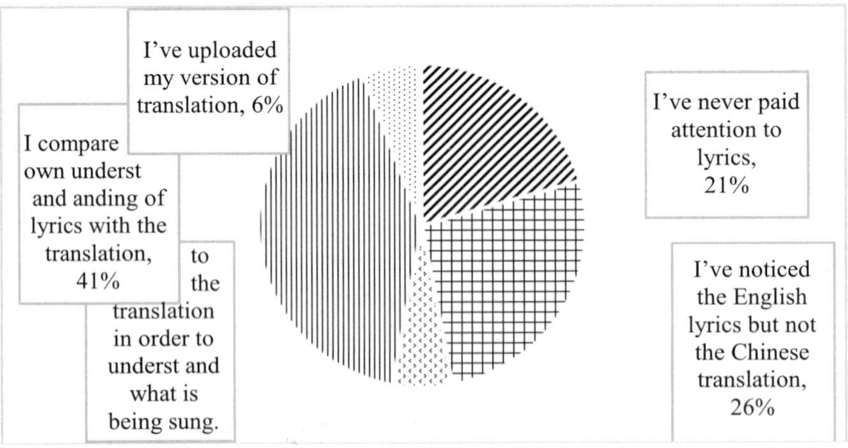

Fig3.2 the result of "Which option you've experienced the most often?"

Obviously, a large proportion of people are exposed to English songs, and more than half of them are involved with lyrics translation in the process of listening to songs. This proves that not only English songs, but also their lyrics translation have already had a great influence on the listeners who use music apps now. Lyrics translation has become an unavoidable part of listeners' music life. It is not only due to the increasingly close cultural exchanges between China and Western countries, but also to the growth of Chinese listeners' demand for music. English songs are not only different from Chinese songs in the styles of tunes, but also have unique Western characteristics in lyrics. These differences have prompted Chinese people to have the desire to know more about western culture. However, English education is not one hundred percent promoted in China, and there are fewer people who can do deeper research in English. As a result, many people have to learn the meaning of English lyrics by the translation of the lyrics, so that they have some contact with western culture. One research from *Music and Letters* had shown the relationship among music and culture. (Chadwick 358) Therefore, under the stimulation of this environment, the lyrics translation field is developing rapidly, and there are some non-standard phenomena.

In the following questions, I asked the respondents to choose the typical translation irregularities, which they had encountered before, and permit to choose a number of them. From the result, each phenomenon appears almost in the same frequency. Moreover, I also associate this question with the previous Q2, trying to figure out whether the familiarity with English songs will be related to the number of problems.

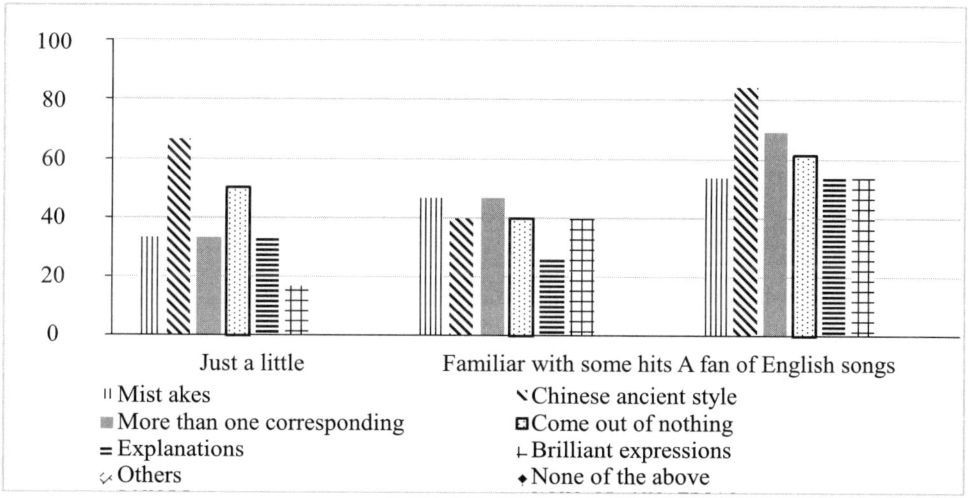

Fig3.3 the relates between Q2 & Q4

From Fig 3.3, in general, the more English songs the people listening to, the more irregular lyrics translations are found. That is to say, the special lyrics translation is not a single case, but a positive correlation with the number of songs. For fans of English songs, the average probability of these phenomena has been over 50%, while those listen to fewer English songs have an average of about 40%. The data also reflects a possibility. The reason why those who have heard a few hits have fewer problems may be the more popular the songs is, the more people view the lyrics translation of it. This requires these lyrics translations to meet the requirements of more people, so that these translations are more ordinary, with few special expression. Those who have heard many English songs may have heard some songs which are not that popular. Compared with those popular songs, the lyrics translation of these songs will not be seen by so many people, so fewer people will question it. Therefore, these songs allow for the existence of special lyrics translation.

Of course, I've also asked the respondents whether there is a must to build up a set of standards to regulate the field. 59.26% of people believe that the styles of translation are so various that tend to be a little disordered. It is better to have a set of standards to regulate. The rest of them believe that the current state is actually good, reflecting the vitality of the translation field. No one thinks the situation is so chaos that there must be a rule to change it.

From these questions, I find that Lyrics translation is indeed a part of people's daily entertainment which cannot be neglected. And this area involves many people's participation: listeners, translators, censors, and the management of music apps. The public is also more inclined to set up a standard to see more professional translation results. However, both the listeners and the translator hope that this field is creative and inspiring. In other words, people tend to think that this set of standards is used to help the development of translation, rather than restricting the creativity of translation. The way and purpose of establishing standards must also be clear and very important.

3.2 Possible Methods to Improve

Because there is a lack of career of professional lyrics translation in academia, or in other words, there are few professionals in music field. Thus, the lyrics translators on the Internet are usually a group of common people. They only need to upload their translated texts to certain websites, and guarantee there is no illegal information, the texts can be seen by the public. It can be concluded that both the creators and censors lack certain standards to check these texts. In this way, they make people feel confused and misunderstood the original meaning. What's more, western culture pays attention to individualism and spiritual pursuit (even including social concerns), which leads to a great difference between foreign culture and Chinese culture. (Capra, Ganga, Moore518) It is very unrealistic to use the content of Chinese culture to generalize the content of western culture, or to ignore those elements that exist in western culture deliberately. And in my thought, on the basis of the lyrics translation standard, cultural communications between China and foreign countries will be deeper. This will also encourage more people to develop interest in the career of lyrics translation.

As a result, I designed Q6 and Q7, and the results comes from the charts below(Fig 3.4).

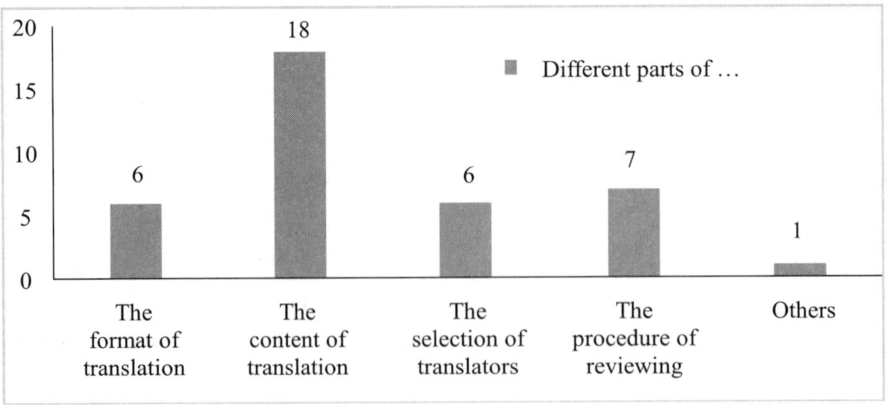

Fig 3.4 the result of "Which part from the options below should be regularized?"

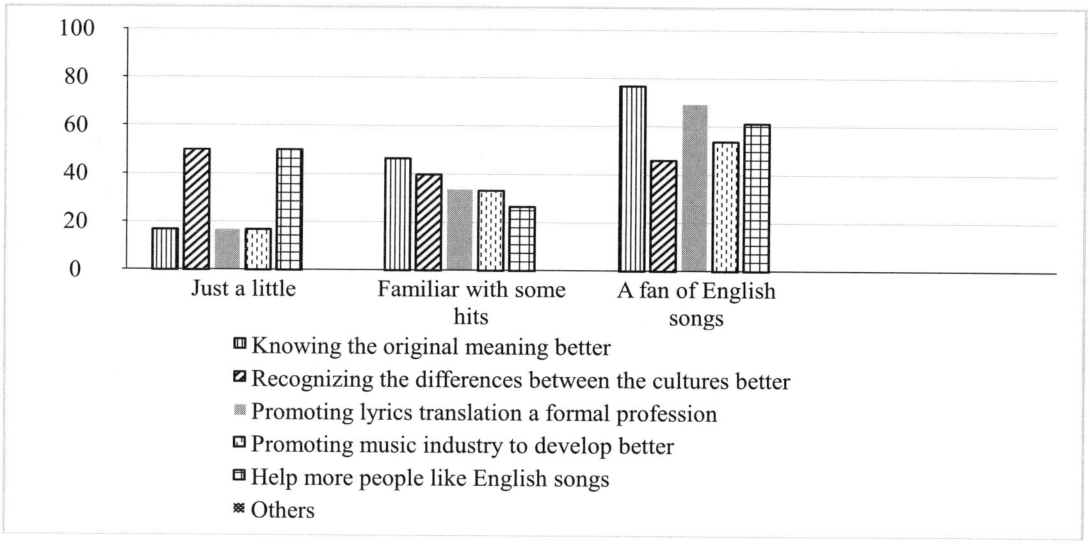

Fig3.5 the relation between Q2 & Q7

From Fig 3.4, it is easy to find that the most important concern is the content of translation. In the various music apps, every lyrics appears in the form of one sentence. In fact, it has restricted the format of each sentence and should be translated as close to the original sentence as possible. You do not need rhymes, you don't need to use idioms to highlight the neatly arranged vision. Similarly, since lyrics translation is a relatively new linguistic and cultural field, more people should be allowed to try. The characteristics of language are generally reflected in the content of translation, so the content requirements should be stricter. For example, it is not allowed to change the image of the original lyrics, not to allow the use of too vulgar, local language, and cannot deliberately create the atmosphere that the original song doesn't have, and so on. Moreover, the standard of lyrics translation once mentioned that it can be referenced by the criteria of poetry translation, and on this basis, we can transform and innovate (Cintrão 814) However, people who are engaged in traditional translation field should be willing to devote themselves to the development and research of new disciplines.

Fig 3.5 shows people's outlook on the functions of this standard. Just like before, the fans of English songs look forward to the future of lyrics translation, and put forward more requests. Among all the functions, eliminating misunderstandings is the most frequently chosen. In fact, it reflects one of the most basic functions of translation, which is interlingual translation. That is translating one language signal into another language signal, and thus it cleans misunderstanding and confusion. This asks that the translator cannot forget the most basic skills and principles while creating. No matter what type of translation is, including lyrics translation and the translation in other fields, the most basic function is to be a vehicle to convey the meaning of one language completely and accurately to the people who use another language.

4 Conclusions

I noticed this question about the translation of lyrics at the time of listening to music. As a person who always listens to English songs, I think the translation of lyrics is closely related to my life. This field has not received much attention at home and abroad, and there are few academic researches and articles. After the investigation, lyrics translation is indeed an indispensable part of entertainment life. The public's attitude to it is also positive, and it also puts forward the need to standardize the field. It shows that it is not necessary to establish this standard in such a hurry, but a suitable standard can definitely help the translation of the lyrics grow better. This requires that the norm of lyrics translation, especially the content norms, should be strictly designed by academic fields and the various music app platforms. Today, with the increasingly permeating of Chinese and foreign culture, songs have been regarded as an important medium. Professional people should strive to reduce the confusion and misunderstanding caused by lyrics translation. This is not only a respect for one's own work, but also a respect for different cultures.

References

[1] Chadwick Nick. Berg's Wozzeck. By Patricia Hall. pp. xi + 211. *Studies in Musical Genesis, Structure, and Interpretation* [J]. Music & Letters, 2013, 94（2）：358-360.

[2] Capra, Gian Franco; Ganga, Antonio; Moore, Allan F. Songs for our soils. How soil themes have been represented in popular song[J]. *Soil Science and Plant Nutrition*, 2017, 63（5）：517-525.

[3] Cintrão, Heloísa Pezza. Translating "Under the Sign of Invention": Gilberto Gil's Song Lyric Translation[J]. *Meta*, 2010, 54（4）：813-832.

[4] 卢明玉. 以中西文化差异探析中英歌词翻译[J]. 河北学刊，2009，29（6）：194-196.

[5] 张琛. 中西文化差异下的中英歌词翻译原则及方法[J]. 教育现代化，2018，5（5）：308-309，316.

[6] 胡凤华.“歌曲译配”与“歌曲翻译”辨[J]. 安徽大学学报，2007，31（5）：96-100.

语言研究

Reasons for the Existence of Vague Advertisement Language

颜淑芳

摘　要：模糊的广告语给予消费者特别的产品体验和独特的感受，为了进一步明确模糊语在广告中如何运用，对产品和消费者产生何种作用，如何正确地将模糊语植入广告中。本文将根据收集的数据举例说明，并通过模糊集理论、接受美学理论等从现象、作用及运用方面对广告模糊语进行解读。通过分析发现，模糊广告语主要分为语音、语义和语用模糊三种类型。模糊的广告语有着一定的艺术特性，具有幽默感，提升了表达效率，让产品更具有吸引力；广告语以读者的认知心理为导向，含蓄的表达顺应思维的模糊性，读者易对产品产生误解。本文旨在探究更科学有效的广告语言，为广告制作者提供一些参考，也让读者有意识地欣赏和理解模糊广告的内涵。

关键词：广告语；模糊性；艺术特性；认知心理；内涵

Abstract: The vague advertisement language gives consumers a special experience to products and a unique feeling when they hear or see those advertisement slogans. This paper will further clarify how vague language can be used in advertisements, what effects it causes to products and consumers and how to implant vague language into advertisements correctly. Meanwhile, through the fuzzy sets theory and reception aesthetics theory, vague advertisement language will be analyzed from the aspects of the phenomenon, the function and the use. By analysis, it is found that vague advertisement language is mainly divided into three types, phonetic vagueness, semantic vagueness and pragmatic vagueness. Vague advertisement language has a certain artistic characteristics, with a sense of humour, which enhances the efficiency of expression, making the product more attractive. Advertisement language is guided by the cognitive psychology of advertising readers. The implicit expression not only conforms to the fuzziness of human thinking but also makes readers misunderstand the products easily. The purpose of this paper is to explore more scientific and more effective advertisement language, providing some reference for the advertisement producers, as well as making readers more conscious of appreciating the connotation of vagueness in advertisement.

Key words: Advertisement language; Vagueness; Artistic characteristics; Cognitive psychology; Connotation

1　Introduction

Advertisement language is a unique language with strong practicability in modern information age, which reflects the demand of consumers and the information of products. It also has become a powerful tool to disseminate economic, politic and cultural information in today’s life. Vague language is largely used in advertisement because it can achieve better publicity for products and manufacturers, and create an interesting phenomenon in journalism and communication through a series of marginal disciplines.

At home and abroad, there are some researches on the phonetic, grammatical, semantic and pragmatic aspects of vague language. American linguist Black (1937) proposes a method for the formal processing of vague words; an American linguist Lakoff put forward that vague conceptual logic can be built up systematically, and that it has its own internal structure(1972). There have also been the theory of fuzziness of Russell, the family similarity of Wittgenstein, the theory of language game and the modern category theories represented by American psychologist Rosch. In China, the research of fuzzy linguistics is mainly based on the foreign introduction. Wu Tieping defines "fuzzy concept" in the *Preliminary Study of Vague Language* (1999), which probes into the difference and relation between fuzzy language and fuzzy concept. Chen Zhi'an and Wenxu points out that vague language has broad and narrow sense in *Retrospect and Prospect of Fuzzy Linguistics* (1996).

There are also some studies about the translation of vague language and vague literary language, but clear studies on vague advertisement language are rare. The significance of the research on this topic lies in not only its innovation but also the practical application value.

2 Vague Phenomenon in Advertisement

2.1 Phonetic Vagueness

Voice is heard by auditory sense, then into mind. According to the auditory masking effect, people are only sensitive to the most conspicuous voice. In advertisement, many slogans takes advantage of this feature, repeating some important parts or imitating some already existed homophones, thus attracting consumers' attention and impressing them a lot. For instance, a tea factory shop uses "good-buy" as its slogan which sounds like "good-bye". (Yang, 2017) It makes consumers confused, attracted and interested with certain popularity. A slogan of GOLGATE that "Good teeth, good health" is repeating the same phoneme, rhyming the sounds, more like "Smell smelly, taste tasty!""J'adore, Dior." the rhythm sensation cater to our pursuit of beauty.

2.2 Semantic Vagueness

A word has plenty of meanings. Located in different cultural environments, owning distinct experiences and cognitive levels, people will understand the same word or phrase diversely, which means a special slogan can resonate with some people inordinately. Such vague similarity in meaning can also make its products more popular. For example, the slogan of Cdirac which is "Dare to be the first" is to advocate consumers, which is also connected with a Chinese allusion—*Gan wei tian xia xian*. The slogan "I never read the China Daily" makes consumers think about it, leaving a question like "Have I read it?" or "Does it really worth reading?" in people's minds. Thinking about semantic vagueness needs our vision sense, feeling and thought used together, so it is more complicated in cognitive psychology.

2.3 Pragmatic Vagueness

A typical phenomenon is that the comparative and superlative degree is applied in advertisement on vagueness. When expressing some food is of great safety, we use the word healthy or green. A slogan of juice is that "If you want to be healthier, body will have to eat more natural food, more natural than ordinary suburban orchard", which mainly concludes the comparative degree. Even if we know little about the food and its authenticity, we would like to try it and we want to upgrade our health level because the product is compared to others implicitly and it wins. Another advertising slogan of makeup is "The excellent craft, the most authentic quality, the most can meet the nutritional needs of human skin."(Sheng, 2015) Seeing a series of superlative degree, our agog psychology will be aroused that we are willing to "take adventure" to use it. Phonetic vagueness is not always based on facts but the slogan structure in order to create a visual impact then a soul shock.

3 Functions of Vague Advertisement Language

3.1 Improvement of Expression Effect

The most typical feature of most advertisement slogans is brief and to the point, but brevity just brings one or two advantages of some product, while the uncertainty or implicitness of vague advertisement language can convey as various meanings as producers want to or improve the effect of slogans. Vagueness may bring us trouble of understanding about its real intention. It is this confusion or so-called misunderstanding that results in a spark of idea among different people in the world and reflects different language circumstances. Then it can achieve their goal of interaction with a diversity of people range gender from age. Take Nike for example, its slogan "just do it" is like the vague externalization of dream so that it becomes popular among generation after generation across the national boundary. According to Leech (1981: 30), "An expression is said to be ambiguous when more than one interpretation can be assigned to it." No wander using vague advertisement language can reach a better propaganda effect through proper affix, blending, abbreviation and some homonyms or polysemy efficiently.

3.2 A Sense of Humor

Phonetic, rhetoric, lexical and syntactic vagueness sometimes cause ambiguity, which may form black humor. It may result from adaption of proverb, a fairy tale or some key words of important persons. Certainly, each person's acceptance degree or comprehension level is different, so the definition of humor can't be certain.

There are several types in advertisement: put the seemingly unrelated things together, through association and imagination to arouse the resonance of the advertising language, after thinking you will smile, like a mobile phone slogan-make yourself heard which seems to mean listening to one's own heart by the phone; use exaggeration to pretend to belittle or deliberately enlarge the good quality of the product, like the functions of the juice and makeup already talked above; or use positive imperative sentences to prompt you to consume as if it is very popular, like the slogan of Cdirac. As happiness is the source of power, to some degree, humorous vagueness in advertisement can be beneficial.

3.3 The Artistic Characteristics

Aristotle ever said "there are still people today for whom the word 'rhetoric' means empty words, misleading arguments, and appeal to base emotions"(2007). It is believed by whom doesn't use it. But for those created slogans, there appear positive effects. On one hand, the attraction of vague advertisement slogans lies in its rhetoric application, on account of the feelings it brings, such as euphemism, metaphor, pun, parody, irony and the like. These vague methods is full of artistic characteristics, some with phonological rhythm beauty, some with organized visual beauty, some with depth-meaning and some being easy-understood but unconventional. On the other hand, people's motivation plays quite an important role in one's purchasing behavior that can trigger a chemical reaction with rhetoric, like the slogan of SWATCH which is "Time is what you make of it", where the word *time* is a pun, both in connotation and in denotation, leaving a memorable impression. In the field of motivation psychology, people may be attracted by only one aspect of a advertisement slogan, such as the quality or the popularity. A motivated person is ready to act at any moment. The use of implicit language can not only make advertisements meaningful, tempting, but also make consumers accept the information of products in the mood of relaxation and cheer, even indulge in uncertainty. Combining artistic beauty and people's motivation psychology, numerous producers add rhetoric into advertisement slogans in large amounts to promote and publicize the features of goods or create vivid images for consumers.

4 Ways to Design Neoteric Vague Advertisement Slogans

4.1 Brevity and to the Point

Advertisement slogan should avoid complicity and lengthy expression. To first catch consumers' eye, it should be brief and to the point because the attraction length is limited. What's more, brevity can leave enormous space for imagination and full feeling. Vagueness has the same effect to rouse consumers' imagination because both of them are lacking in explanation about details of products. Besides, it should refrain from monotonous repetition in advertisement slogans, encouraging phonetic, semantic and pragmatic change with vagueness.

4.2 Hint and Association

From the layer of perspective of cognitive psychology, whether advertisers or consumers, their "cognitive expectations" are the pursuit of "inexpensive" goods, but the two "cognitive expectations" focus on different cultural connotation of the word *inexpensive*. For advertisers, the intention is to create novel product images, such as unique background, belle color or charming stories in it, all of which beautiful things are hoped to be inexpensive; for consumers, the word *inexpensive* is to the buying process, the packaging and the price. How to convey abundant advantages of the product needs extraordinary slogans first to enlarge popularity and publicity, thus stimulating the consumers' desire to purchase it. Their ultimate goal is to buy goods of high quality. Therefore, the slogan must imply both the beautiful things and the cheap price to seek the ideal point of combination. Besides, associating seemingly different things in advertisement properly, consumers' imagination and seeking psychology will be aroused by some ambiguity on the basis of traditional cognition. Concerning the regeneration of traditional culture, ad. slogan should contain some traditional elements through some vague images.

4.3 Catering to Consumers' Common Psychology

Acceptance is the crucial process of creating works, which is in need of and reveals readers' aesthetic experience. Readers' acceptance degree is limited by their own historical conditions, cultural environment and conventional wisdom, so weighing and analyzing all of this is of great importance before making a slogan. In advertisement, it is necessary to comply with consumers' taste and psychology. When slogans are fit for their expectations, it is close to succeed. For different types of people, they are consistent with one point, that is, the products count as much as its slogans and deserve buying. Now that the artistic distance among different consumers is hard to grasped and controlled, it is wise to put emphasis on complying the common psychology, other information as supplement.

5 Conclusions

This paper is to explore more scientific and more effective advertisement language, which can not only help enterprises obtain certain economic benefits, but also contribute to the regeneration of traditional culture, making social benefits, and enable the advertising readers to learn to appreciate and understand its connotation. By analysis, guided by the cognitive psychology of consumers, vague advertisement language has certain artistic characteristics, with a sense of humour, which helps enhance the popularity and positive effect of product, making the product more attractive, so it is useful to apply vagueness for advertisement language.

There are several ways to create more excellent vague advertisement slogans, but the range is very large. This is one of shortages of the paper, not enough to be professional and detailed. Besides, the reference books are a little limited and my comprehensibility need improving. A deeper and more comprehensive research can be conducted on a broader database and keener awareness of this area.

References

[1] Aristotle, *On Rhetoric*, second edition[M]. New York Oxford: Oxford University Press, 2017.

[2] Lakoff, G Hedges: A Study in Meaning Criteria and the Logic of Fuzzy Concepts[C]. *Chicago: Chicago Linguistic Society*, 1972: 458-508.

[3] Mr. Fahd Mohammed Sagheer Eid, Functional Analysis of Clause Complex in the Language of News Websites Texts: A Comparative Study of Two Article[J]. *International Journal of Scientific and Research Publications*, 2016, 6（6）：323-334.

[4] 陈治安，文旭. 模糊语言学研究的回顾与展望[J]. 上海外国语大学学报，1996（5）：29-34.

[5] 端木义万. 从广告心理学角度看广告英语特色[J]. 山东外语教学，1987（4）：3-13.
[6] 刘贺. 模糊语言学在国外的发展状况研究[J]. 经济师，2013（2）：57-58.
[7] 沈雯静. 企业广告营销中英语模糊性词语的使用及翻译[J]. 商场现代化，2015（18）：60-61.
[8] 吴世雄，陈维振. 中国模糊语言学：回顾与前瞻[J]. 外语教学与研究，2001（1）：7-14.
[9] 王佳琦. 论英语广告语言含蓄性和读者认知间的互动[D]. 江苏科技大学，2011.
[10] 杨铭. 茶叶企业广告英语中模糊语言的语用功能及翻译[J]. 福建茶叶，2017（3）：45-46.

Pragmatic Study of the Chinese Contronym Word "Chen"

朱珈璇

摘　要："臣"字最早是以甲骨文的形式出现在中国历史上的，经过时间的推移，其词意发生了巨大变化。直到现代，"臣"字具备了反义同形的特征。在当代，有部分学者虽为分析反义同形词而对"臣"字的字意变化稍有所涉猎，但该字只是作为反义同形词的例证之一出现在文本中。本论文首先将对反义同形词的概念、何兆熊的著作《语用学》中的语境概念进行简要介绍，紧接着将站在前瞻的角度，以部分"臣"字相关文献的考订为基础，来对"臣"字字义用法加以分析。最后本文将从语境的角度上得出结论：社会形态的变化是导致"臣"字字义变化成为反义同形词的重要原因。

关键词：臣；反义同形词；语用学；变化成因

Abstract: The Chinese word "chen" showed up in ancient China as the oracle bone script. As time went, the meaning of it changed a lot. Up to now, the word "chen" is of the character of contronym. In the modern time, some scholars have paid attention to the changes of the meaning of "chen", but the word represents in their texts as one example of contronym. First of all, this paper makes a brief introduction to the definition of contronym context, one of the two important conceptions in Pragmatics written by He Zhaoxiong. And then we will analyze it from the prospective viewpoint based on some "chen"-related references. At last, this paper finds the reason for the change of the meaning from context aspect that the changes of the social formation is an important reason for the changes the meaning of "chen" and making it a diachronic contronym.

Key words: Chen；Autantonym；Pragmatics；Reasons for change

1　Introduction

1.1　Contronym

An auto-antonym or autantonym, also called a contronym or contranym, is a word with multiple meanings of which one is the reverse of another. In the western country, the terms "autantonym" and "contronym" were coined by Joseph T. Shipley in 1960 and Jack Herring in 1962, respectively (Tinakimmel) and in China, the conception was coined by Guo Pu in Jin Dynasty which is 1600 years ago. He generalized the phenomenon as

"义相反而相通" and "美恶不嫌同名" (郭璞, 2013: 61)

("Yi xiang fan er xiang tong" and "mei wu bu xian tong ming")

("The meanings of one word were totally contrary" and "The meanings of beauty and ugly monster shared the same word")

And there is another way in China to name this kind of phenomenon—反训(fanxun) (antonymous gloss).

1.2 Pragmatics and Context

Pragmatics as a field of linguistics inquiry was initiated in the 1930s by Morris, Carnap, Perice, for whom syntax addresses the formal relations of signs to one another, semantic deals with the meanings of signs of what they denote, and pragmatics addresses the relation of signs of their users and interpreters. (Morris, 1979) In this regard, pragmatics is the study of those context-dependent aspects of meaning which are systematically abstracted away from in the construction of content or logic form. (Verschueren, 2006)

Context is one of the two important conceptions of pragmatics mentioned by He Zhaoxiong in his book *Pragmatics*. Context plays an important role in the interpretation of meaning; different contexts often influence the understanding of addressees. (Zhang zhaoxiong, 2011) In his book, He Zhaoxiong quoted W. Downes' representation of the various kinds of "contextual information" involved in the course of comprehending an utterance:

Background knowledge (i) Knowledge of the language .
(ii) Metaconversational rules, norms, conventions.
(iii) Participants' biographies.
(iv) Metassocial rules, norms, conventions.(situation types)
(v) The encyclopedia.

Mutual knowledge Each participants' knowledge that the other knows that a person inferred d on some basis.

Context of utterance (i) Previous utterances in same conversation.
(ii) Immediate setting of speech
(iii) Previous conversations of participants
(iv) Background knowledge, accessed by (i) — (iii).

(Lyons, 1981, p. 25)

And the "contextual information" mentioned above will be used for the analysis of the word Chinese "chen" (臣).

2 Pragmatic Study of "chen"

2.1 Original Meaning

"Chen" is the word with a very long history. At the very beginning, the word "chen" was found among oracle bone scripts and it was used as verb and noun at that time. When it was used as verb, it referred to the action that the slaves obey the commands of their owners. And when the word was used as noun, it was used to name the slaves. The two different usages could be considered as the original meaning of "chen".

臣：甲骨文象箕坐之形，身手都被束缚。(黄现璠, 1979, p. 71)

（chen: jiagu wen xiang ji zuo zhi xing, shen shou dou bei shu fu）

（chen: The oracle-bone inscription of “chen” looks like the action that people sit like the dustpan with his extremities bound)

According to the example mentioned before, it is obvious that “chen” is the special belonging of the slaves. And as we know that, the oracle-bone inscriptions were used by some slaver's owner who were literate in slavery society which complied with the low productivity. There were a great number of the poor, while there were a few rich men. And at that time there were three kinds of people: the slaves, the commoners and the slave owners. Among the three kinds of people, they belonged to different social ranks. The slaves belonged to the lowest social rank because they were owned by the slave owners. They should obey to comments of their owners unconditionally. Commoners were the individuals who belonged to nobody and nobody belonged to them, which means that they were the middle social rank. And according to the historic records, we can know that the kings of that time tried their best to inject the idea to listen to the higher class into the individuals and to make them to believe that they were born to be slaves. So the slaves were used to the situation that they served for their owners and obeyed to the commands of them. Their owner s could kill any one of them casually. Of course they did not have the right to talk to their owners to decide whether they should be picked out from the crowds with the word “chen”. Under that case, their ultimate goal was to live. And because lacking of money and awareness of breaking the barrier of changing the social statures, although the the power were passed to anther family who were slave owners before the power change, they never made they social rank or the way they were called change.

2.2 The Development of Original Meaning

The first time that the meaning of “chen”changed was when it came into the feudal society. It was used by the people who served for the kings specially, for instance,

然则侍卫之臣不懈于内。(诸葛亮, 2005, p. 1)

(ran ze shi wei shi chen bu xie yu nei)

(Bearing the late king's special favor in hearts, the officials at court who guard Your Majesty dare not to slacken in their vigilance) (罗经国, 2005, p. 1)

诚国家爪牙之吏，折冲之臣。（班固, 2005, p. 983）

(Cheng guo jia zhao ya zhi li, zhe chong zhi chen)

(He does just like the claws of our country and he is the one who can help to defeat the violations of foreign.)

The two examples mentioned above both happened at the time that one remonstrates with the king. And “chen” in the two examples referred to the individuals who served on the position for the king or we can say for the king's family. And we can know that people use “chen” to name that kind of people in feudal society. In this kind of society, the productivity was higher when compared with slavery society. To make the kingdom more flourishing, the hierarchy changed the way to choose the people who could help them to rule the kingdom. That is the imperial examinations which was one kind of exams' system in which the young male students who learned something about value, the way to rule the kingdom and the way to write great articles should pass the exam And their minds were emancipated in some aspects for their enriched knowledge and their understandings about the meaning of life. And because of the imperial examinations, the individuals found the way to change their social class and earn much more money. Although they only needed to serve for the king or emperor, in essence, they were still the salve of the king or emperor. The king could kill any one of his "chen"s. Because of the mind emancipation, the idea that someone was born to be someone changed. During the feudal society period, there r were some people who killed his emperor became the emperor of the next dynasty.

And when it comes to the meaning of "chen", in the feudal society, the usage of "chen" had changed a little, but the profound meaning of it was just like before.

2.3 The Original Opposite Meaning

Not only the development of original meaning of "chen" happened in feudal society, but also the original opposite meaning appeared. And the symbolic example happened in the conversation between emperor Gaozu and his father.

高祖奉玉卮，起为太上皇寿，曰："始大人常以臣无赖……" (司马, 2009, p. 81)

(gaozu feng yuzhi, qi wei tai shang huang shou, yue: "shi da ren chang yi chen wu lai...")

(Emperor Gaozu stood up with a cup of Yuzhi to make a toast for his father on the birthday party, and then he said: "when I was young you think I am a good-for-nothing guy...")

This example happened in the birthday party of emperor Gaozu"s father. "chen" was used to refer to emperor Gaozu himself. As we know that the emperor was the noblest one in the feudal society, it was not a proper usage for him to call himself. But this conversation happened between father and son. According to the thoughts of the ancient people, the "jun-chen" relationship which was the relationship between the emperor and individuals who helped to rule the country was premier than the relationship between father and son. But emperor Gaozu's family had been commons for a long time before this conversation and during that time he was the good -for nothing guy in his family members' minds. He paid more attention to the father-son relationship. And there were two aims that he said the words. The first aim was to toast for his father's birthday. The second aim was to say that they gave the wrong judge to him and he was the one whose achievement was great. So, actually, he said these words with proud even though "chen" was not a proper usage.

2.4 The Final Opposite Meaning

The forth time that the meaning of "chen" changed was when it was the modern time in the socialist country. And it always appears in the articles about foreign political situation. And "chen" refers to some positions in the government, for example,

新华社快讯：据外电 9 日报道，英国外交大臣约翰逊辞职。(新华网)

(xin hua she kuai xun: ju wai dian 9 ri bao dao, wai jiao da chen yue han xun ci zhi.)

(Xinhua News Agency: According to foreign reports on the 9th, British Foreign minister Johnson resigned)

From the example, we can know that "chen" is used to refer the ministers. Since our country came into the socialism, "chen" hasn't been the word which referred to the ones whose social class is lower than the people they served for. And with the productivity developed fast, the thoughts have been changed. There is not the idea that one is born to be someone. In stead, we do believe that we are created equal, which means we can choose to be who we want be and there is no prejudice about the jobs. Although “chen” serves for the public, they are respected by them. And for themselves, they are proud of their job.

3 Conclusions

The meaning of a word relies on the context which includes social, cultural and contextual factors. The context changes and the meaning will also change. In general, one word represents the most normal things while people always use it to refer to the special and specific issues in different contexts. In this situation, one word is of different meanings or even opposite meanings.

In the slavery society, “chen” referred to the slaves. And there were two kinds of usages in the feudal society. One was naming the individuals who helped the emperor to rule the country. And the other was Emperor Gaozu calling himself when in front of his father. The usage in feudal society can be considered as the passing way of that in slavery and socialist society. In the socialist society, it refers to ministers who work for the country and the public and receive great respect.

And function of “chen” as noun, which refers to the slaves or the ministers, makes it a contronym. The meaning of “chen” referred to the salves earlier than to minister, which implies that the two different meanings were formed through a historical period of time which is the reason why we can analyze it from the diachronic linguistic aspect. Slaves were the people who served their owners and observed their commands. While although the ministers were the individuals who belonged to the higher social class, they were not the chiefs of the state and they have to work for them and serve for them. Besides, the social functions of the government, the ministers can be regarded as on kind of “public servant” who serve for the taxpayers. The way the ministers serve for people and their social recognition and are totally different from the slaves. The “servant” character of ministers is a metaphor.

From what we have analyzed in the former chapter, we can conclude that the usages of “chen” change as the changes of the society. The development of productivity changes the society. And the society helped to emancipate the minds of the public which change the idea people are born unequal. They figure out the way to change their social class and rank. And ultimately, “chen” becomes the word which makes people be of equal social class but of great proud of themselves and respect from others.

References

[1] Lyons, John. *Language and Context*[M]. London: Fontana,1981.

[2] Morris, Charles. *Logical Positivism, Pragmatism and Scientific Empiricism*[M]. New York: AMS Press, 1979.

[3] Tinakimmel. *Auto-antonym*[OL]. <https://en.m.wikipedia.org/wiki/Auto-antonym> 2 June, 2018.

[4] Verschueren, Jef. *Understanding Pragmatic* [M]. Oxford: Blackwell Publishing, 2006.

[5] Zhang ,Zhaoxiong. *Pragmatics* [M]. Shanghai: Shanghai Foreign Language Education Press, 2011.

[6] 班固. 汉书[M]. 杭州：浙江古籍出版社，2005.

[7] 郭璞. 尔雅注[M]. 郑州：中州古籍出版社，2013.

[8] 黄现璠. 我国民族历史没有奴隶社会之探讨[J]. 广西师范大学学报，1979（3）：71-79.

[9] 罗经国. 古文观止[M]. 北京：外语教学与研究出版社，2005.

[10] 司马迁. 史记[M]. 北京：中华书局，2009.

[11] 新华社. 快讯：英国外交大臣约翰逊辞职[OL]. https://news.china.com/internationalgd/10000166/20180709/32657803.html, 2018 年 12 月 5 日获取.

[12] 诸葛亮. 出师表[M]. 北京：外语教学与研究出版社，2005.

浅谈汉语词汇意义历时演变中的常规与非常规表现

贾 淞[1] 汤朝菊

摘 要：从本体论来说，汉语词汇也是汉语语言结构中非常活跃的要素之一，其词汇的意义特征也随着语言的变化而变化，表现为词汇意义的增加与减少等其他意义转换的特征。本文通过一些词汇的具体案例，对汉语词汇意义历史演变过程中出现的常规与非常规的表现进行讨论。

关键词：词汇；历时演变；引申；非常规表现

Abstract: From the perspective of ontology, Chinese lexicon is also one of the most active elements in the structure of Chinese language. The semantic characteristics of Chinese lexicon is also changeable along with the change of language, which is manifested as the polar increase and decrease of lexical meaning, and other characteristics of meaning transformation. This paper discusses the conventional and unconventional expressions in the historical evolution of Chinese lexical meaning through some specific vocabulary cases.

Key words: Vocabulary；Diachronic evolution；Extended meaning；Abnormal performance

1 引 言

语言三要素中随时间变化最大的就是词汇，相比较而言，语法和语音的变化就要小得多。作为一个高语境的语言，汉语语句中词汇顺序的变动空间很小，更加强调使用汉语的人对汉语词汇的理解和运用。

汉语词汇脱胎于生活又影响我们的生活，其丰富词意的形成深深植根于中华文化几千年的发展之中。但词汇的意义绝非一成不变。在汉语词汇大爆炸的当今，词汇意义的每一次微小变化都会引发语句使用习惯的巨大变革。深入了解汉语词汇的历时性变化，能够更好地促进我们对于词汇的理解和运用。（闫从发，2008）

2 汉语词汇意义的演变常规与非常规变化

汉语作为世界上最古老的语言之一，它的构词特点、词汇意义都远不同于拉丁语体系下的其他语言，词汇意义的产生与演变也有其独具的特点，许多词语的历时变化极为丰富。而这些词汇意义的变化包含常规变化与非常规变化，这里分类讨论一下词汇意义的不同变化形式。

---

① 作者为电子科技大学外国语学院英语专业二年级本科生，本论文在"英语词汇学"课程论文基础上修改，指导老师为电子科技大学英语系教授汤朝菊

2.1 词汇意义的常规增加

词汇意义的增减是人们实践发展的客观需要，一种事物的兴起与消亡必然带来相关词汇的创造与废弃，久而久之其背后的词汇意义也就相应地增大或缩小。词义的常规增加包括词意引申带来的词义变化和特殊条件引发的词义变化两种。这种由常规词义增加形式引发的词汇意义改变占整个词义改变体系的绝大部分。

2.1.1 词意常规引申导致的词意扩充

词意常规引申形式包括放射型、连锁型和综合型三种基本形式。放射型即以词的基本义为中心，其他次要的意义像光芒一样从中心向四周放射出来，每个次要意义同时来自中心的基本意义，彼此又是相互独立的（常用语比喻义的引申）。例如：从“头”这个词的基本意义“头部”引申出“头状物体”“头脑；才智”“脓头”“名单最前面的部分”“河流的源头”“著有头像的硬币”等等含义，均是由其基本义向外发散产生的各种意义。

连锁型是指从一个意义出发产生第二个意义，然后不顾第一个意义而从第二个意义出发又产生第三个意义，最后产生的词义与第一个词义毫不相干，这种演变过程叫作连锁型。如“绿”这个词的本义：通“菉”。一种野菜。该义即是该词的核心意义，我们根据这种植物的颜色引申出“蓝和黄混合成的颜色，一般草和树叶呈现这种颜色”这一如今常用的意义——绿色。连锁型的引申形式虽不易看出本义，但却一定能够从该词汇的本义寻到这种词义转变的过程。

而许多词的演变过程是十分复杂的，不一定按照单一的方式进行。词意的演变多数情况下是两种方式的交叉结合进行，这便是综合型词义引申法。如“脸”这个词通过词意的放射引申出“人”“表面”“事物的正面”等词意，而再次将“人”这个词意进行词意的连锁，引申出“人的外表”，并进一步引申出“表情”“尊严”等等。

2.1.2 由其他原因导致的词意扩充

词汇意义的增加还有许多其他的因素，包括社会的发展与环境的改变、民族情绪与种族情绪的影响、社会价值观的改变等等。（刘兴容，2015）这里以社会发展对词意扩充的影响为例，仍以“绿”的词汇变化为例：元朝统治者对妓女及在妓院里做工的男人着装的规定使得“绿帽子”中“绿”的含义应运而生。这种词意的引申受到政治环境、社会发展的影响。

2.2 词汇意义的减少

减少的含义也称为泛化，是扩大词义相反的意思。本文所述的“减少”并不等同于“缩小”，前者是多义词词汇意义的减少，后者是指多义词中单个意义所指范围的缩小，如：“禽”在古代指“鸟”和“兽”，后来专指鸟类（包括飞禽和家禽）。“子”原义包括“儿子”和“女儿”，现在却只能指“儿子”等等。

词汇意义的减少主要体现在单个词义使用率下降而逐渐被遗忘的现象和社会、政治、自然等因素的综合影响两方面的影响。现就前者给出例子，如：“互”字，其原本有“挂肉的架子”的意义（张衡《西京赋》：“置互摆牲”），但这个意义随着历史环境的改变而逐渐被淘汰。还有一些词语的意义处于即将被淘汰的边缘，如：“花”这个字，在古代有“某些幼嫩微细的东西”的意思，如：刚孵出的幼蚕成为蚕花，称鱼苗称为鱼花，这种意义现在在我国南部地区还偶尔使用，但随着时间的变化或许最终会淡出历史舞台。再如“花”这个词作为“痘”的含义（如天花）也逐渐被人们弃置。

2.3 词汇意义的非常规增加与转换

汉语中许多词的表意在直接和间接的引申过程中出现了不同于以上常规演变的变化形式。这种演变很难找出一条演变历程中的内在线索。长期以来，对这部分词义演变的描述多停留在对引申原因的一股猜测和引申结果的分类说明上。新的理论、方法始终未能建立起来。（董为光，1990，1）L. R. 帕默尔在他的《语言学概论》序言中说道：学者们早已认识到，对意义变迁做出纯逻辑分类是徒劳无功的，因为两种或更多的不同过程可以得到完全相同的语义结果。（L.R.帕默尔，1983）前人对于这种词义非常规增加的现象做了大量的探索和考证，力图梳理出其中的脉络，下面浅谈一些个人不同的看法和观点。

2.3.1 单语素词表意的非常规增加

以词意演变的历时观点来看，汉字的演变总是从单语素词开始的（葛本仪，2006）。汉语词汇中单语素词的引申过程一般遵循上述常规形式，但也有一些词的表意过程存在争议。词语双本义的现象就是表现形式之一，如：“良”的名词本义是“首；头；首领；首长”的意思，但在其向形容词的引申过程中却出现了完全不同于其名词本义的特点，其形容词的意义为“善；良好；美好；优秀；和悦；和善；吉祥……”其形容词一类的意义可以说是在循着一个背后的独特的本义引发而来的自引申，其引申的意义均具有“美好；善”的基本义（但不能确定“美好”和“善”的意义即为其形容词本义）。而根据“良”的副词意义为“很；极；非常；确实……”来看，其副词的引申义是在形容词词意的基础上合理衍生的，是对形容词本义及引申义的意义附加，其词意中包含有对形容词词意的正面情感期待。这种对本义的溯源最终得到两个基本意义，违背了词义诞生时“一词对一义”的理论基础。

引申过程的缺失也使得一些词义的产生非常规。例如：“架”的本意是“棚架”，在其引申义中为“框架；建造；支撑；支起；搀扶”等意义，均是由“棚架”这一原始意义进行联想产生的其他意义。而其另一个表示“殴打；争吵”的意义却让人起疑。这个意义不同于常规的引申形式，一种说法是说该义来自“人们击打棚架，或在架起棚架的时候需要击打来树立木桩”，也有人认为该意来自典故“大禹治水”的故事，故事中提及“水来土掩”即是将水架起来打，故得此义。而该词词意的具体来历现已无法考证，这种对引申过程考证的缺失使得该词意的变化被并到词义引申的非常规表现的范畴。

词语的“相因生义”现象也是词语意义演变中难以解释的一部分。“相因生义”即是指一个词由于受另一个与之相关词意义的影响而产生新的义项。罗积勇曾给出一个简单明了的例子，即：“信”与“引”原本为同义词，两者的引申义均为“伸展”，在这个意义上两者互通，而“信”在汉代产生的另一个意义“凭证”则在使用的过程中慢慢影响到“引”的使用，使得“引”慢慢也具有“凭证；符契”的意义。（罗积勇，1985）这种意义的产生无论是用引申还是假借都无法解释，这种演变形式在单语素词中表现得最为典型。

2.3.2 多语素合成词表意的非常规表现形式

大多数汉字多语素合成词的表意是两个单语素词意的直接叠加或进行合理的引喻引申。（吴毅安，2008，3）但有极少数的合成词具有非常规的结合形式，即词意完全无关或轻微相关。造成这种现象的原因之一就是取自生活约定俗成事物的原型缺失。这种情况多发生在名词上，比如“活套”这个词，现代汉语的解释是“精装书封加工的一种形式，常见于塑料软面的精装书籍和本册上使用”即是将该词“活”与“套”的单个词意义进行结合。但古汉语词典中，该词的意义为“俗语杂谈”。黄宗羲的《柳敬亭传》中有言：“敬亭耳剽口熟，从委巷活套中来者，无不与宁南意合。”说的即是柳敬亭耳朵经常听到的，口里经常说的，都是从僻陋里巷俗语常谈中得来的。而这个词的意义却与其组合成词的单字意义关系甚浅。在历史上也并没有典故、俗谚能对其进行溯源的解释。诸如此类的还有“东西”作为“泛指各种具体或抽象的事物”的意义，大多数学者认为该种词意产生的原因与相关物品的代指或相关事物的假借有关，（曾石飞，2010）许多考证仍停留在对物体原型的探索之中。

另一种重要的表现形式是特殊环境与特殊心理因素的共同决定，这类词在词义引申过程中产生了意义的“断崖”。例如“感忽”这个词，该词中“感”通“憾”意为“恨；不满”，“忽”有“迅速；辽阔的样子；忽然”等不同词性的意义。但两字合二为一却为“恍惚”的意思，在《荀子·议兵》中有：“善用兵者，感忽悠暗，莫知其所从出”的句子，（《古汉语常用字字典》2003，1）其产生的原因与个人瞬间的情感获得密切相关。

不同字之间的通假也是重要的形式，但这种形式的使用极为少见。如在汉代，“大家”这个词出现了和字面义相去较远的含义：①对妇女的尊称。②妇女称丈夫之母。这样的称呼始于班昭，“帝数召入宫，令皇后诸贵人师事焉，号曰大家。”由此，往后许多妇人都被称为“大家”。（秦峰，2014）这个词义的产生即是因为“家”字与“姑”字发生了通假，从而出现与本义相去较远的现象。

3 结　论

汉语词汇意义的历时演变具有相当的复杂性，汉语词义的转变带有浓厚的民族色彩、民族个性。词义的常规引申是词意扩展的重要原因，人们在使用词汇的基础上依据词义的相关特征对现有词义进行合理联想和引喻，以增加新的意义。但对于汉语词义演变中非常规的形式，我们应该高度关注。目前对这种词义历时演变的考证仍停留在猜测的基础上，其背后的原因仍值得我们深度探索。我们应在合理扬弃的基础上加深对汉语词汇意义历时演变的理解，更好地应用到我们的日常生活中。

参考文献

[1] L. R. 帕默尔. 语言学概论[M]. 北京：商务印书馆，1983.

[2] 董为光. 词义演变过程中的心理因素[J]. 语言研究，1990（1）：1-10.

[3] 葛本仪. 汉语词汇研究[J]. 北京：外语教学与研究出版社，2006.

[4] 本书编委会. 古汉语常用字字典[M]. 长春：吉林大学出版社，2003.

[5] 刘兴容. 浅析词汇意义变化之原因[J]. 校园英语，2017（29）：210.

[6] 罗积勇. 论汉语词义演变中的“相因生义”[J]. 武汉大学学报（社会科学版），1985（5）：71-75.

[7] 秦峰. “大家”词义的演变过程[J]. 北方文学旬刊，2015（2）：136-137.

[8] 吴毅安. 汉语词义引申研究中的几个问题[J]. 社会科学战线，2008（3）：183-185.

[9] 闫从发. “商量”的意义演变[J]. 西北大学学报（哲学社会科学版），2008，38（6）：187-190.

[10]曾石飞. “东西”的词义演变历程及其原因探索[J]. 现代语文：语言研究版，2010（2）：68-69.

句末句号的缺失：网络社交礼仪

柳　依

摘　要：随着互联网与移动设备的普及，社交软件成为人们日常生活中必不可少的信息交流方式。新的网络语境下，人们的“书写”通过社交软件发生了巨大的转变。本文主要讨论这一转变中网络聊天句末句号的缺失现象。文章以微博和微信为主要的语料来源，对缺失句末句号的不同情况进行整理与分析。同时通过调研社交软件用户对句末句号的使用方式，文章将从语言学角度对缺失句末句号的现象予以分析和解释。本文认为网络交际中，句末句号会发生缺失，往往相当于被替换为零符号或表情符号，这一变化使网络聊天信息更加经济、简洁，有利于为聊天情境注入更多的情态要素，使表达生动形象。信息因此得以更准确地传递，降低产生误会的风险。对大多数用户来说，句号象征着完整单位意思地表达与传递，但过于冷漠严肃，不足以满足网络时代人际互通的需要。网络用语中句号的缺席意味着信息情态化是网络社交的重要礼仪。与标准书面用语进行比较，我们可以重新审视传统标点符号的规范形式与社交功能。

关键词：标点；句号；网络交际

Résumé: Avecla démocratisation d'internet et de l'appareil mobile, des logiciels sociaux deviennent un mode de communication indispensable dans la vie quotidienne. Dans l'environnement numérique, les façons d'« écrire » ont connu un glissement important. Cet article s'intéressera spécifiquement à un phénomène — le manque du point final dans la communication médiée électronique (désormais CME). Pour organiser et analyser les différents cas de l'omission du point final, nous prendrons Weibo et Wechat comme corpus et collecterons les points de vue des utilisateurs. Enfin, nous traiterons des données dans une perspective linguistique. Nous faisons l'hypothèse que dans les CME, la disparition du point final est remplacée par « rien » ou des emojis. Ce changement rend les échanges d'informations plus économiques et efficaces, de plus, il aide aussi à recadrer le contexte affectif d'un message et à rendre l'expression plus vivante. Par conséquent, des informations peuvent être transmises fidèlement et le risque de malentendu baisse. Le point traditionnel signifie la clôture d'une transmission d'une unité de sens complet. Cependant, pour la plupart des utilisateurs, il est trop froid et sérieux qu'il ne peut pas toujours satisfaire le besoin des communications interpersonnelle dans l'ère d'internet. Le manque du point final illustre que la modalité des informations est un élément de sens important dans les CME. En comparaison avec le standard de la langue écrite, nous pourrions réexaminer la forme normale des ponctuations traditionnelles et aussi ses fonctions sociales.

Mot clés: Ponctuation；Point final；Communication médiée électronique

1 引 言

随着社交软件的普及，人们的书写由于互通媒介的改变也随之发生了巨大变化，大量“不标准”的标点符号用法开始涌现。汉语书面语中的标点符号主要有三种功能：表示停顿、气，或词语的性质和作用。但对比传统标点符号的定义，网络环境下标点符号则有新的形式与功能。例如，网络聊天语境下句末句号的缺失就是一类典型现象。

网络语言持续在国外学术界得到普遍关注，已有专门针对 Facebook 与 Tweeter 为研究对象的诸多成果。国内网络语境下的标点异化研究也取得了相应进展，但对汉语标点符号在社交媒体中的情态用法与社交功能的探讨还可以进一步完善。因此，本文以网络聊天过程中，汉语句末句号的缺失为切入点，通过分析句末句号形式与含义的转变，配合调研社交软件用户对句号使用意图的看法，试图概括出句号在网络语境下的新意涵。文章对网络语言的关注也能够为人们在新时代重新审视传统标点符号的定义提供参考。

2 句号的传统定义

根据中华人民共和国国家标准标点符号用法的规定，标点符号是辅助文字记录语言的符号，是书面语的有机组成部分，用来表示停顿、语气以及词语的性质和作用，其中句号用于陈述句末尾（例 1）或语气舒缓的祈使句末尾（例 2），表示停顿。

例 1：春天来了。

例 2：请勿乱扔杂物。

句号是表示句意完结的点号，象征着完整意义单位的传达。与其他标点符号相比，其停顿时间最长。

3 书面语与网络用语比较

书面语是指书面上交际使用的语言，与口语相对，书面语是写和看的语言，要求比口语精确、严谨、规范。

例 3：正在热闹哄哄的时节，只见那后台里，又出来了一位姑娘，年纪约十八九岁，装束与前一个毫无分别，瓜子脸儿，白净面皮，相貌不过中人以上之姿，只觉得秀而不媚，清而不寒，半低着头出来，立在半桌后面，把梨花简了当了几声，煞是奇怪：只是两片顽铁，到他手里，便有了五音十二律以的。（刘鹗《老残游记》）

在例 3 的描写中，作者按照视觉顺序依次从年龄、装束与面容对王小玉进行刻画，逻辑十分清晰。然而，在网络聊天过程中人们的表达则相对随意。

例 4：A：一起去上课吗

B：不去了，肚子疼

在例 4 中，B 所说的“不去了，肚子疼”省略了因果关系，其完整的逻辑表达应当是“因为肚子疼，所以我不去上课了”。但在网络语境中，缺乏逻辑关联词以及零碎的表达是被允许且能够被理解的。因此，网络语境下的无声文字交流是对听和说的模拟，所以要求快，讲求效率，用词范围相对较窄，句子短小且结构简单，有脱节和颠倒等现象，与口语有相通之处。

4 句末句号的替代者

4.1 零符号

用空白代替句末句号即不在句子末尾添加任何符号。

例 5：A：成都天气好吗

B：挺冷的，这里下雨了

A：多穿点，别感冒啦

B：好的

在例 5 的聊天记录中，除逗号用于表示停顿以外，所有短句都存在句号缺失现象。但即使句中不含句号，两位对话者依然能够有效理解双方的含义，这是因为对话双方在即时交换信息的过程中共享同一个语境，有着明确的聊天目的与主题。除此以外，中文中的语气助词“吗”和“啦”也有效地帮助读者自动为这段聊天信息补充上与语气相符的标点符号，如下文所示。

A：成都天气好吗？

B：挺冷的，这里下雨了。

A：多穿点，别感冒啦！

B：好的。

除却语言层面的因素，网络这个特殊的交流环境也是句末句号缺失的重要原因。虽然人们是通过打字，即非语音的形式在网络环境中进行交流，但短频快的交流特点与口头交流有极大的相通之处，因而可以将网络聊天内容视作是笔语化的口语，这也是人们将网络环境中的文字交流生动形象地称作“聊天”的原因。人们在说完一句话之后的停顿，即话语的空白与零符号在形式上有异曲同工之妙。实际上，通过社交媒体软件的文字交流并不是传统意义上的书写，而是文字对口头交流的模仿。网络用语的形式符合口头聊天时短频快的特点，也符合话语经济原则。（Marie-Anne Paveau, 2013：139-176）这不仅仅是句末句号的缺失，多数情况下人们也会用零符号代替其他标点符号以示停顿，（方艳，2015：4）使网络聊天更加方便快捷。

4.2 表情符号

4.2.1 表情符号发展梳理

表情符号是指对面部表情进行模仿的符号，通常用来传达感情。在表情符号出现之前，人们通常使用传统的标点符号来表达感情，例如，感叹号能够用来表达惊讶或者激动之情，问号则用来表达疑惑与疑问。有时人们甚至会将同一标点符号多次叠加使用以强化情感的表达。然而这些传统标点符号逐渐难以满足社交软件用户们的社交需求，一种新型的表情符号——颜文字出现了，如表 4.1 所示。

表 4.1 颜 文 字

^_^	微笑
T^T	伤心
^_-	眨眼
?_?	疑惑

起初这些符号通常是字母与传统标点符号的组合，这些组合通过模仿眼睛和嘴巴的形态以描绘面部表情。虽然颜文字还算不上真正的表情图标，但它们是将面部表情简化和符号化的宝贵尝试。随着社交软件的快速发展，每一个社交平台都设计有专属的系列表情图标，而这些表情图标与颜文字相比更加复杂，更加富有表现力，通常以动画的形式出现，如图 4.1 与图 4.2 所示。所有的社交软件用户都能够在各自的平台免费使用这些表情图标。

图 4.1　微信系列表情图标

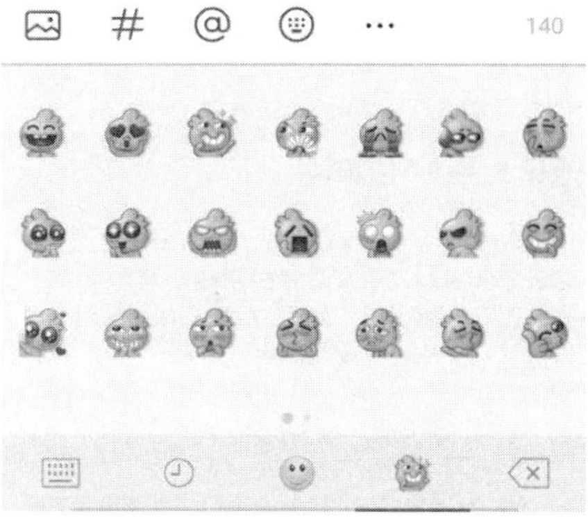

图 4.2　微博系列表情图标

4.2.2　表情符号的作用

交流最重要的目的是准确有效地传达信息。在网络聊天的环境下，为达到这个目的人们通常需要文字之外的更多信息。美国心理学家 Albert Mehrabain 把信息传达的总效果概括为一个公式：7%的有声语言+38%的语音语调+55%的态势语言，其中占比最重的态势语言包括表情语、姿态语、动作语和目光，而表情符号正是在无声聊天的过程中填补了态势语言的空缺（Pier Halté, 2013: 46）。

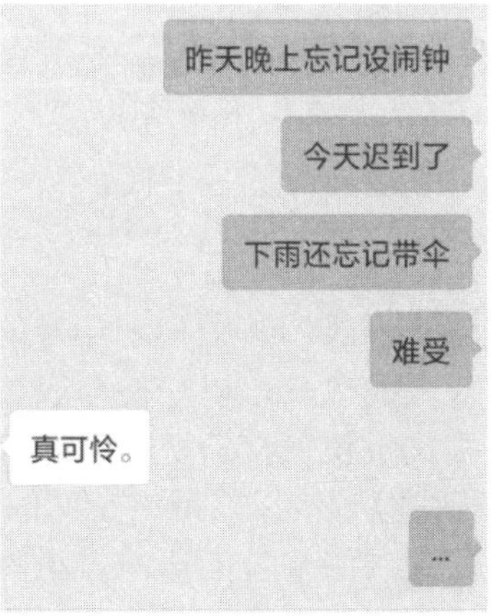

图 4.3　微信聊天截图

如图 4.3 所示，“真可怜。”容易被接收者理解为冷漠，或者理解为对象想尽快结束对话。但倘若删掉句末句号，换做一个“哭脸”表情，则为这段聊天定下了“感同身受”的情感基调，而不至于产生误解。

表情符号是文字的延续，它们能够在纯文字交流中重新定位语境的情感基调，（Barrier Guy, 2010：51）而这种功能是句末句号难以体现的。倘若缺乏表情符号，那么在交流过程中极有可能产生误解。

5　句末句号的缺失：价值与情感的体现

如今对于多数社交软件用户来说，句末句号在网络聊天过程中通常带有负面的含义，（Danielle N. Gunral&Celina M. Klin, 2015）因此网络聊天过程中使用空格或者表情符号来代替句末句号已经成为一种网络社交礼仪。在中国，短消息的本质是口语化交流，而句号会将这种口头表达固定为一种正式的书面表达，容易使接收者认为对方情绪不佳（如图 5.1、图 5.2 所示）。

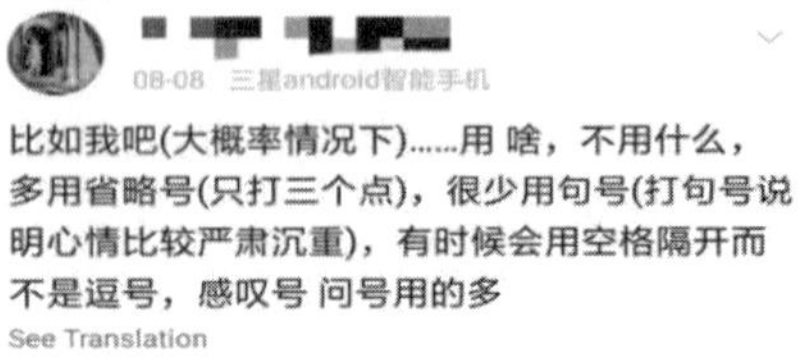

图 5.1　微博截图

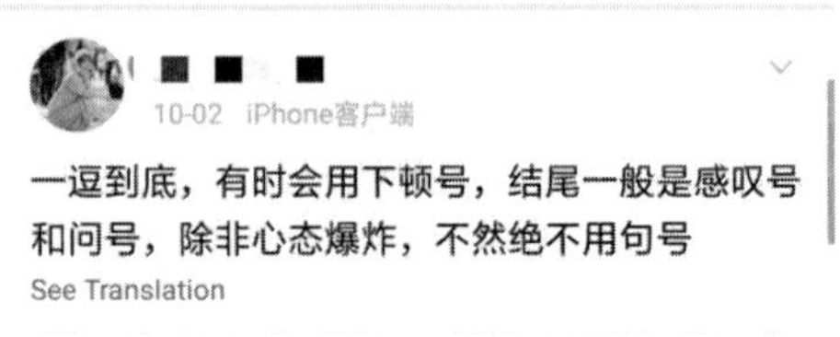

图 5.2　微博截图

然而，比起在交互性的网络聊天过程，在个人动态发表中使用句末句号则代表发表内容的重要性以及发表者态度的严肃与肯定（如图 5.3 所示）。但与此同时，作为短频快的交流工具，微博与微信上的动态字数通常相当有限，而短消息中的句号尤其会因为极度有限的信息容量容易使人产生生硬粗暴之感。（Antoine Gautier, 2016）

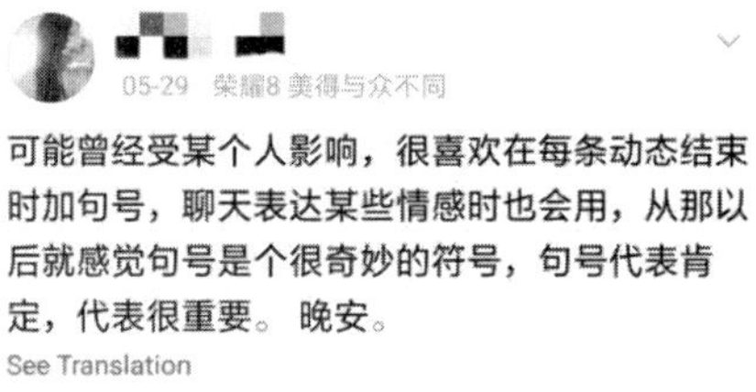

图 5.3　微博截图

6　结　　论

互联网的发展颠覆了我们的交流方式，其中句末句号的用法巨大变化就是一项证明。在网络交流中，句末句号的形式与含义的改变，以空格与表情符号取代句末句号几乎已经成为一种通行的网络社交礼仪。这种礼仪不仅使交流更加迅捷，而且能更准确地传达说话人的真情实意。这两个原因又与网络交流的短频快以及网络空间的无声化的情态缺失紧密关联。

句末句号在网络语境的使用受到网络情境的影响，虽然对于大多数使用者而言，他们对句号的“规范”用法具有清晰意识，但对网络上相应的“不规范”用法持有包容态度。网络环境下的标点符号异化现象还有许多情形有待跟进研究。网络用语的快速发展对传统的标准标点符号的定义也提出了挑战。两者之间原本“标准-非标准”的二元关系将有待以新标准来进一步统一探讨。

参考文献

[1] Antoine Gautier. La ponctuation à l’aube du XXIème siècle: Perspectives historiques et usages contemporains[M]. Éditions Lambert-Lucas, 2016.

[2] Barrier Guy. La communication non verbale: comprendre les gestes : perception et signification[M]. Issy-les Moulineaux, ESF éditeur, 2010 (1996).

[3] Danielle N. Gunral, Celina M. Klin. Texting insincerely: The role of the period in text messaging[J]. Computers in Human Behavior, 2015.

[4] https://fr.wikipedia.org/wiki/Albert_Mehrabian?wprov=sfla1. 2018 年 11 月 23 日获取.

[5] Marie-Anne Paveau. Technodiscursivités natives sur Twitter. Une écologie du discours numérique[J]. Séoul : Revue internationale de sciences humaines et sociales appliquées, 2013.

[6] Pier Halté. Les marques modales dans les chats : étude sémiotique et pragmatique des interjections et des émoticônes dans un corpus de conversations synchrones en ligne[D]. Luxembourg: Université du Luxembourg, 2013.

[7] 方艳. 网络标点符号使用现状探析[J]. 北京邮电大学学报，2015，17（6）：1-6.

教育研究

A Case Study of Translation Teaching through MOOC

曾楚奇

摘　要：慕课作为互联网与教育相结合的学习平台，逐渐成为时代的热门话题。它具有大规模、在线、免费和开放性的特点，为广大学生和其他学习者创造了一个前所未有的“网络大学”。本文针对慕课平台的课程设计和教学模式展开研究，挑选了两门翻译课程进行案例分析，并将其与传统教学模式进行对比，借此探索慕课的发展前景及其面临的挑战。

关键字：慕课；教学模式；发展前景

Abstract: As a learning platform which combines education with Internet, MOOC has gradually become a hot topic in recent times. MOOC is massive, online, free and open, and it has created an unprecedented online university for students and other learners. This paper mainly is focused on the teaching model on MOOC platform. We picked out two types of courses about translation in MOOC to make the case study, and then compared them with the traditional teaching mode, from which we have seen MOOC's prospects and challenges in the future.

Key words: MOOC；Teaching method；Prospect

1　Introduction

MOOC is a technology-based online education. MOOC is for some universities to offer classes online to share educational resources with millions of learners in the world, which is massive, open and flexible. (Wang, 177) The appearance of MOOC is a kind of educational innovation, but it also incurs some disputation.

On the one hand, MOOC can meet the needs of different learners and their various learning demand, to make the more people have the chance to contact with multicultural education resources, to provide more convenient platform for learners to discuss and communicate. (Chen, 7) On the other hand, due to the characteristics of the course and the limitation of objective conditions, MOOC rarely provides feasible practical courses for learners. The educators in MOOC like to provide basic theory courses according to their interests and expertise, without considering the actual needs of the learners, which resulted in the low finishing rate in MOOC. However, MOOC is a technological innovation in education, and it is not mature enough by now.

2　Translation Courses in MOOC

Up to now, there have been 214 cooperative universities on MOOC in China, such as Peking University, Nanjing University and Zhejiang University and so on. There are various kinds of courses in MOOC (there are 14 types of courses by now), such as Computer Science, Economic

Management, Psychology, Foreign language and so on (Fig. 2-1). The courses are so rich and varied that everyone can choose them based on their interest. (Carolyn et al., 26) When you choose a course, you will find that many of the courses have already been over, of course, there are also some courses about to begin. I have chosen the two on-going courses: *Translation in Practice* and *Consecutive Interpreting*. Although I went to class halfway, I could also review the previous courses, which is also the advantage of MOOC. On the one hand, as English major, I am more inclined to study the courses of foreign languages. On the other hand, these two courses are very representative in translation studies: translation and interpretation. And they are offered by famous teachers from the key universities in China.

Fig. 2-1

Translation in Practice is offered by Yao Yuan, associate professor from the School of Foreign Languages of Nanjing University. This course emphasizes on analysis and practice. The lecturer likes to share some examples and experience from some literary works, academic works and other materials to make the comprehensive and detailed analysis, to show the process of translation, and some translation skills, which can lay a solid foundation for learners to become good translation talents. *Consecutive Interpreting* is offered by two teachers, OuYang Qianhua and Yu Yi, from Guangdong University of Foreign Studies. This course selects the core skills in consecutive interpretation training, such as information analysis, memory and notes, which led us enter into a world of consecutive interpretation through principle explanation and practice display.

In the course of *Translation in Practice*, we mainly study the similarities and differences between MOOC and traditional classes. In the course of *Consecutive Interpreting*, we focus on comparing the advantages and disadvantages of them. We do some concrete analysis of the two courses on MOOC, and by comparing MOOC teaching style with the traditional teaching mode, it is found that they can absorb the quintessence, remove the dross and make their respective advantages complementary to each other.

3 Case I: Translation in Practice

3.1 Courses Description and Teaching Method

In the browsing interface of MOOC, we can find that the course is divided into eight sections (Fig. 3-1), and each consists of video teaching and discussion tasks (Fig. 3-2). By observing the study titles of each section, we can see that this course involved in many fields. For example in the lesson 1: "Why Translate", "What Is Translation", "What Is Good Translation". At the same time, you can observe that there are a wide range of translations involved. For example, in the lesson 3, there are Scientific Writings, Legal Documents, Translating Public Speeches, and Translating Literary Works. In Lesson 5 there are Adding or Omitting Words, Phrases, and Clauses, Considering Connotations and Tones, Being Flexible in Translation. This also talks about the problems that need to be paid attention to in translation, and introduces the process of translation, and explains and practices in the order of words, sentences, paragraphs and chapters, from simple to complex, from easy to difficult. (https://www.icourse163.org/learn/GDUFS-1002493010#/learn/content)

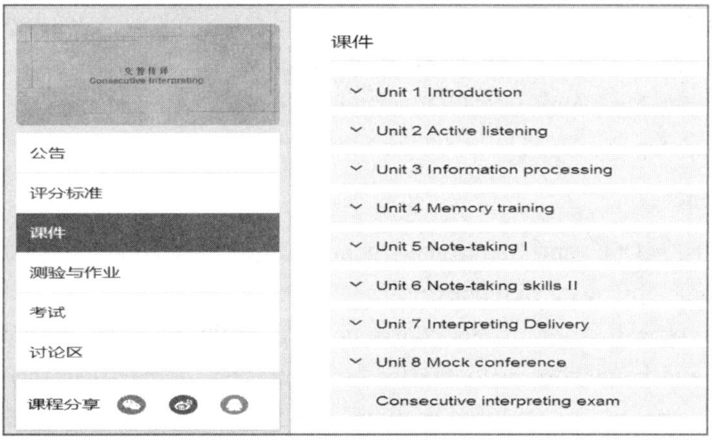

Fig. 3-1

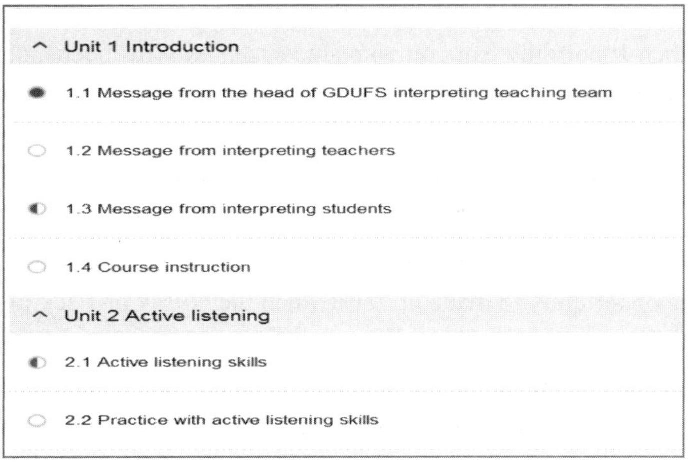

Fig. 3-2

Translation teaching requires an amount of practical experience, and some researches on translation. Practical experience, theoretical guidance and teaching method are the basic guarantee to complete the translation of education. (Liu, 50) In the process of the course, the translation examples all are derived from the literary works, academic works, and social science, law, science, technology, medicine, government documents and other materials translated by the teachers over the years. Teachers do the comprehensive and detailed analysis, help learners to take command of the ideas and methods of translation, show the flexible skills. This kind of practical experience can effectively help learners to get hold of the methods and skills of English-Chinese translation.

3.2 Compared with Traditional Translation Courses

3.2.1 Similarities

We find that this course on MOOC is very similar to the traditional class. For example, in the assessment aspect, the final result is composed of several sections. If the total score reaches 60%, students can obtain the certificate of qualification. When we are learning translation at ordinary times, teachers always teach translation skills by interpreting examples. It is the same with MOOC. In the interaction, MOOC pays more attention to the discussion between students, which is also attached great importance to traditional class. In terms of knowledge, learning is a process from the shallower to the deeper. No matter in MOOC or the ordinary classes, teachers always start from the simple and go deeper step by step. These are the Similarities.

3.2.2 Differences

In many aspects, MOOC and traditional teaching styles have some characteristics in common, but there are also some obvious differences.

First of all, the overall grade of this course consists of three parts: discussion, homework and exams. Discussion and homework accounts for 40% and test scores 20%. In traditional class, the final result is also composed of multiple sections, but the traditional exam takes up a very larger proportion, which is a typical exam-oriented education in China.

Second, MOOC focuses more on class discussion, and even the way of homework check is corrected by each other. It not only can cultivate students' ability of independent thinking, but also can help with each other between students.

Thirdly, during the study of this course, I found that the homework time is very strict, and the submission deadline, the time for mutual evaluation is arranged already and fixed. As it is a machine operation, once missed, there will be no chance for students do make up, which can promote the learning progress of students. However, the traditional model is different. It is humanized, so students will have the opportunity to make up for it when they delay or slack off. Finally, this course involves in wide things. For instance, when talking about translation, the teacher will enter the theme through stories, and in this process, the teacher will expand a lot of knowledge, such as cultural influence. In the traditional education mode, most teachers directly go into the theme and start theory: the word is the word, the sentence is the sentence. They speak out formally and systematically, some even give the frame structure and let students exercise by themselves.

4 Case II: Consecutive Interpreting

4.1 Courses Description and Teaching Method

About the *Consecutive interpreting*, there are eight small videos, the contents of which go from the easy to the difficult and complicated, from the listening skills, information processing, memory training, notes taking, to the final consecutive interpretation task. The time of each video is very short, only a few minutes or so. But the teacher can grasp the key point within a limited time, which is also the biggest characteristic of MOOC. Finally, the teacher will arrange the homework for the students after the lecture. In this course, the discussion section has a great feature, which is divided into three sections: comprehensive discussion section, teachers' answers section and class communication section. In this way, we can not only see the homework submitted by students, but also see everyone's own questions and teachers' answers, which can be good for others to think and learn. At the same time, if you have any comments, you can also leave a message. For example, the teacher adopted the students' suggestions about subtitles in the screen, so that it would be easier to carry on the course in the future.

4.2 Compared with Traditional Teaching Courses

In China or in the world, we mainly go to class in the classroom instead of online. But with the rapid development of information technology, the learning demand becomes more and more, the online education like MOOC has risen in response to the proper time and conditions. (Zheng, 58) So now is there any impact generating between the two different patterns? Next, we will compare the differences between MOOC and the class education to figure what advantages and disadvantages on earth they have.

4.2.1 Advantages

From the view of the design, MOOC is a public beneficial class, and it is of great scale, open to all people and the time is free and flexible. MOOC platform is various, and not only the students at different ages, but also those who have not got education or have already work in society, all of them can enter MOOC to study what they really like. The time is not like the class in school with the fixed time and fixed classroom. MOOC is for you when free to study online, and the video time is very short, knowledge are more essential and complete. (Wang, 141)

In content, although MOOC is video teaching, teacher still uses image to express meaning vividly. For example, she says the memory training is like building a house with the paining, which actually attracts the interest of students. After learning these video, I found MOOC teaches more skills, which requires students to practice on their own after class. However, in the offline class, maybe our teachers pay more attention to exercises instead of theory. So MOOC is really a goof platform for us to supplement knowledge and improve ourselves, which advocates that combining the advantages of traditional teaching with the advantages of digital teaching can complement each other and achieve better teaching results. (He, 17)

In the video, the teacher also invited some students to talk about their own experience, indicating that the online class is not mechanical and monotonous. There is also a friendly interaction between teachers and classmates. The last thing that impressed me most is the teacher's oral speech sounds, which sounds comfortable and smooth, because the teacher always will make adequate preparation for the recording.

4.2.2 Disadvantages

However, it is obvious that this class also has some disadvantages, which is the commonality of MOOC. For instance, the students cannot communicate with the teacher face to face so that the problems cannot be solved in time. Though the teacher is full of rich experience, it is still hard to teach students in accordance of their own aptitude because there are a larger number of learners. If students have no time, they will not listen to the class; if they have no time, they will not do the homework. This kind of phenomenon is very casual and universal. MOOC has no hard and fast administrative mechanism like schools, and students are easy to give up and drop out of it.

5 Conclusions

Through the case study and analysis of the two courses, and the comparison of MOOC with traditional teaching model, we find that they have many similarities, have their own advantages and disadvantages. (Li, 65) In fact, as for the study of translation, whether online or offline education, the teacher is a guide and inductor. If we want to improve ourselves, we have to practice and practice. Education has been developing with the times. Different teaching modes can absorb the quintessence, remove the dross and make their respective advantages complementary to each other. The development of MOOC is also an embodiment of the connectivism theory, which has the internet and digital characteristics. Information technology always keeps pace with The Times, so online education such as MOOC is the inevitable result of Internet development. (Zhao, 142) Though there are some defects in MOOC at present. (Zhai, 264) For example, some teachers' lack of deep research on effective learning, which cannot meet the demand of learners, is not easy to inspire learning motivation. Students cannot get reasonable effective detection and teachers cannot receive the feedback. In fact, MOOC can continue to draw on its strength in the field of science and technology, and combine the traditional teaching mode to create a good learning experience for learners.

References

[1] Carolyn, King, et al, Online education: Targeted MOOC captivates students [J]. *Nature*, 2014, 505（2）：26.

[2] Li Jing. MOOC: A Crisis or an Opportunity for Chinese General Education Curriculum? MOOC's Implications for Chinese General Education Curriculum Development [J]. *Cross-Cultural Communication*, 2015（11）：64-69.

[3] Zhai Xuesong & Lin Lilan, Research into Development Dilemmas of MOOC in China's Higher Education and Its Countermeasures[J]. *Academics*, 2014（3）：262-268.

[4] Zhao Ying, On the Instructor Role in Online Education[J]. *Overseas English*, 2013（10）：142-145.

[5] Zheng Xinyi. The Enlightenment of MOOC for the College English Teaching in China[J]. *Higher Education of Social Science*, 2015（6）：57-60.

[6] 陈坚林. 大数据时代的慕课与外语教学研究——挑战与机遇[J]. 外语电化教学，2015（1）：3-8.

[7] 何志伟. 国外 MOOC 研究现状可视化分析[J]. 扬州大学学报，2016（2）：15-19.

[8] 刘和平. 翻译教学模式：理论与应用[J]. 中国翻译，2013（34）：50-55.

[9] 王国卫. 线上教育的优势与不足[J]. 都市家教（上半月），2016（8）：141.

[10] 王秀丽. 慕课发展困境与路向[J]. 江淮论坛，2017（1）：177-181.

Cooperative Learning in English Major's Classes at UESTC: Problems and Solutions

仇筱萱

摘　要：随着合作学习法的开展与实施，其在大学文科课程尤其是英语专业教学方面的问题逐渐浮现出来。通过参考学术论文、数据和调查研究、实际案例等方法，可以总结出合作学习法最为主要的两个问题：很多教师受到传统教育模式影响导致合作学习法无法发挥其作用；学生在参与合作学习的过程中也出现诸多问题，引起学生群体对小组合作模式的不满，"小组恨"也作为一种校园现象出现。而美国作为合作学习法的发源地，在合作学习法的研究与应用方面硕果颇丰，因此学习和借鉴对发展完善中国的合作学习教学是非常有必要的。本文以电子科技大学为例，系统地总结了合作学习法在英语专业课堂上遭遇到的误解、误用以及面临的困境，并探讨了如何借鉴美国合作学习法特别是拼图合作法来开展英语教学活动。

关键词：合作学习法；英语专业；电子科技大学；问题；办法；拼图合作法

Abstract: With the implement of cooperative learning methods, problems surfaced gradually, especially in courses for liberal arts and English majors. From practical examples and findings in research papers, we find that due to misunderstandings from teachers who often stick to some Chinese traditional teaching methods so that CL cannot come into play. Based on surveys, we find that students are not satisfied and complain a lot about the cooperative homework. As the birthplace of CL, the United States is famous for its systematic and scientific education system. The research and application of CL have been fruitful there, so it is necessary for us to incorporate their advanced knowledge and concept. The paper systematically surveys the misunderstandings, misuses and dilemma of cooperative learning in English majors' classes in UESTC, and then discusses the Jigsaw way as one of the many effective CL methods.

Key words: Cooperative learning；English major；UESTC；problems；solutions；the Jigsaw method

1　Introduction

1.1　What is Cooperative Learning (CL)?

Cooperation is one of the fundamental modes of inherent viability of human beings. However, until twenty centuries, people found its precious value in education. In 1930s, Kurt Lewin established the relationship between group members in order to successfully carry out and achieve the learning goal. And in the 1940s, Deutsch improved Lewin's theory and he first proposed that compared with the continently inter-dependence of competition, the promotive inter-dependence of cooperation is much better. (李家黎, 2005: 6) His theory did a great contribution to the cooperative learning. In the next few years, cooperative learning gradually has been well established and comprehensive. And now, cooperative learning method is a kind of mature educational approach and idea which aims to organize classroom activities into academic and social learning experiences.

1.2 CL in China

In the 1990s, China began to introduce cooperative learning into class teaching, which aims to change the stiff traditional Chinese education technique. It began with the teaching experiment in Hang Zhou university of Zhejiang province. Then in 2001, the ministry of education introduced relevant policies to promote the implement of cooperative learning. Until now, cooperative learning is widely used in Chinese middle schools, high schools and universities.

1.3 CL Problems

1.3.1 The lack of participation

Firstly, because of the lack of participation in panel discussion, the teacher missed the best time to solve the students' problems and give directions. Without being enlightened, students' understandings just stay on the surface. So the result of group discussion is superficial and scanty. Also in one group, there exist some incontinent talkers and the silencers. Without the intervention of teacher, the discussion can easily lose control. It is necessary that teachers come to every group to give timely help. But not every teacher is conscious of this point.

1.3.2 Teachers' wrong position

Though cooperative learning is the way that students learn by themselves, teachers play an important role as guide. Some college teachers tend to give much time to students for group discussion whatever they need or not. Studies have shown that twenty minutes for strong concentration is the maximum. If a teacher cannot distinguish the priorities, the class is destined to failure. The class is in low efficiency.

1.3.3 Low efficiency

The proverb: "There is strength in numbers." doesn't show his power in cooperative learning. Without the scientific points system and the teachers' participation, students in group do not treasure the time and the project. They do not take the group work as serious projects as exams, which inversely is also a significant component of their final grades.

2 CL Problems in English Major's Classes in UESTC

Despite the general problems of cooperative learning method and some mistakes, college students also complain about the cooperative learning method. Recently a survey conducted almost 560 undergraduate students from five universities about their opinions of cooperative learning method①. 93.61% students have the negative attitude towards the cooperative spirit of the modern

① The five universities are: Central South University, Hunan University, Hunan normal university, Hunan Agricultural University, and Central South University of Forestry and Technology.

college students. 57.71% students refuse cooperation for fear that they cannot do great contribution to group. And 55% students refuse cooperation for lacking communicative competence. (李家黎, 2005: 6) From the data, we can see the social appraisals to cooperative learning method are not so satisfying.

2.1 Misunderstandings

Cooperative learning is not only a simple teaching method that teachers ask students to do group work. It is more complicated than we imagine which has many limitations. Sharan describes the constant evolution of cooperative learning as a threat. (Sharan, 2009: 8) Because cooperative learning is constantly changing, there is a possibility that teachers may become confused and lack complete understanding of the method. Unfortunately, the prediction really happens in Chinese college classes.

The traditional teaching method in China is forced feeding teaching method. The dominant right is held by the teacher and the only thing that the students can do is listening. Obviously, if no interactive communication, there is no enthusiasm. So when cooperative teaching method was introduced in China, Quite a few of Chinese teachers realized that the dominant right should be handed over to the students. But the fault is that sometimes they hand over all the class to students and forget that they are also a part of class. I am an example, in a common course, the teacher asked us to make groups and talk about a certain project. And she gave us 20 minutes. Without doubt, she wanted to make students the leading role of class and help us do something about cooperation. At the first five minutes, everything is fine. Someone did the data collection and someone took notes. Each airs his own views. However we students do not have enough knowledge reserves to have our own viewpoints and make the data theoretical. So after the first five minutes, my group member got tired and bored, with nothing to do. Spontaneously they began gossiping. I observed the other groups around, same with us. So it seemed like a classroom was full of activity, but everyone was bored. But is that the students' fault? And as to the teacher, she didn't say any words during the twenty minutes. Her misunderstandings of cooperative learning method are the cause of this fail class.

2.2 CL in English Major's Curriculum Provision

Based on the "Undergraduate Education Plan of English majors in UESTC", cooperative learning method exists in 47 courses during the four year study. For example, "Ideological and Political Theory Courses" are the input courses which focus on what we have learned and how we keep the knowledge in mind. So the way of cooperative or group work must be group presentation and paper writing. On the contrary, basic disciplinary courses like "Comprehensive English" and "Disciplinary Extensive English" and "English Speaking" attach more importance to output. So the students have more choices of group work—video shooting, project report, group presentation and paper writing. Basically, every semester, English majors have 7 to 9 classes with group work, and the number reach the peak at 11 in the 5th semester. The data shows that cooperative learning method play a really important role in English majors' study.

2.3 Questionnaire for Students

In order to see directly and clearly, I had an interview with about fifty students (most of them are English majors) in School of Foreign Languages UESTC. The followmg four tables record their opinions of cooperative learning.

Table 2.1 In which kind of class do you have group work?

Major compulsory course	50
Major elective course	46
General Course(despite major compulsory course)	50
Courses on B platform	0

From Table 2.1, we can find that the cooperative learning method has already been a part of English majors' study. Despite the course for interests, almost all the interviewees have to do group work in different kinds of courses. Also, the students said that the proportion of group work reach up to 20% of the final grade, which is much higher than the Attendance (10%), Classroom performance (10%) and Quiz (10%).

Table 2.2 What kind of group work you have done?

Project presentation	50 (the most common way)
Paper writing	50
Video shooting/Scene play	50
Practice report	29

These four kinds of cooperative learning are all the choices for English majors in UESTC. It's not multiple and flexible.

Table 2.3 Are you satisfied with your past group work?

Satisfied	Unsatisfied	So-so
10	28	9

For instance, in UESTC, the regular grades account for a great population in the final grade. Especially in most liberal arts like English, Japanese and French, the regular grades account for fifty percent. And cooperative learning method is the most common way. Take the Comprehensive English as an example, seminar account for ten percent, penal time account for thirty percent, and partner work account for twenty percent. And every unit the teacher asked us to have a special activity such as debate which also needs cooperation, so we know that cooperative learning method really plays an important role in students' life. But now over eighty percent of the students are dissatisfied with this kind of learning method. And their discontentments are quite unified.

Table 2.4 Which kind of group work do you think is the best way to evaluate your work?

Video shooting/Scene play	31
Practice report	12
Project presentation	5
Paper writing	2

Unexpectedly, only 7 students choose “project presentation” and “Paper writing”, which are the most common way of cooperative learning in English majors’ class. However, 31 students have mentioned that the way of “Video shooting” is the fairest way since that the teachers can see you work and contribution directly through the video and play. The teacher knows that you are a main character or a director so she will give you a higher grade. “That’ the real group work”, a student said, “I want my work pay off. But in the cooperation of paper writing, my efforts are not worth.”

Table 2.5 Please write down your opinions about cooperative learning method

NO.1	Contemptible, untrustworthy and loathsome partner	41
NO.2	Unfair scoring system	30
NO.3	It may hurt the friendship between group members	17

2.4 The Main Problems in Cooperation

“The degree of participation in one group cannot be the same”, a student who helped me finish the survey told me. And she speaks out, more or less, some truth of the status quo of cooperative learning method in today’s classes. Everyone students participated in my survey complained about the unfair situation. And I summarize their complaints into three points.

2.4.1 Students’ problems

Firstly, there must be at least one group member who seeks to evade their responsibility. Those kinds of students are called “loafing”, they do not take responsibility for their own role, and even it is the smallest role in the group. They don’t do any preparations or they care only for themselves. They didn’t show up when the group are discussing. “Once a group presentation, a man kept quiet all the time and didn’t actively ask for something to do. So we asked him to so the final speech. We made ready all the PPT, the material and the speech, but he told us that he doesn’t have time at the last gasp. So finally he did nothing but got the same grade because we are a group!”

“The fear that some members of the group will act as passengers or social loafers and derive a benefit (generally a good grade) from the group activity undermines the effectiveness of the group. Some students hoard their intellectual capital to make sure that no one unjustly benefits from it. Ironically, some of the students most indignant about ‘slackers’ or ‘freeloaders’ make immediate assumptions about their peers and insist from the outset that they will have to take care of everything in order to maintain control.” (吴颖, 2014: 210) The original aim of cooperative learning method was to have common progress with the group member. However it seems like it now becomes the burden and drag of those active and serious students who really make efforts. “It’s really unfair, why we need to work hard for others grade!”

Secondly, even everyone participates in group work, the tasks cannot be appointed very impartially. Based on the policy in China, most college students are the only child in their families. We can seldom find the selfless spirit from them. So everyone wants to enjoy the fruits of others’ work without toiling. Students know that the data collection is the easiest wok. And the PPT making is almost the hardest one. When appointing the tasks, it’s easy for them to have conflicts with each other. And always, the final result is charitable students take charge of the hardest work and the bossy person gets the easiest work. It isn’t fair because everyone gets the same grade but the charitable students have to spend much more time and energy than others.

To sum up, students will easily get “Group Hate”. (Sorensen, 1981, p. 11) It is defined as a feeling of dread that arises when facing the possibility of having to work in a group. Cooperative learning originally aimed to promote the cooperation among students. Compared with individual work, studying pressure may release a lot. However, when I gave the choice to interviewees for learning activities (group based or individual work), more than half students chose individual work, which reflect that the Group hate is common in Chinese universities. And if the misunderstandings and wrong use cannot be banned in class, then “group hate” will happen in more and more groups. Students gradually loose the confidence of cooperation with others. From cooperative learning they learn nothing about share, dedication and team spirit. Incorrect cooperative learning habits force students to become self-centred, individual and closed.

2.4.2 Teachers’ mistakes

Group member assignments is also a big trouble for students. (高丽梅, 2014, p. 49) For the most part, college students won’t receive excessively interference and they may prefer to emphasize their right of freedom in handling things. But the reflection that I have collected is not so satisfying. In the first place, if students are allowed to make groups freely, the average students will come to the outstanding students for help. For fear of hurting classmates’ feelings, the outstanding students they generally say yes. However, there are big differences between their language proficiency, spoken English and capability. So generally it cannot reflect the true level of the outstanding students. What worse, at the beginning, the aim of some students is to rely on their capable group member. So the other group member has no choice but to complete most the missions. In another, birds of a feather flock together. Students with good grades and outstanding performance like to be together. But when one group includes all the top students, the competition can be also unfair. The others feel frustrated and give up early.

The fact that cooperative learning is such a dynamic practice means that it cannot be used effectively in many situations. (Angawi, 2014, p. 825) Simpler, not all the class, project and teaching content are suitable for cooperative learning method. I am also an example; there was a professional course last semester. The teacher would leave us some questions as after-class assignments that were obscure and dense and asked students to make groups to find the answer. I ensured that all my group members worked really hard and spent much time on that course. Helplessly, we didn’t make the teacher satisfied. Because the only way we had was to find some information online, but usually the teacher would give us a “F” because what we had searched are too simple that everyone can have it only if searching online. So we were forced to understand some scholarly papers that are not related to my major. With the situation being tough and urgent, some students chose to file the class because they didn’t want to dedicate all their energy and time to only one course. It can be said a failure. Cooperative learning doesn’t mean students should take charge of all things. The original intention is to inspire students to cooperate with each other to figure out things. Obviously, the questions are totally beyond students’ ability. This kind of cooperative learning doesn’t make any sense because students learn nothing. Also the teacher didn’t provide timely help.

2.4.3 The lack of supervision and management

Without the supervision and management of cooperative learning method, marginalized characters appear in college group work. (周静, 2015, p. 1) Due to the degree of the importance, group member can be divided into core members and marginalized member. The marginalized members have to do the work of supplementary property and with low involvement of group work. It’s hard for them to get to the core of group work. In other words, they are in the borderland. With the lapse of time, marginalized members feel so frustrated that they keep disinterested attitude towards the cooperation. However, it is their disinterested attitude and low involvement proves that what the major members’ choice is right. The gap and estrangement become larger and larger. Because of the barrier, the marginalized members cannot get the instant information and their rights are not guaranteed. So when doing presentation, they have few chances to speak. After a group work, the confidence and enthusiasm of marginalized member get hardly hit. Without the supervision and management, the cooperative learning method easily loses trust since the students feel that their work and effort get no pay off. Just like the opinion of No.2 (Table 2.5), the unfair scoring system is the shortcut for lazy students to get good score. That’s not fair.

3 Jigsaw Method: A Useful Way of Overcoming CL Problems

Frankly speaking, there are so many different methods for us to adopt to maintain an effective cooperative learning in English classes. But here I would like to introduce a very special method—Jigsaw method—which has been widely used in other fields.

3.1 What is Jigsaw Method?

The Jigsaw method is a way of cooperative learning method firstly advocated by the famous American educator and sociologist, Elliot Aronson, and his colleagues. It was first initiated in 1978, when the apartheid had just lifted. But in the same class, the lack of communication between students from different ethnic and trust often makes the normal teaching activities difficult to carry out. So Elliot first started this teaching method in Texas and finally got success. So this method popularized gradually, from primary school to university, from language teaching to other subjects. (百家号, 2018, p. 1)

3.2 How to Use Jigsaw Method?

Step 1: Grouping

The first thing is to group the students. According to the number, divided the students into several groups, each group had better number of 4-6 people. These learning groups are called the Jigsaw Group. Also, the overall level of each group is basically the same, ensuring fair competition between groups.

Step 2: Define teaching objectives and assign learning content

The learning content should be divided into relatively independent parts.

Step 3: Each student in the puzzle group is responsible for one part

At this time, each student temporarily does not interact with other members of the group.

They learn the projects by themselves.

Step 4: Students who learn the same content form a "expert group"

After self-study, students who learn the same content will gather together to form a content "Expert Group".

In each group, students communicate with each other about what they have learned, and work together to prepare what they will learn from the puzzle group. During this time, students will fill gaps in knowledge, clarify concepts and misunderstandings, and consolidate important concepts.

Step 5: restore the "puzzle" and share the learning content in turn

After communication in the expert group, the students returned to their puzzle groups. Then, take turns sharing what they have learned.

When a student is teaching, other students listen carefully, take notes, and ask questions.

Step 6: Teacher's summarize and evaluation

The teacher gives suggestion and point out some of the mistakes that students often make.

The Jigsaw method cultivate the students' autonomous learning ability, communication and coordination ability and team cooperation spirit, also very helpful to the students' development and growth.

The truth is that the cooperative learning now in China is immature, single and rigid. We just copy the teaching method without considering the reality of China, updating and checking. We still have a long way to go. And the teaching systems in some developed countries are the lighthouses.

3.3 A Practical Way of Using Jigsaw in English Major's Classes

Comprehensive English is one of the most important course of the four year's study since the course include all the basic aspects—Listening, Speaking, Reading and Writing. Obviously, English majors do various group works in class. So what if teachers take the Jigsaw method into Comprehensive English classes?

When it comes to a new text, there is always a casual and free group talk. The teacher gives students about 10-20 minutes to let the students share their ideas or their preview results. Then every group elect one people to do short and brief report. This is really a boring way with low efficiency. The students do not take the group work as a formal thing, and then the group talk becomes a gossip chat. Scientific grouping as the Jigsaw method is necessary. Firstly, limit the number of group member of the "puzzle" group not form teams according to the seat position. Students easily go to their close friends as always. Teachers should encourage students step out the comfort zone. Also, group number limitation is good for task division. Second step is that teachers should assign the task to each member in the group rather than give a topic or question to the whole group. With the task, everyone is responsible for one part and the sense of responsibility pushes the students to take the job seriously and do their best. Then the whole activity becomes more valuable, interesting and competitive. After study for a while, English majors who learn the same part gather together to form an "Expert Group" and share their points of view and understandings since everyone has its own preoccupations and understandings. During this part, we see the collision of thoughts and the process of learning from each other. Later, students go back to the "puzzle" group and have to be the teacher in turn to teach what they have learned and the final result of the communication. The purpose of this section is to save precious class time as every student has to learn the entire topic now which is time consuming. However, with the Jigsaw method, all students only have to spend time on part. The Jigsaw method still need teacher's participation as a mentor and judge who guide the direction of the communication, give suggestion and point out the error.

The cooperative learning method has been widely used in English majors' class at UESTC, but not various and innovative. We cannot mire in stalemate. Maybe it's time to move forward and pick new method.

4 Conclusions

We have to admit that there are several problems of cooperative learning existing in English majors' class teaching. But at the same time, we cannot ignore the great contribution that CL had done. It not only practices and improves the ability of students in group work, but also builds bridges between teachers and students. The future is a world with cooperation. People who can cooperate with others well will be highly regarded, which means the cooperative learning method will play a more and more important role in our growth. The advantage cannot be ignored. So the key is how we can make up and fix the flaws. It's a truth that CL method in China is immature. By contrast, this teaching method in some developed countries is very mature. So we have to take them as examples and introduce the advanced management system and scientific teaching method like the Jigsaw method to better the cooperative learning in China. However, despite the Jigsaw method, there are still many new things waiting us to explore and learn. But what really important is that we should take action right now—to start the application of the new method in Chinese English majors' classes.

References

[1] Angawi, Rihab F. Using a Problem Solving-Cooperative Learning Approach to Improve Students' Skills for Interpreting[J]. *Journal of Chemical Education,* 2014, 91（6）：823-829.

[2] Gillies, Robyn M. and Michael Boyle. Teachers' Reflections on Cooperative Learning: Issues of Implementation[J]. *Teaching and Teacher Education: An International Journal of Research and Studies*, 2010, 26（4）：933-940.

[3] Nam, Chang Woo. The Effects of Trust and Constructive: Controversy on Student Achievement and Attitude in Online Cooperative Learning Environments[J].*Computers in Human Behavior,* 2014（37）：237-248.

[4] Sorensen, Susan M . Group-Hate: A Negative Reaction to Group Work[J]. *Classification,* 1981: 27

[5] Tsay, Mina; Brady, Miranda “A case study of cooperative learning and communication pedagogy: Does working in teams make a difference?[J]. *Journal of the scholarship of Teaching and Learning*, 2010, 10（2）：78-89.

[6] 董琪. 拆拼法——大学合作学习探究[D]. 华东师范大学，2015.

[7] 高丽梅，沈娟，李辉. 基于建构主义理论在大学英语教学中推行合作学习法的策略与研究[J]. 海外英语，2014（3）：49-50.

[8] 李家黎，谢芳. 合作学习：历史发展、现状及展望[J]. 湖北第二师范学院学报，2005，22（6）：76-77.

[9] 邵钦瑜，何丽. 基于网络与课堂混合环境下的大学英语合作学习模型构建及实证研究[J]. 外语电化教学，2014（2）：31-35.

[10] 吴颖，庄秀华，马云晓. 建立团队合作的大学英语自主学习模式[J]. 山西师大学报（社会科学版），2014（4）：210-211.

[11] 周静，刘勤. 小组合作学习中大学生边缘者现象探究[J]. 理论观察，2015（1）：153-155.

[12] 百家号“风靡全球的合作学习法，走进‘拼图式’教学”[OL]. 2018.0502.<http://m.baidu com/sf_baijiahao/s?id=1600800103287920769&wfr=spider&fpr=pc2018.07.10.

文化研究

The Fatalism Narrative Model in Films: *Kung Fu Panda 2* and Posey Jackson and the Sea of Warcraft

韩子钰

摘　要：宿命论是电影中惯常出现的一种情节模式。宿命论认为，在人类诸多的神秘变化的命运现象中存有一些定数。而《功夫熊猫 2》与《波西杰克逊与魔兽之海》在大体上有着十分相似的主题和方向，不管是从人物安排上，还是在情节的叙述上来看，这两部电影都有共通点。我们发现，这种共通点在作品中可以归纳衍生出一种宿命论模式叙述方法。本文将以《功夫熊猫 2》与《波西杰克逊与魔兽之海》为例，讨论这两部电影在叙述过程中人物和情节的异同，探讨宿命论这一电影叙述手法的艺术效果和运用方法。

关键词：宿命论；《功夫熊猫 2》；《波西杰克逊与魔兽之海》；叙事模式

Abstract: Fatalism is a plot pattern that is commonly seen in movies. Fatalism believes that there are some fixed patterns in the fate of many mysterious changes of human beings. *Kung Fu Panda 2* and *Posey Jackson and the Sea of Warcraft* have quite similar themes and ideas, whether in the setting of characters or in the arrangement of the plot, both have striking similarities. This similar fatalistic theme derives a modeled narrative approach from the work. This article will use these two movies as examples to compare the two works in terms of stories and plots as well as character settings, and explore the similarities and differences between the fatalistic narratives in *Kung Fu Panda 2* and *Posey Jackson and the Sea of Warcraft*. Then reveal the use of this model and its application effects in the performance of the film.

Key words: Fatalism; *Kung Fu Panda 2*; *Posey Jackson and Sea of Warcraft*; Narrative mode

1　Introduction

The film is a continuous image frame developed by the combination of motion photography and slide show. It is a visual and auditory modern art. It can also accommodate drama, photography, painting, music, dance, writing and sculpture. However, it has its own characteristics. In terms of artistic expression, the film not only has the characteristics of other arts, but also has the ability to use artistic montages like Montage to surpass all other arts. The creation of movies often have rules to follow, there may be fixed plot pattern, common human relationships, telling orders or other customary tactics. By watching some of the movies, we could find that there is a fatalism narrative model in a series of movies. In the movie *Kung Fu Panda 2* and *Posey Jackson and the Sea of Warcraft*, we could easily notice this two movies shares same patterns of story. The protagonist, prophet, guide and the ending in these two movies has a lot in common. Considering these two movies follow different categories and were released at different time, we think that typically shows that in fact the fatalism narrative pattern was widely used in movies. And by further analyze these common points, we wish to reveal the use of this model and its application effects in the performance of the film, and analyze the cultural connotation contained in this narrative model. Then apply it to other film and television analysis.

2 Common Points

In the movie *Kung Fu Panda 2*, as a continuation of the first story, *Kung Fu Panda 2* tells the life of the main protagonist Po and the process of beating the biggest enemy Lord Shen, which is the scion of a peacock clan that rules Gongmen City in ancient China, seeks to weaponize gunpowder. After discovering from the court's goat soothsayer that "a warrior of black-and-white" will defeat him if he does not change his ways, Shen leads an army of wolves to exterminate the panda population to avert the prophecy. (https://en.wikipedia.org/wiki/Kung_Fu_Panda_2)And as for Po, however, is easily distracted by the symbol of Shen's scion because the memory of his infant. After several battles and guided by soothsayer, Po learns to embrace his past and attain inner peace, realizing that he has lived a happy and fulfilling life despite this early tragedy.

And for the plot of *Posey Jackson and the Sea of Warcraft*, similarly, as the second work of the Posey Jackson series, a story of the protagonist Posey surmounting the challenge to save the tribe is still told. At the beginning of this movie, Posey was told by the spirit of Delphi that "the evil soul, cursed blade shall rape." Although didn't understand at that time, he remembers this at the last confrontation and win. His voyage starts to save the protection of their camp, but during the process of he gradually realizes that the process of the story has already been arranged. With the help of his friends, Annabeth and Grover, and his brother, he got the fleece, save the tree of protection and banished Kronos's remains in the depths of Tartarus.

As is mentioned above, these two films shares similar story patterns. To further prove this, we will discuss the common points from four perspectives—protagonist, prophet, guide and support group and the ending.

2.1 Protagonist

In *Kung Fu Panda 2*, Po is an ordinary panda who has the desire to help others and become heroes. He is kind, independent, and determined, but has inevitable weaknesses. Although he became the Dragon Warrior by chance, he had never lived up to this name. In fact, as early as in the first part, the audience felt the fate of Po has already been arranged. On the face of it, Po, who has great skills, protects and keeps the valley safe, which is the masculine side of his character. But the subconscious memory of his mind chaotic, and let him show the emotional "feminine" side. (王筱竹 & 吴冠英, 2012) In the second part, this fatalism has been more evident. According to Po's memory, he has already met the Lord Shen when he was a infant.

This ambitious and brutal peacock almost destroyed the whole village, and Po's parents sacrificed for saving Po's life. As the story progressed, Po's memory became clear. He realized that he was the key figure in defeating Lord Shen. He was obliged to end the tragic memory of the past and eradicate the villain that was linked to his destiny. From the movie's timeline, the beginning of

Po's Life closely linked to the end of Lord Shen's life, giving the audience a feeling of destiny.

In the movie of Posey Jackson and Sea of Warcraft, the protagonist Posey also has a very similar character set. He is an ordinary student, experiencing all kinds of unpleasant things in life. But he was wrongly regarded as a thief of the lightning and learned his true identity— the son of Poseidon, and began his life in the halfblood camp. At the beginning of the film, his fate was announced by the prophet, and it was a seemingly unrelated thing to promote this fate. At the same time, in the adventure journey, the three eyeless witch sisters also casually revealed his destiny. Although seemingly ridiculous, these prophecies have finally been realized one by one, and people have been surprised at the power of destiny.

The protagonists of these two stories did not subjectively act in accordance with the so-called "preliminary settings", and sometimes even went against them, but their extraordinary ability often enabled them to turn around. (吴智龙, 2012) In the end, their powerful driving forces for the story make the plot develop into a "preliminary setting".

2.2 Prophet

"Prophets" is a symbol of the power of God in the works. The goat soothsayers and the spirit of Delphi are tellers of secrets in movies. They already set an end for the story as soon as they appear. In other words, they represent an irresistible force and the development of the plot points to this set outcome. (吴智龙, 2012) This seemingly stifling suspense treatment, to the contrary, adds more suspense to the story, because the reader's desire for suspense is not only reflected in the outcome of the story, but also reflected in the process of achievement. Telling audiences in advance results in giving them an understanding of the story. Instead, they want to know more about the progress of the story.

In *Kung Fu Panda 2*, the goat soothsayer told Lord Shen at the early stage of the story that if he continues to do thing in that brutal way, he will be defeated by "a warrior of black-and-white". This character, although appeared in the movie for just a few minutes, means a lot to the core topic. And her words were undoubtedly the punchline of this story. The first was for the villains. From the beginning of knowing this prophecy, he began to pay attention to who is the black and white warrior, and tried to get stronger first, but his approach had accelerated the future. For the protagonist, when he understood that he had become an important part of the great career, his confidence and perseverance had grown tremendously, and he became even more fearless. For the audience, this prediction is undoubtedly an indirect way of telling the audience that there will be a fixed future, but there are many ways to achieve it. This made the audience unconsciously become participants in this fate runner, witnessing the "arranged" story.

In Posey Jackson and Sea of Warcraft, the spirit of Delphi also directly told the protagonist Posey what is his future. Although the prophet's words are a little bit more sloppy to the audience due to the influence of cultural, it can be known that this story must ended with the win of Righteous side. According to the prophet, the sons of the three great gods will save the entire Olympus. And Posey, as the only surviving son of Poseidon, undoubtedly believes that this person is himself. However, in the end, the daughter of Zeus was resurrected, and the prophecy was verified. The fate of Posey became more confusing but made the audience found this story even more magical. In addition, the three blind witch drivers encountered on their way out of the hybrid camp also greatly contributed to the development of the story. At first, Posey did not understand the four figures they gave. However, when they reached the sea, he was surprised to find that these figures were the longitude and latitude of their destination. Such an arrangement was undoubtedly unexpected but also expected. Fatalism has again been reflected, but the interest in the story has not diminished.

2.3 Guide

In the two films, the guide was the duck father and Poseidon. Although these two roles appeared soon in movie, they play a decisive role. They made it possible for the protagonists to grow in another worldview and learn to get used to a widely different dimensions. To some extent, they have played the role of the protagonist's character cultivators and educators, and played a decisive role in the formation of the protagonist's outlook on life and values. And in this story of fatalism, "guide" is a symbol of revenge, and is a prerequisite for the completion of fate.

In Kong Fu Panda 2, the duck father found and adopted Po. He treated Po like his own son. If it isn't for later that lord Shen's mark reminds Po of his past, Po will never doubt whether this is really his own biological father. As Po's father, he taught Po to be a kind and enthusiastic person, helped him form a persevering character, and laid a good foundation for him to overcome difficulties in the future. And in the first part, it was the duck father's words that made Po see the secret of the wordless scroll and defeat the enemy. When Po is stuck in painful memories, it is the comfort and encouragement of the duck that allows Po to understand that only accepting the past and working towards a better future is the best thing that he should do. If not adopted by the duck father, Po may not grow like he is today, or if it is not because the duck father found him, Po may died in the flames of war, and this story was impossible to happen. The met of them is a fatalism.

In Posey Jackson and Sea of Warcraft, Posey, son of Poseidon, never knew his identity until he entered the halfblood camp and began to understand that he was actually a hybrid. However, although Poseidon rarely appeared, he always helped Posey secretly. (郑莉, 2012) There are two main points in this movie: Posey's brother and Poseidon's heart voice. At the beginning of the movie, a Cyclops who claimed to be the son of Poseidon found Posey and stayed with him along the way to adventure. This role may seem dispensable, sometimes even encumbered the protagonist, however, played a key role and saved Posey's life in the end. This person can be seen as part of Poseidon as a "guide." On the other hand, Poseidon often gave them assistance, which indirectly promoted Posey's understanding of his identity and power then eventually leaded his triumph.

2.4 Ending

In *Kung Fu Panda 2*, Po and Lord Shen fought repeatedly. Sometimes Po has the upper hand, but sometimes he loses. Even the Furious Five were once captured by Lord Shen. But at the end of the film, Po still used his power to repel the enemy and save the Valley of Peace from being destroyed. From the encounter between baby and Lord Shen to the first battle, and then to the battle of defending and saving people, finally Po won at the last war. While watching this movie, the most intuitive feeling of the audience is that no matter how hard the process was, the Righteous side will defiantly win. Meanwhile, coupled with the goat's prophecy, the audience can easily gain a feeling that this story should end like this. This sense of fatalism is actually what the director intends to reach, and the purpose is to add some magical color to the story.

In Posey Jackson and Sea of Warcraft, the protagonist's experience seems to be more tortuous. Although the prophet had already told him the prophecy at the beginning of the film, however, as the story developed, this prophecy became less obvious. In their adventure, the protagonist first repulsed the mechanical bull, then found Luke's father, and escaped from the sea of Warcraft. But until the end of the movie, when the golden fleece revived Cronos, he really understoodd the truth of the prophecy and fulfilled his own duty. Unlike *Kung Fu Panda 2*, the story of Posey Jackson and Sea of Warcraft is echoing in a head-to-tail relationship rather than a step-by-step process. The branch line task and the main line mission seem to have little relevance, but it is indispensable. While watching this movie, audiences are easily attracted to the branch story and may temporarily forget the original prophecy. However, when they see the final of the movie, they will be shocked by the strange feeling of fate, and a better viewing effect was thus achieved.

In both films, the protagonists had fulfilled their mission in accordance with established predictions and settings. But in the process, *Kung Fu Panda 2* allowed the audience to have a step-by-step testimony to the results, while *Posey Jackson and the Sea of Warcraft* had a simmering impact. The designs of the two directors have their own considerations, but they all try to use this fatalism narrative model to a fullest extent.

3 Conclusions

Through comparative analysis, it is not difficult to find that *Kung Fu Panda 2* and *Posey Jackson and the Sea of Warcraft* all use the fatalistic narrative mode to tell their story, which is embodied in four aspects—protagonist, prophet, guide and the ending. In addition, in terms of outcomes, the directors adopt different lead patterns according to their own habits and have subtle differences, but in general still follow the fatalism narrative pattern. Although the director and release time of the two films are not the same and the subject matter is also different (animation and science fiction), they adopt a similarly identical fatalism model in terms of narrative methods. The characters of the movies have similar backgrounds (all became a powerful people from ordinary people), have enlightened prophecies of the prophets and fortune predictions, have an inspiration from their mentor, and at the same time also successfully achieved their mission at the end of the film. This model, widely used in the film, was already embodied in the Greek story. For example, Oedipus finally killed his father and married his mother no matter how he avoided it. (张小燕, 2017) This fatalism has long formed a profound cultural habit in the West, and is then used in various entertainment media. In the movie under this mode, viewers usually feel a sense of irresistibleness or a sense of destiny. This art experience fulfills the ordinary real life with a sense of beauty, which is why the fatalism model movie is more prosperous nowadays.

References

[1] *Kung Fu Panda 2*. https://en.wikipedia.org/wiki/Kung_Fu_Panda_2. 2018 年 7 月 7 日获取.

[2] *Fatalism*. https://en.wikipedia.org/wiki/Fatalism. 2018 年 5 月 14 日获取.

[3] 吴智龙. 论《功夫熊猫 2》中的宿命论叙事模式[J]. 电影文学，2012（2）.

[4] 郑莉.《波西杰克逊与神火之盗》赏析[J]. 电影文学，2012（2）.

[5] 张小燕. 透过《俄狄浦斯王》看古希腊人的命运观[J]. 黑河学院学报，2017（6）.

[6] 王筱竹，吴冠英.《功夫熊猫 2》角色塑造分析[J]. 装饰，2012（3）：80-81.

中日女性时尚杂志封面对比研究

杨芷玥　周小萱　欧宇玲

摘　要：处于不同的时代，不同的国家地区的人，他们的心理，性格和对于自我的期待肯定会有很大的不同。这些不同体现在社会生活的方方面面。我们从女性这一历来话题不息的社会角色切入，另辟蹊径的以面向年轻女性的时尚杂志封面为对象，并在此基础上选取样本，将中日两国面向年轻女性的时尚杂志进行了对比。由此得出中国女性大多追求稳重的精英气质，而日本方面更加喜欢具有亲和力的少女气质这样的结果。追求即是一种自我期待，这种差异也反映了中日两国文化上的差异。通过研究我们能够更加深入详细地了解中日文化环境的差异，对于女性的自我定位有更好的理解。

关键词：时尚杂志封面；色彩；女性；心理期待

Abstract : People in different times, different countries and regions, their psychology, personality and self-expectations will certainly have great differences. These differences are reflected in all aspects of social life.We start from the social role of women, which has always been a topic of constant discussion, and find a new way to take the cover of fashion magazines for young women as the object.On this basis, a sample was selected to compare fashion magazines targeted at young women in China and Japan.Thus, it is concluded that most Chinese women pursue stable and elite temperament, while Japanese prefer girls with affinity.Pursuit is a kind of self-expectation, and this difference also reflects the cultural difference between China and Japan.Through research, we can have a deeper and more detailed understanding of the cultural environment differences between China and Japan, and have a better understanding of women's self-positioning.

Key words : Fashion magazine cover；Color；Women；Psychological expectation

1 引　言

时尚是我们生活中一种重要且不可或缺的文化现象，为迎合女性的审美诉求，同时为了引领时尚潮流，中日两国均大量发行以年轻女性为对象的时尚杂志。例如，中国有《ELLE》《VOGUE》《时尚芭莎》《ViVi 昕薇》等；日本有《CanCan》《LEE》《mina》等。这些女性时尚杂志均以年轻女性读者为主要对象，以时尚生活为主要题材的期刊是一种定期的，有固定名称，并用以期号连续不断的形式，间隔地、不断地出版的出版物。随着女性社会地位的提高，女性在社会中的作用不断增强，我们能在社会分工的各个环节中看到女性的身影。因此在当代社会中的女性购买力不断增加，并且大多数女性有了一定的时尚追求[1]。在这样的背景下，以年轻女性为主要消费对象的女性时尚杂志在中日两国发展得如火如荼。而由于中日两国在时尚文化背景与社会文化氛围上的差异，两国的时尚文化杂志封面在风格、配色等等方面都有较大差异，从而也折射出两国年轻女性时尚审美的差异。因此我们在本次研究中将通过对比中日女性时尚杂志封面，浅析两国年轻女性对女性形象的期待与女性心理的不同。

此前，国内外有不少对比中日差异的相关研究，从女性这一角度切入的也不在少数，无论是文学作品还是影视作品，例如《〈世俗女人与纯净女人〉——中日文学中的女性形象比较》（陈丽）和《〈从欢乐颂〉和〈东京女子图鉴〉看中日女性形象的对比》（水源，2017）都能从中窥见社会对于女性心理的塑造。而在《时尚杂志的风格与市场定位——日系和欧美系女性时尚杂志比较》（胡博，何文一，2011：15-18）中对日系女性时尚杂志和欧美系女性时尚杂志的风格做了对比研究，研究认为由于欧美系女性时尚杂志与日系杂志所面向的人群在职业、阶级、生活层次、女性地位上有着巨大的差异，欧美系的女性消费杂志几乎都假定其读者为品位至上的时尚优雅女子，有的还以女权色彩浓重的女性读者为其阅读对象。研究还指出欧美系与日系的文化氛围也是影响其杂志风格差异的原因。而我们在对杂志的筛选中发现欧美系杂志封面和中国杂志封面有很大的相同性。为此，我们以中国女性时尚杂志与日本女性时尚杂志的封面为课题展开新的研究。

2 研究样本

哪种时尚杂志的销量排名靠前，正反映了大多数目标消费群体对于该类杂志所展现的风格的追求，于是我们以销量排行作为选取样本的依据。根据2017年此类杂志的销量排行（中国数据暂不可考，根据杂志订阅-杂志云而选取比较人气的几本；日本杂志销量排行数据来自日本杂志协会：http://www.j-magazine.or.jp/），我们分别选取中日两国销量前三的杂志作为参考样本，再从中抽取每种杂志2018年前六月的杂志封面共计36本（中国18本，日本18本）进行对比分析（如表1所示）。

表1 中日杂志样本选择

中国（共18本）	日本（共18本）
《时尚COSMOPOLITAN》（6本）	《very》（6本）
《时尚芭莎》（6本）	《story》（6本）
《红秀》（6本）	《LEE》（6本）

3 对比研究

在对杂志封面的直观感受下，我们主要分两个方面进行对比：（1）奠定总基调的封面色彩；（2）杂志封面人物，即模特的姿态和服装风格。

3.1 关于杂志封面色彩的对比分析

颜色给人的感受是一种主观的极具个人色彩的体验。它往往与感受主体的成长环境、所受教育以及各方面条件都有密切联系。举个简单的例子，生长在北半球亚热带季风气候地区的人，看到粉色，嫩绿，会不由自主联想到春天的花朵与青草，那么这两种颜色自然也带给他们花朵与青草的浪漫清新的生命之感。而换做生长在常年冰雪覆盖的冰原上的人，他们也许从来没有见过春天娇软的花朵与青草，所以当他们看到这样的颜色，内心的感受一定是有别于季风地区的居民的。而在此，我们对于色彩搭配的研究也只能是基于杂志的大部分受众对于颜色的普遍感受来进行。

色彩搭配是时尚杂志封面设计的一个重点，不同的色彩和搭配能够传递不同的情绪，给人完全不同的视觉感受。以下是针对中日面向年轻女性的36本时尚杂志的色彩运用进行的统计。

3.1.1 模特服饰颜色

在时尚杂志封面中，模特往往是画面的主体，且处于画面的中心，占据面积比例也极大。而模特呈现出的整体颜色是由服饰颜色决定的，所以，为了研究杂志的色彩搭配，我们将模特服饰的颜色进行统计，统计结果如图3-1所示。

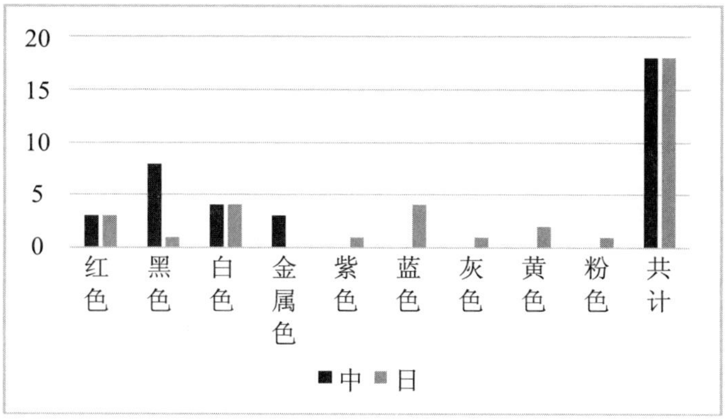

图3-1 中日女性时尚杂志封面模特服饰颜色统计图

通过图3-1数据，我们发现18本中国杂志中，有8本杂志中模特服饰主体色彩为黑色，其次则是白色，有4本，接下来红色和金属色各3本，而其他颜色则没有。中国杂志中身着黑衣的女性形象借助黑色的沉重感，往往表现出强烈的气场和性感，也可以说是压迫感，或严肃感等，给人一种精英印象。

反观日本杂志，模特服饰的主体色彩中白色和蓝色为最，但也只是各有4本，红色有3本，剩下7本杂志分别有黑，紫，灰，粉，黄。由此可见，在颜色种类和丰富度上远超中国杂志，这种丰富的色彩给人的感受也比较多变。相对中国杂志，日本杂志似乎想通过多种多样的色彩来表现年轻女性的活泼可爱和青春靓丽。

3.1.2 封面底色

封面底色在杂志封面中有衬托主体物，奠定基调的作用，它占据的面积也往往非常大，图3-2是关于中日两国女性时尚杂志封面底色的统计。

通过对图3-2的统计，我们发现，中国杂志中，白色有5本，卡其色有4本，这种极浅的色彩一共有9本，占据样本的一半，剩下有2本红色，2本黑色，2本灰色，黄色和绿色各1本。相对于模特服饰的色彩，封面底色相对比较丰富。而日本也是白色为最，有5本，但剩下的13本分别为红、黄、紫、粉、蓝、灰、卡其等色彩。相比于中国的杂志底色，日本的用色更为广泛丰富。

两国杂志都偏好白色，白色作为背景色，往往给人干净空旷的感觉，不会喧宾夺主，能够很好地衬托主体。白色也是中性色，中性色往往不抢眼，非常好与其他颜色搭配，卡其色，黑色，灰色，白色都是中性色，而中国杂志有13本以中性色为底色，日本杂志有10本以中性色为底色，可见两国杂志都利用中性色作为底色低调的特点。不过相比中国杂志，日本杂志底色色彩使用还是略显丰富大胆。

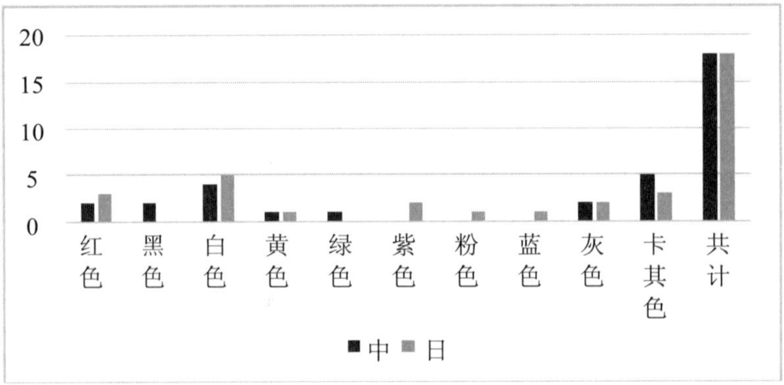

图 3-2　中日女性时尚杂志封面底色统计图

3.1.3　整体的色彩搭配

这里的色彩搭配，我们选取每本杂志封面上肉眼所见占比最大的两种颜色，并以这两种颜色的搭配进行分析。根据奥博斯科的《配色设计原理》，我们将这些杂志的色彩搭配分为四类：同类色搭配、邻近色搭配、互补色搭配以及黑白灰参与的色彩搭配。

分类解释：根据奥博斯科的《配色设计原理》中提到的色彩学原理，同类色即色相盘上夹角为 60 度以内的颜色。比如橙色和黄色、粉色和红色、嫩绿和深绿等等，这些颜色比较相近，搭配起来非常和谐，故同类色搭配是不容易出错的搭配。邻近色则为色相盘上夹角为 60 度到 90 度的颜色。如红色和黄色、绿色和蓝色、紫色和红色。邻近色的搭配相对同类色要跳跃活泼一些，但两色给人的温度感受往往区别不大（比如绿色和蓝色都是冷色），不会给人冲突感。互补色即色相盘上夹角为 180 度的颜色，广义上也可以指冷色和暖色的搭配。如红色和绿色、黄色和紫色、橙色和蓝色。这类搭配将两种相差极大的颜色搭配起来，给人鲜明的对比感，通过调节明度和纯度，有时这种搭配可以达到互补，有时也会造成强烈冲突。而黑白灰是色相盘之外的颜色，我们称它们为“中性色”，他们自身不存在色温，所以与所有颜色搭配都比较容易产生和谐的效果，黑白灰参与的色彩搭配往往比较安全保守，和谐不易出错。

图 3-3 是中日的对比统计图。

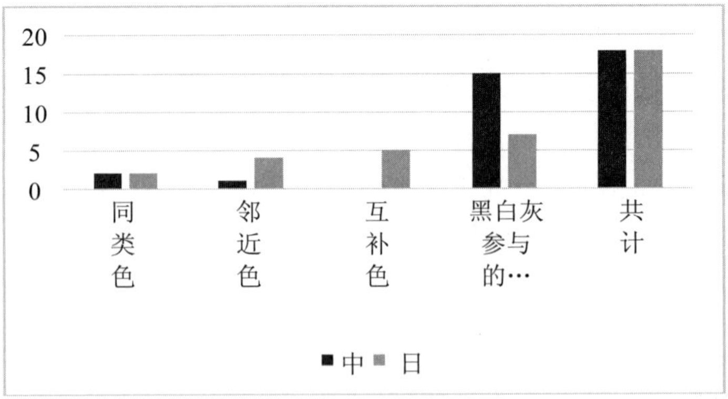

图 3-3　中日女性时尚杂志封面色彩搭配统计图

通过对图 3-3 的统计发现，中国杂志有 15 本采用黑白灰参与的色彩搭配，剩下 3 本也有 2 本选择了同类色搭配，仅 1 本选择了邻近色搭配，互补色搭配为 0，可见中国杂志在色彩搭配上大大倾向于保守低调不易出错的搭配。而中性色的搭配常给人以稳重高级的感受，同时配合模特服饰的黑色、白色、红色及金属色，给人一种高级感和精英感。而日本杂志在利用中性色的百搭之余，有 4 本使用邻近色，5 本使用互补色，用色相对来说可谓大胆跳脱，给人活泼、轻松以及青春感。

中国杂志对于黑色和白色此类中性色的运用非常广泛，中国杂志在使用这两种颜色的时候往往避免彩色与之搭配，而是采用低保护度的一些颜色，如灰色、棕色，所以整体烘托出了黑色的重量感和质感。在这样的配色安排中白色给人洁净和冷清的感觉，整体凸显气质与距离感。而日本杂志在运用黑色时都避免了大面积使用，并且常常利用跳脱俏皮的粉色来中和掉黑色的压抑感，而白色的出现往往伴随饱和度高的彩色，比如白色与大面积蓝色的搭配，避免了单调感，给人以明快的感受。

3.1.4 个例分析

值得一提的是，中国杂志封面的配色多次使用了黑色与红色的搭配，非常具有视觉冲击力。而同样使用红色，我们的研究样本中也有一本日本杂志使用了大面积的红色，但是该杂志采用了黄色与红色的搭配，反而给人以活泼快乐的感觉。我们在样本中抽选两本大范围使用红色的杂志（如图 3-4 左为中国杂志，如图 3-4 右为日本杂志）进行直观具体的分析。

图 3-4　中日杂志

同样是使用红色的情况，我们不难发现日本杂志和中国杂志所展现出的风格大相径庭。中国杂志在使用红色的同时，也大范围使用了沉闷的黑色，以黑色为背景衬托红色，给人强烈的视觉冲击感，主体十分突出。黑色将整个画面的重量感体现出来，显得沉稳高雅，黑红搭配给人以压迫感，是扑面而来的时尚个性的精英女性气场。而右边这本日本杂志，红色与其邻近色黄色的搭配显得大胆跳脱，且红色明度明显高于左边的中国杂志，加之黄色也是明度很高的颜色，所以给人一种活泼明快之感。

上面就中日两国女性时尚杂志封面的色彩进行了分析，下面我们就封面人物进行对比，该对比研究主要从两个方面展开，一是人物表情，二是人物服饰风格。

3.2 关于杂志封面人物的对比分析

从杂志主体（即封面人物）来看，不管是人物表情还是人物服装风格中日两国都存在较大差异，下面我们分别从这两个方面进行比较。

3.2.1 人物表情对比

这一节里我们就模特的面部表情进行分析，主要从三个维度来展开：（1）微笑（不露齿）；（2）露齿的笑；（3）无笑容（高冷表情）。下面先看看中日两国的封面模特儿的表情特征（如图 3-5 所示）。

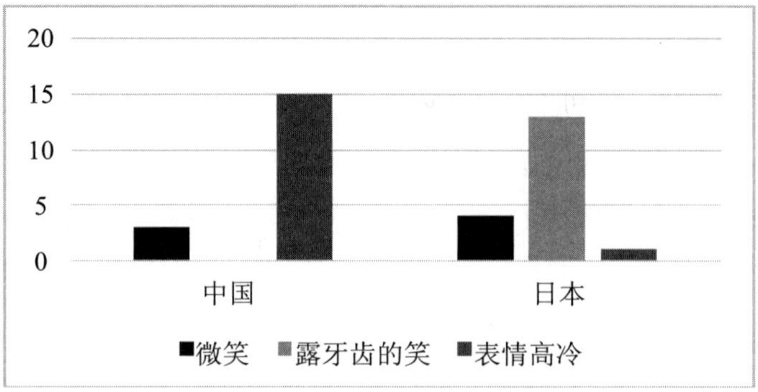

图 3-5　不同国家杂志封面人物表情

首先从人物表情来讲，表情作为人物主观心情的客观表达，无论是对杂志封面的人物塑造，还是对杂志封面整体风格的定位都有较大影响。而笑作为人们日常生活中用于传达友好，表示亲近的标志性表情，在日本杂志封面中大量运用，但在中国的此类杂志封面中却很少见。在我们所选取的样本中，日本时尚杂志封面女性表情是笑容的为 17 本，其中露牙齿的笑为 13 本，模特大多表情活泼而生动。但中国时尚杂志封面女性表情是笑容的仅为 3 本。而在中国时尚杂志封面中，模特大多下颚微扬，嘴唇微抿，给人一种高冷不可亲近之感。

3.2.2　人物气质特点对比

从模特的气质和特点来看，与日本杂志的模特相比，中国的封面模特大多为国内知名演员或国际模特，个体性非常强，面容精致，在不同的杂志封面有各自不同的个性，古典或性感。而日系女性时尚杂志的封面模特大多为较为生活化的本土普通女性模特，她们不一定长相明艳而精致，但是却让人看上去很舒服，很容易让人产生亲近感。

3.2.3　人物服装对比

再从人物服装风格来说，在我们所选取的样本中日本时尚杂志封面服装大多为日常服装，而礼服类服装仅占 2 本；而中国时尚杂志封面女性服装则是以礼服或造型夸张的服装为主，占 17 本（如图 3-6 所示）。

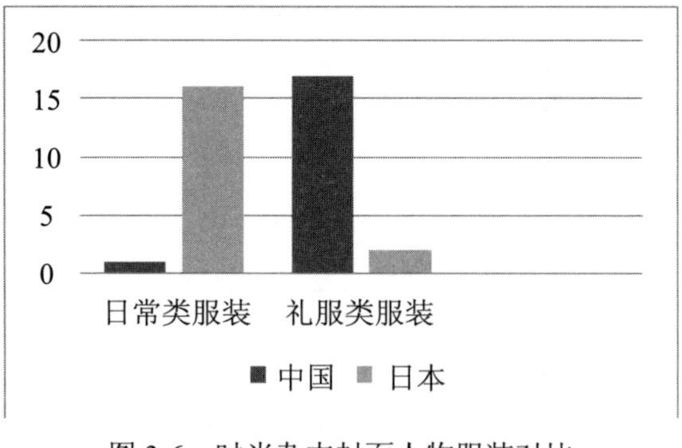

图 3-6　时尚杂志封面人物服装对比

礼服类服装从表现形式上来看更加浮夸,能给人更大的视觉冲击力，再根据服装的各自不同的特点能塑造出一个或冷峻或妖艳的人物形象,有很强的艺术性，或许让人认为这样的女人确实只能出现在杂志中。而日本封面人物的着装就大有不同。她们只穿着普通的日常类服装，一条花边连衣裙，又或者是一件有设计感的衬衫，她们让你觉得好像她们就是你身边那些生活精致的女孩，虽然美丽可爱，但不会产生距离感。

3.2.4 人物对比总结

综合模特特点、表情和服装可以看出，中国女性时尚杂志封面所推崇的女性形象为“品位至上的时尚优雅女性”，她们大多高冷而性感，给人一种高高在上不可亵渎之感。此类封面也能反映出这类女性往往具有很高的艺术性，是干练的精英女性形象。日本的杂志封面塑造的则是可爱至上的自然活泼的少女形象，让人感觉容易接近与相处，也许往往能让我们想起某个就住在自己邻家的小女孩。

4 时尚杂志背后的文化

以上从色彩和模特两个方面对比研究了中日两国女性时尚杂志的特点，结论为中国女性时尚杂志封面强调质感、设计及配色保守稳重，突出精英气质，意在突出独立、优雅、成熟和性感的女性形象。而日本女性时尚杂志封面更为生活化，设计跳脱活泼，表现出的是邻家、可爱、有活力、具有亲和力而少女感突出的年轻女性形象。那么，这两种不同的表达形式背后有着什么样的文化背景呢？下面我们将对中日两国的女性文化做一简单探讨。

4.1 欧美时尚影响下的中国时尚杂志

中国近现代意义上的时尚杂志是 20 世纪 80 年代自第一本法国时尚杂志《世界时装之苑——ELLE》传入中国才开始发展起来的。在中国时尚杂志尚处于萌芽之际，欧美时尚杂志通过与中国出版社进行合作，占领了大部分的中国市场。在这样一个背景下，中国又掀起向国外时尚杂志学习的澎湃浪潮。“本土的所有时尚杂志要么与国际时尚杂志进行版权合作，要么以这些时尚杂志的编辑形式为标准进行改版，时尚杂志同质化现象达到了前所未有的高度……也有不少探索，但是这场学习与改造的过程仍然在艰难进行当中，中国时尚杂志走出自己的民族特色仍是步履维艰。”（赵云泽，2011：109）据此，中国的时尚杂志可以说是由外向内的发展，若要深究中国的时尚杂志风格就要从欧美风格入手。欧美女性往往懂得追求自我价值，展现独立自主的形象。这同样也是许多中国女性的追求。

提到欧美女性独立自主就不得不讲到女权主义，这种产生于欧美资本主义革命时期所说的人权只是男权而不包括女权这样的背景下的主义表达了女性对于男女平等的期待和追求。平等就意味享有相同的权利，拥有独立自主的地位，不再附属于男性。中国女性受到传统社会“男主外女主内”的社会分工的历史惯性以及儒家“男尊女卑”思想的影响，几千年来女性一直是男性的附庸。直到近代，思想启蒙的近代知识分子寻求救国之路，借由西方思想的影响，开始为女性争取地位和权益。经过数代先辈的努力争取和解放，中国女性才有今天的地位。有着长期被压迫的历史的后果就是当代的女性在追求独立自主上拥有更加强烈的期待。在时尚杂志这一能够起到引领潮流的领域正好能够表达女性的这一追求。而在欧美杂志的影响与助推下，这种女性的追求更加深刻。即中国杂志在依托国际杂志发展的同时，也很好地迎合了中国女性的期待。

根据 2014 年 The World Bank 中关于女性就业比例的调查，中国男性和女性就业率仅相差 14%，其中男性就业率为 78%，女性就业率为 64%，与美国在这项指数上表现相似。根据 2015 年国际经济论坛发布的全球性别不平等报告，中国在“女性受高等教育比例”和“女性技术和专业工作者”两项指标上均为世界前三名。由此可见，中国在世界范围来看也是女性就业率很高的国家之一。而女性的社会参与必定给女性带来竞争意识、精英意识，追求卓越，追求高薪是生活在我们周围的绝大多数女性的梦想，可以说女性时尚杂志的封面设计（或选择）也是这种意识的充分反映。

4.2 日本文化社会渊源

日本杂志业方面十分发达，他们的发展立足于“守住本土市场的基础上进行国际化”。这是一个由内向外的过程，因而日本杂志带有比较浓厚的本土色彩，关于这一点，我们首先谈谈日本的“男主外，女主内”的社会分工现象。众所周知，日本是个大男子主义的社会，职场是男人的战场，而家庭是女人的阵地。做一个贤妻良母，为在职场拼搏的男人带去温柔似乎是日本女人的天职。在这样的社会文化背景下，整个社会期待的女性形象是柔和、温暖，不具攻击性。由此，女性杂志的封面设计也是这一种文化的体现。

其次，我们联系到日本的“可爱文化”来做一分析。在日本追求可爱已经成为一种大众的心理趋向，也是日本的一种特有的文化现象。在日本，年轻女性是追求可爱的主要群体，对于她们来说“可爱是一种确认自我的工具”。而“……日本传统美学崇尚谦逊、纤弱和童真。而可爱的服装和装饰品普遍造型小巧、设计简洁、色调柔和，恰好是日本传统美学概念的最好诠释。”（张彦萍，2012：41）从女性的角度来看，给予自身活泼可爱而邻家的定义，其实希望得到更强大的对象的照拂。而男性对女性的期待也是“可爱”。比如，在日本男性对女性最大的赞美词不是“きれい、美しい（漂亮、美丽）”，而是“かわいい（可爱）”。所以，不管从女性角度也好，还是从男性角度也好，对可爱的追求是一种普遍的文化诉求，而日本的女性时尚杂志也是这一文化的反映。

5 结　语

中国受到欧美女权主义的影响以及自身对于独立自主的强烈诉求，使得时尚杂志迎合女性这一诉求而体现出独立自主的精英范；日本的历史以及社会诉求，使得其具有亲和力的可爱女性形象大行其道。其实，杂志等出版物为了自身的市场需求也罢，为了社会责任也罢，为了某种情怀也罢，它一定是一个社会文化的反映，它会按照女性想要成为的样子去塑造自己的产品，在引领潮流的背后，迎合社会女性的期待和定义。当然，社会是变化的，随着经济的发展，在未来的中国有可能会出现更多的家庭主妇，而在日本，女性的就业率也可能会增加，那么，女性时尚杂志的封面又会发生怎样的变化呢？我们将会一直关注下去。

参考文献

[1] 日本奥博斯科编辑部. 配色设计原理[M]. 暴凤明译. 北京：中国青年出版社，2009.

[2] 胡博，何文一. 时尚杂志的风格与市场定位——日系和欧美系女性时尚杂志比较[J]. 出版与印刷，2011（1）：15-18.

[3] 水源. 从《欢乐颂》和《东京女子图鉴》看中日女性形象的对比[J]. 文艺生活，2017（9）：82-83.

[4] 张静. 从可爱文化看日本人的逃避心理[J]. 科技视界，2017（12）：129，148.

[5] 张彦萍. 论日本的可爱文化[J]. 成功（教育），2012（11）：40-41.

[6] 赵云泽. 中国时尚杂志的历史反思[J]. 国际新闻界，2011（5）：108-112.